DESCENDING STORIES

SHOWA
GENROKU
RAKUGO
SHINJU

Haruko Kumota

THE STORY SO FAR

YOTARO'S ODYSSEY

Yotaro falls in love with Yakumo Yurakutei's *rakugo* when he hears it in prison. Once free, he becomes Yakumo's apprentice and is soon made a *zenza.* As his appreciation for *rakugo* grows, the incredible *rakugo* of the late Sukeroku takes hold of him and he commits an unthinkable faux pas at a solo recital by his teacher. Facing expulsion, Yotaro begs forgiveness. Yakumo relents, but extracts three promises from his student. Then he begins to tell the tale of his own promise with Sukeroku...

YAKUMO AND SUKEROKU

Yakumo Yurakutei VII takes two apprentices on the same day: Kikuhiko and Hatsutaro. Promoted to *shin'uchi* together, the two are soon popular *rakugo* artists, with Hatsutaro adopting the name "Sukeroku," and Kikuhiko finding his own style at last.

But Sukeroku argues with his shisho and is expelled from the lineage. Wounded, he disappears with Miyokichi, Kikuhiko's former lover. Not long after, Yakumo makes a deathbed confession to Kikuhiko of his secret connection to the Sukeroku name. Bereaved and alone, Kikuhiko goes in search of Sukeroku at a hot springs town in the countryside, in order to make him inherit the Yakumo name. Sukeroku has abandoned *rakugo*, but, at Kikuhiko's insistence, the two Yurakutei disciples put on a successful joint show.

CAST OF CHARACTERS

Yakumo and Sukeroku

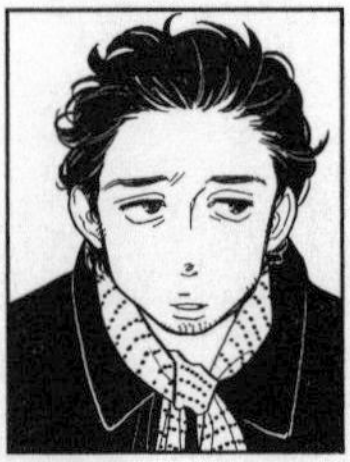

Sukeroku
Apprentice of Yakumo VII, making him a brother apprentice to Kikuhiko, until his expulsion.

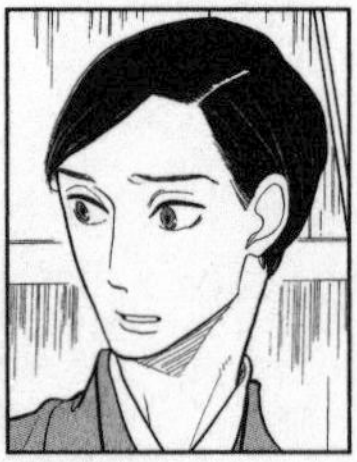

Kikuhiko
Yakumo Yurakutei VIII as a young *zenza*. The same age as Sukeroku.

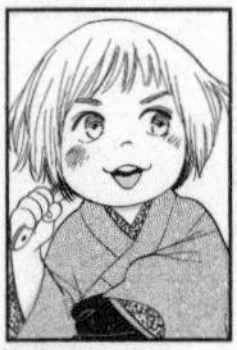

Konatsu
Konatsu in her youth. Daughter of Sukeroku and Miyokichi.

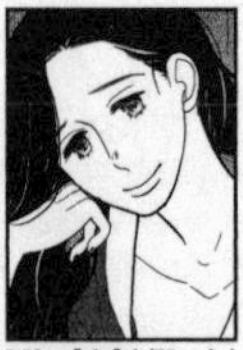

Miyokichi (Yurie)
Konatsu's mother. Dies falling from a window with Sukeroku.

Yotaro's Odyssey

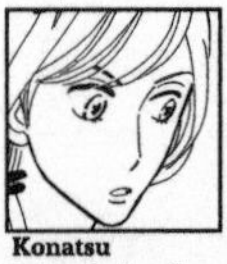

Konatsu
Sukeroku's only daughter, taken in by Yakumo.

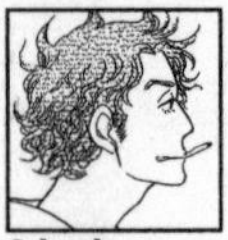

Sukeroku Yurakutei
Legendary *rakugo* artist hailed as a genius before his untimely death.

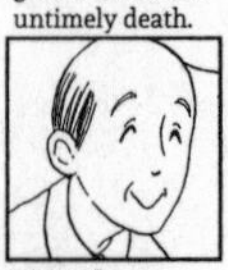

Matsuda-san
Faithful servant and driver of Yakumo VIII, and Yakumo VII before him.

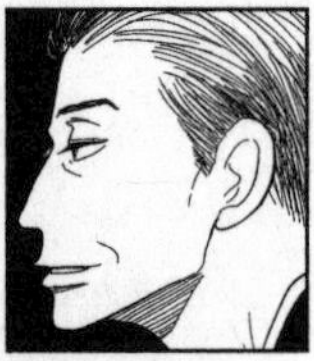

Yakumo Yurakutei VIII
Renowned as the Showa period's last great master of *rakugo*.

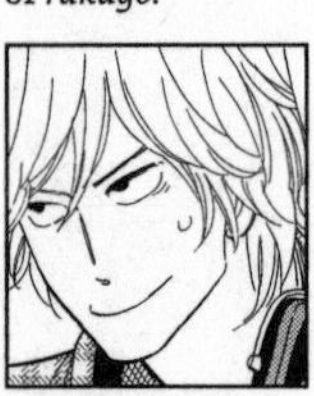

Yotaro (Kyoji)
Reformed street tough who became Yakumo's apprentice.

That night, however, Miyokichi reappears, hinting at a joint suicide with Kikuhiko. Driven by a hunch, Sukeroku bursts in to stop them, and the scene ends in tragedy as Sukeroku and Miyokichi fall to their deaths together. Taking in their child Konatsu in memory of the two, Kikuhiko inherits the Yakumo name himself, in order to put an end to the story...

SUKEROKU AGAIN

Taking the promises he made to Yakumo to heart, Yotaro diligently polishes his craft. With the *rakugo* world fading and only one *yose* left in Tokyo, he is finally promoted to *shin'uchi*—adopting the name "Sukeroku III." At nearly the same time, Konatsu reveals that she is pregnant. Determined to keep Sukeroku's bloodline alive, she refuses to identify the father and soon becomes a single mother—until Yotaro marries her and becomes father to her child.

For his shisho...for his wife...to change the Sukeroku that comes between them...can Yotaro find his own *rakugo* at last?

Cast of Characters

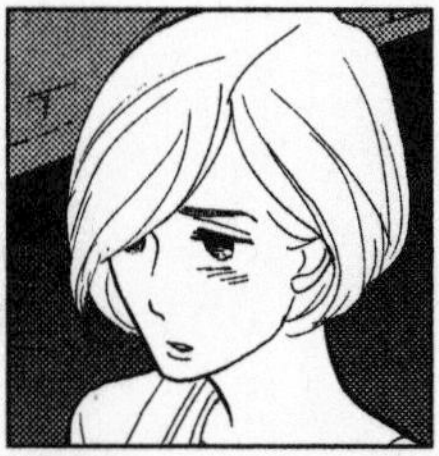

Konatsu
Only daughter of the late Sukeroku II, taken in by Yakumo. Had a child without revealing the father. Now married to Yotaro.

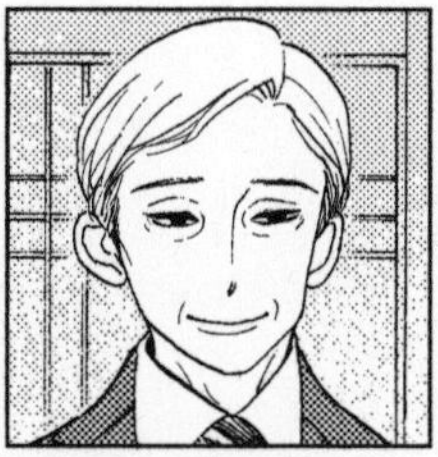

Yakumo Yurakutei VIII
Now the most powerful figure in the world of *rakugo* and president of the *Rakugo* Association. Accepted no apprentices except Yotaro, leaving nobody to inherit the Yakumo name.

Sukeroku Again

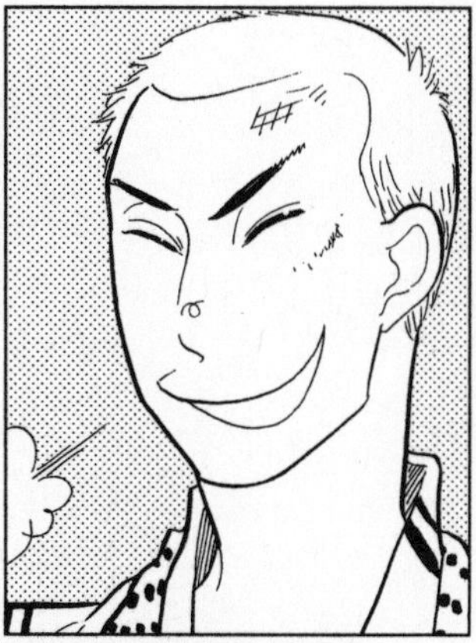

Sukeroku Yurakutei III (a.k.a. Yotaro)
Promoted to *shin'uchi*, Yotaro inherits the Sukeroku name and marries Konatsu to form a family. Loves *rakugo* with all his heart.

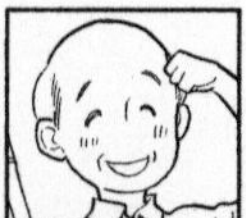

Matsuda-san
Faithful servant and driver of Yakumo VIII. Part of the Yurakutei family in all but name.

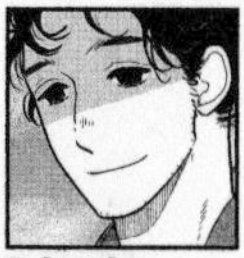

Sukeroku Yurakutei II
Konatsu's deceased father, whose *rakugo* remains legendary.

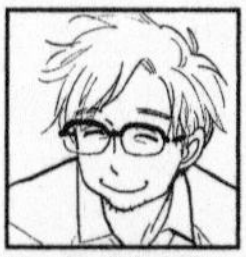

Eisuke Higuchi
A.k.a. "Sensei." Popular writer and fan of Yotaro.

DESCENDING STORIES | SHOWA GENROKU RAKUGO SHINJU

Contents

Sukeroku Again

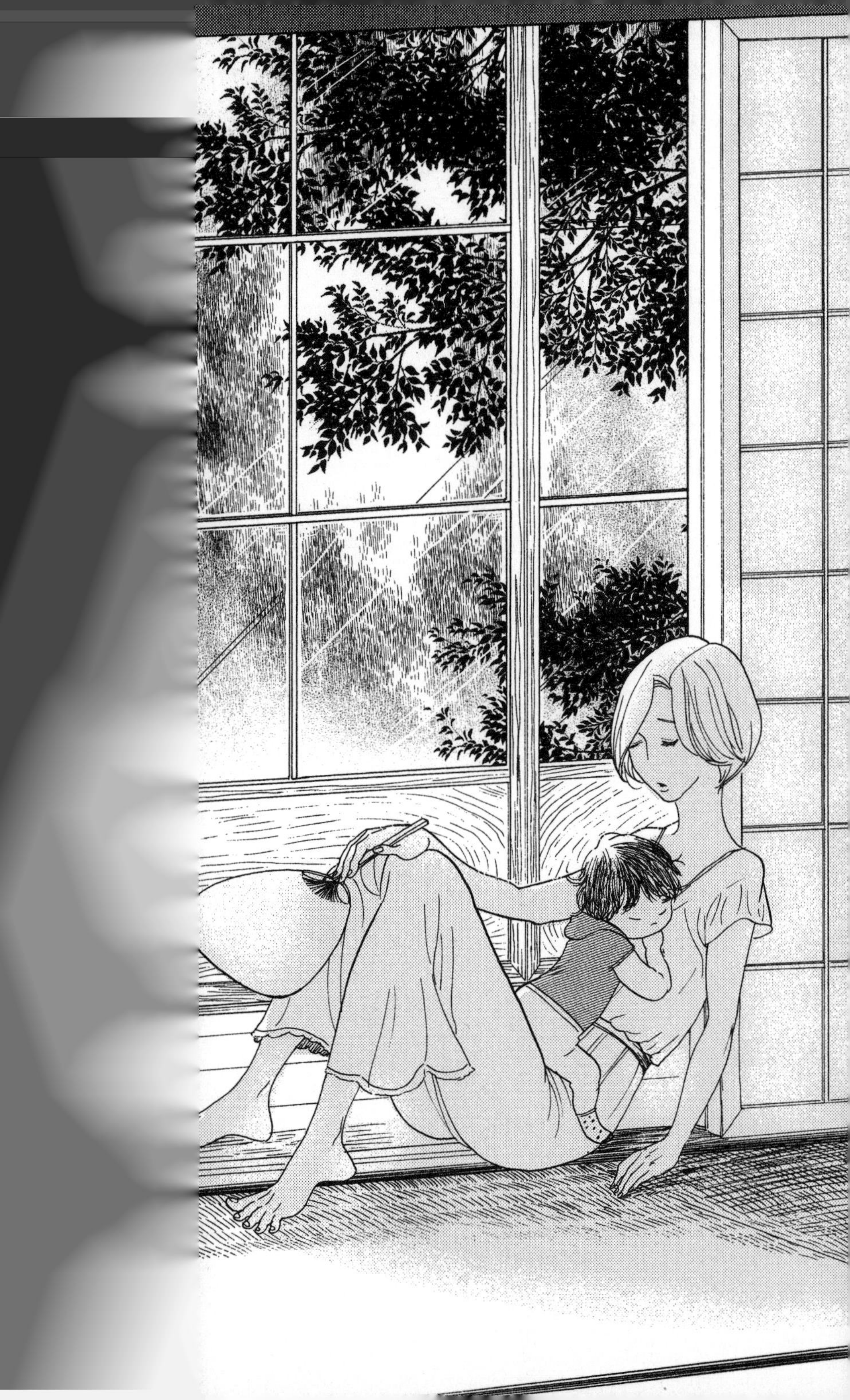

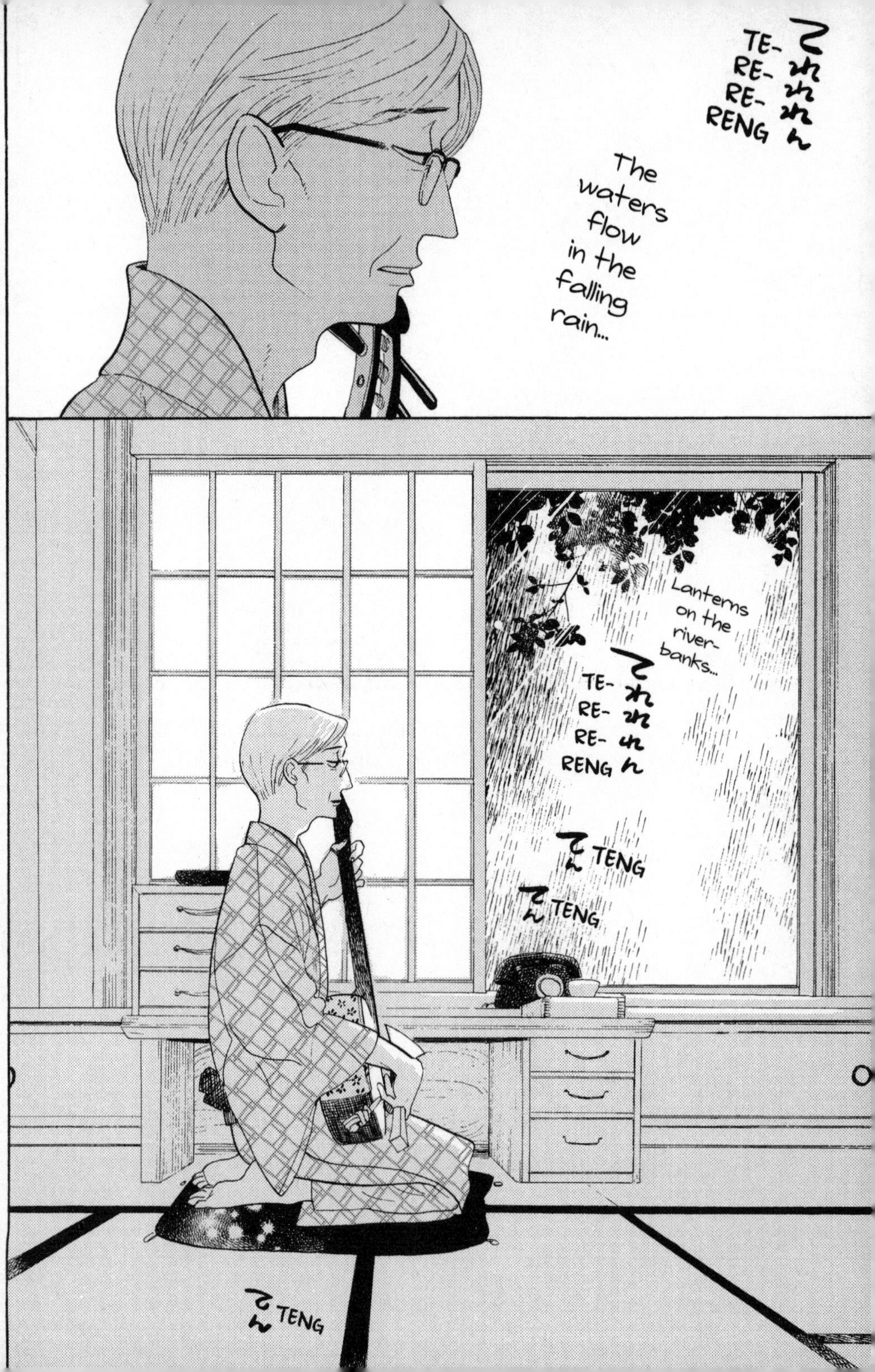
てれれれん
TE-RE-RE-RENG
The waters flow in the falling rain...
Lanterns on the river-banks...
てれれれん
TE-RE-RE-RENG
てん TENG
てん TENG
てん TENG

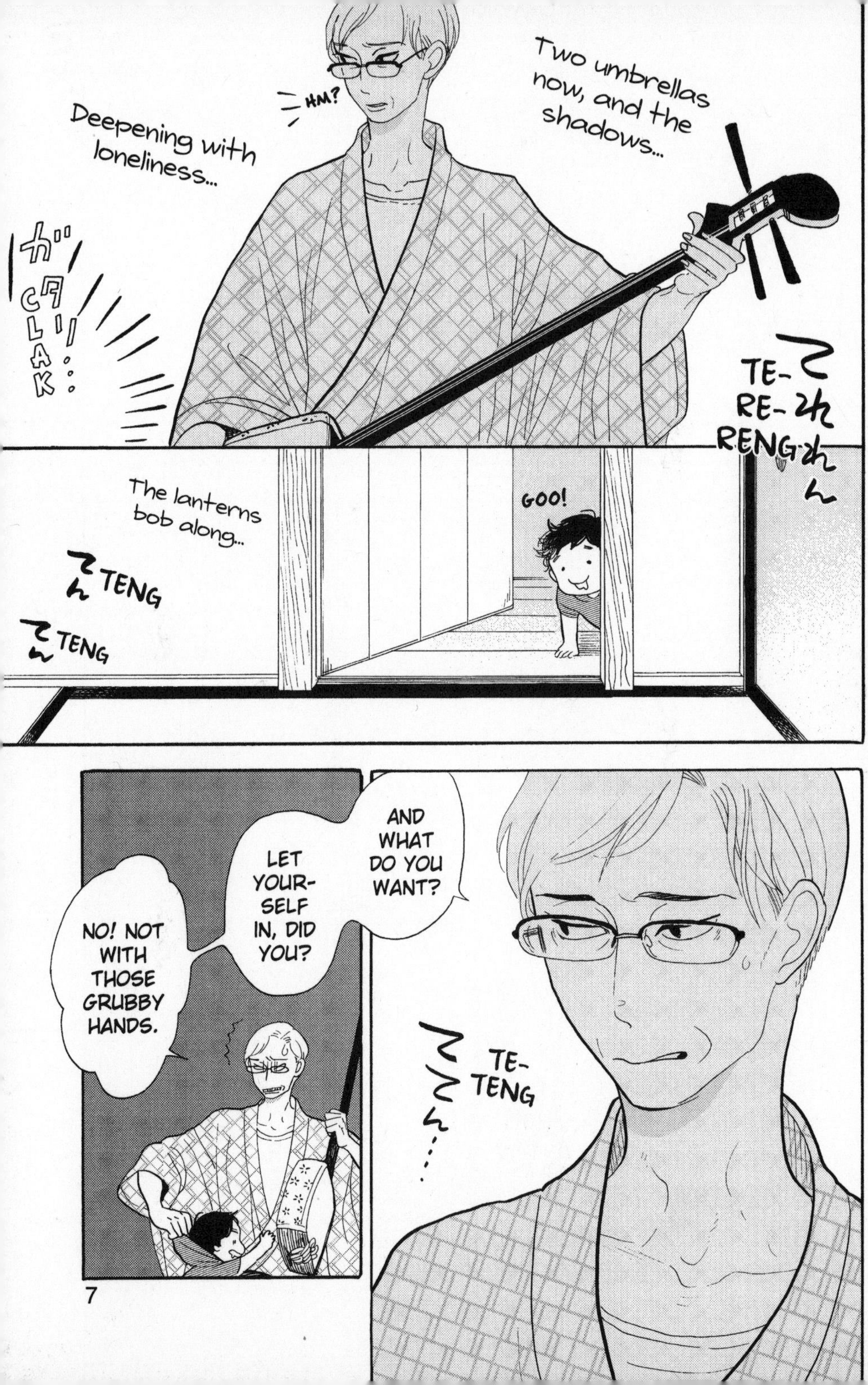
Two umbrellas now, and the shadows...
HM?
Deepening with loneliness...
TE-RE-RENG
CLAK
GOO!
The lanterns bob along...
TENG
TENG
AND WHAT DO YOU WANT?
LET YOURSELF IN, DID YOU?
TE-TENG
NO! NOT WITH THOSE GRUBBY HANDS.

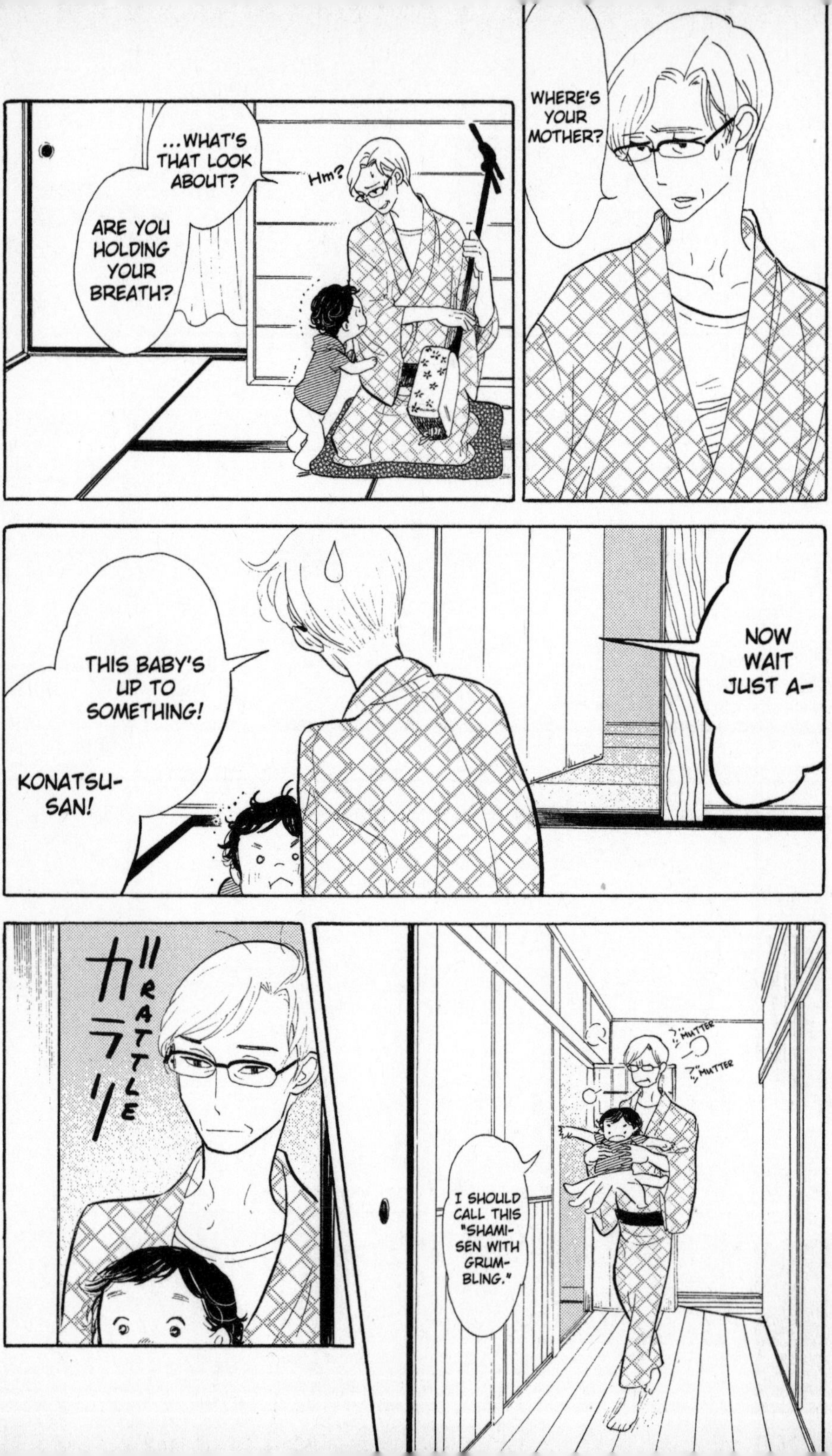
WHERE'S YOUR MOTHER?
Hm?
...WHAT'S THAT LOOK ABOUT?
ARE YOU HOLDING YOUR BREATH?
NOW WAIT JUST A-
THIS BABY'S UP TO SOMETHING!
KONATSU-SAN!
MUTTER
MUTTER
I SHOULD CALL THIS "SHAMISEN WITH GRUMBLING."
ガラリ
RATTLE

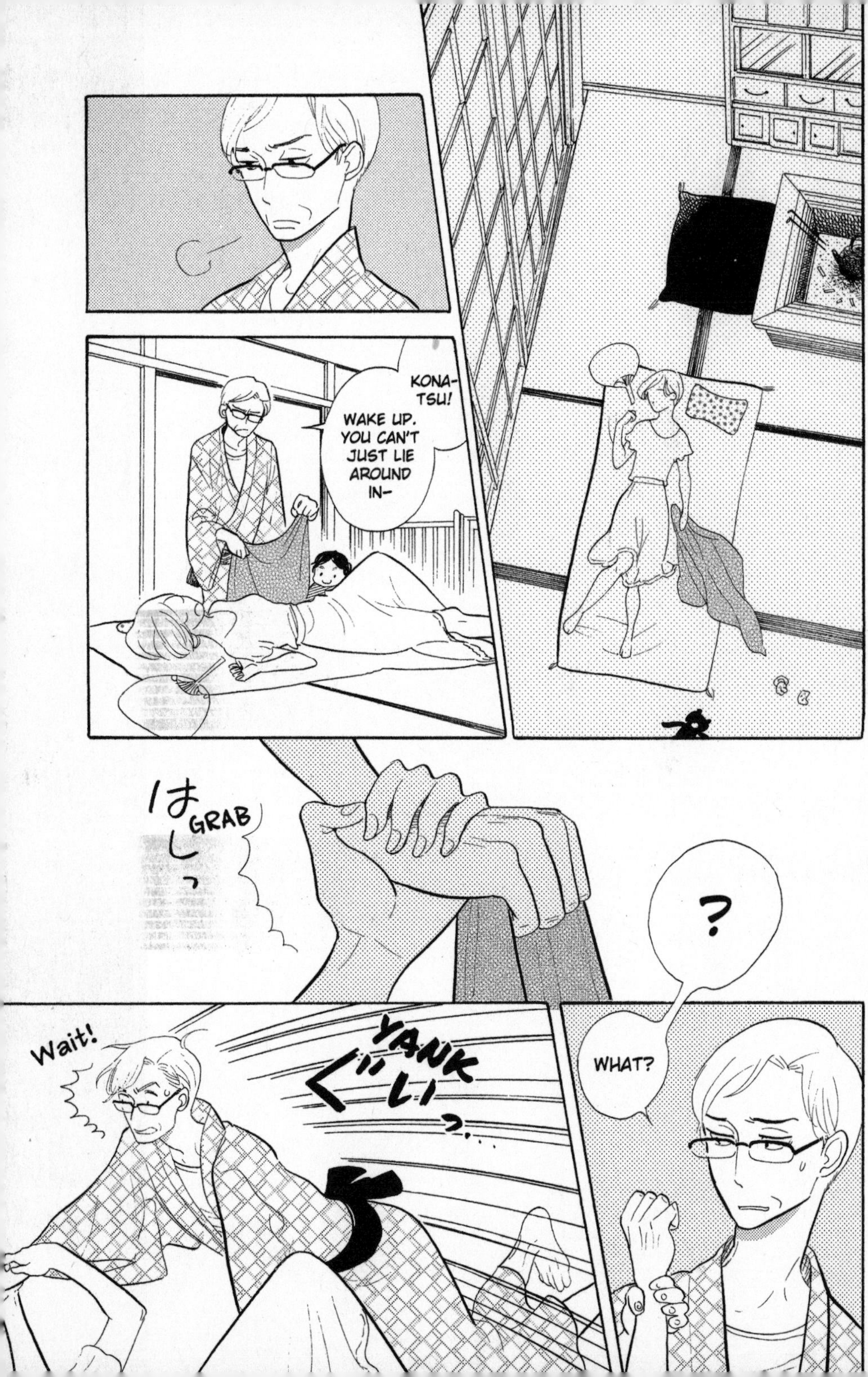
KONA-TSU!
WAKE UP. YOU CAN'T JUST LIE AROUND IN–
はしっ
GRAB
?
WHAT?
YANK
ぐいっ
Wait!

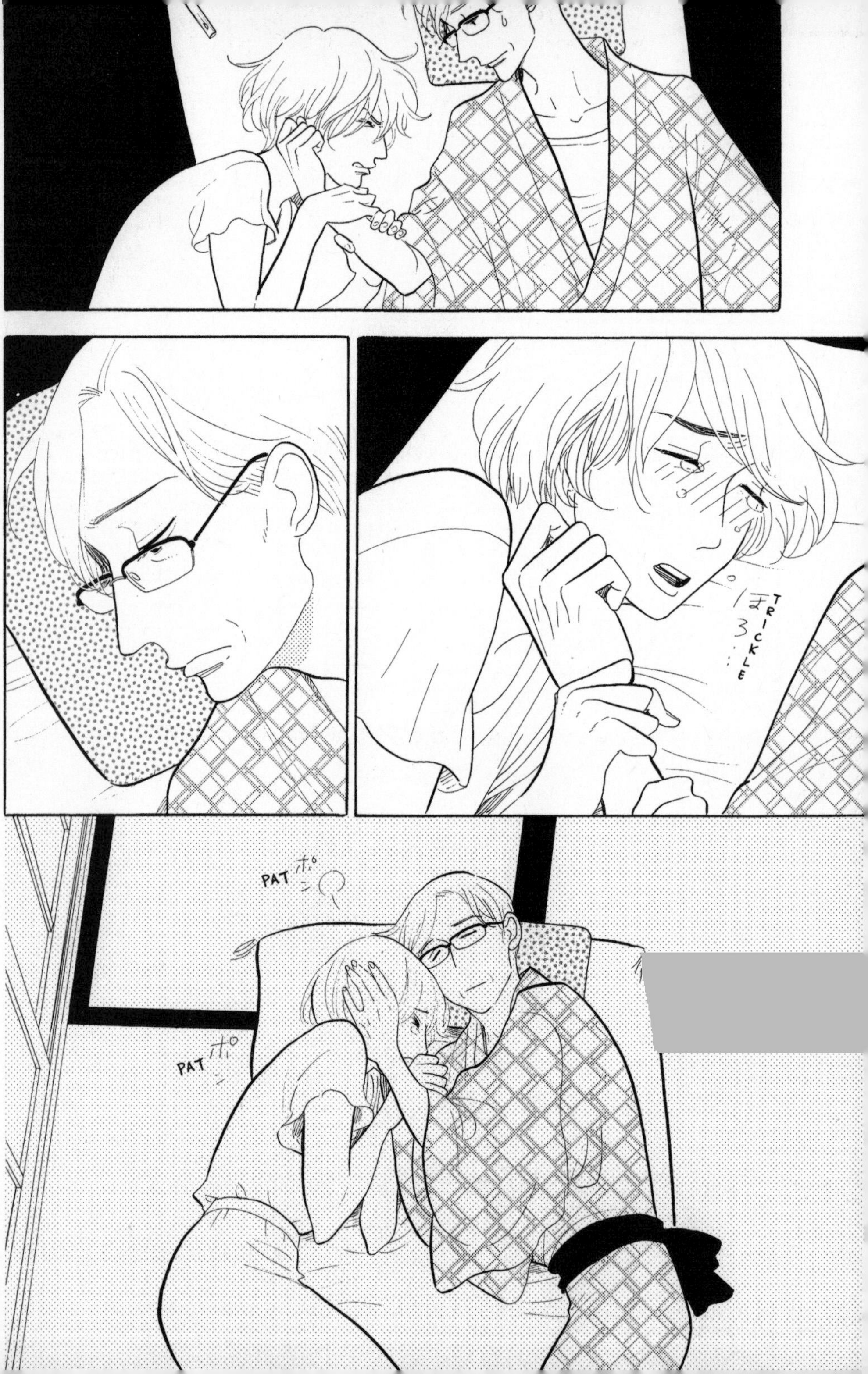
ほろ…
TRICKLE
PAT
PAT

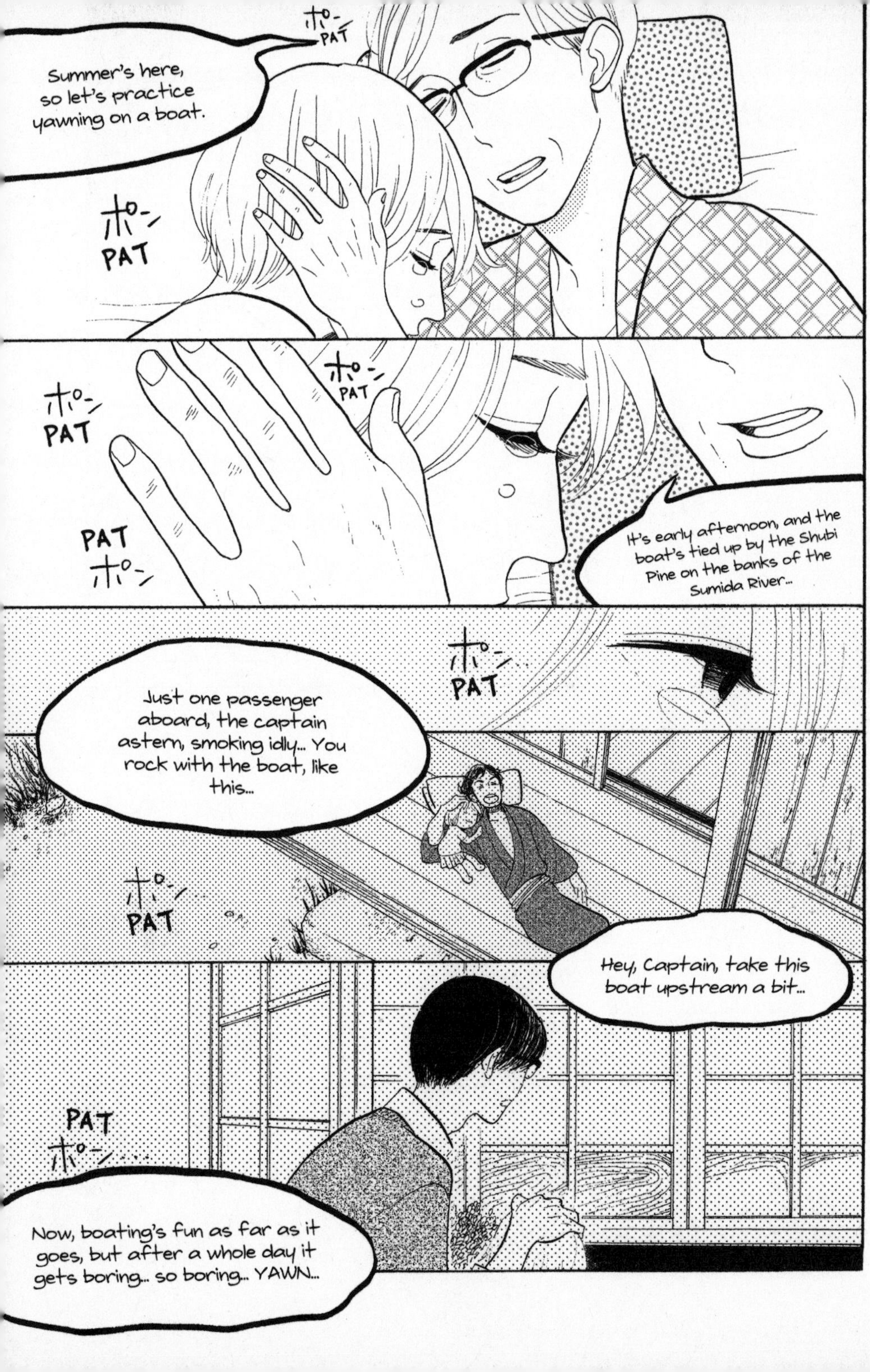
PAT
Summer's here, so let's practice yawning on a boat.
PAT
PAT
PAT
PAT
It's early afternoon, and the boat's tied up by the Shubi Pine on the banks of the Sumida River...
PAT
Just one passenger aboard, the captain astern, smoking idly... You rock with the boat, like this...
PAT
Hey, Captain, take this boat upstream a bit...
PAT
Now, boating's fun as far as it goes, but after a whole day it gets boring... so boring... YAWN...

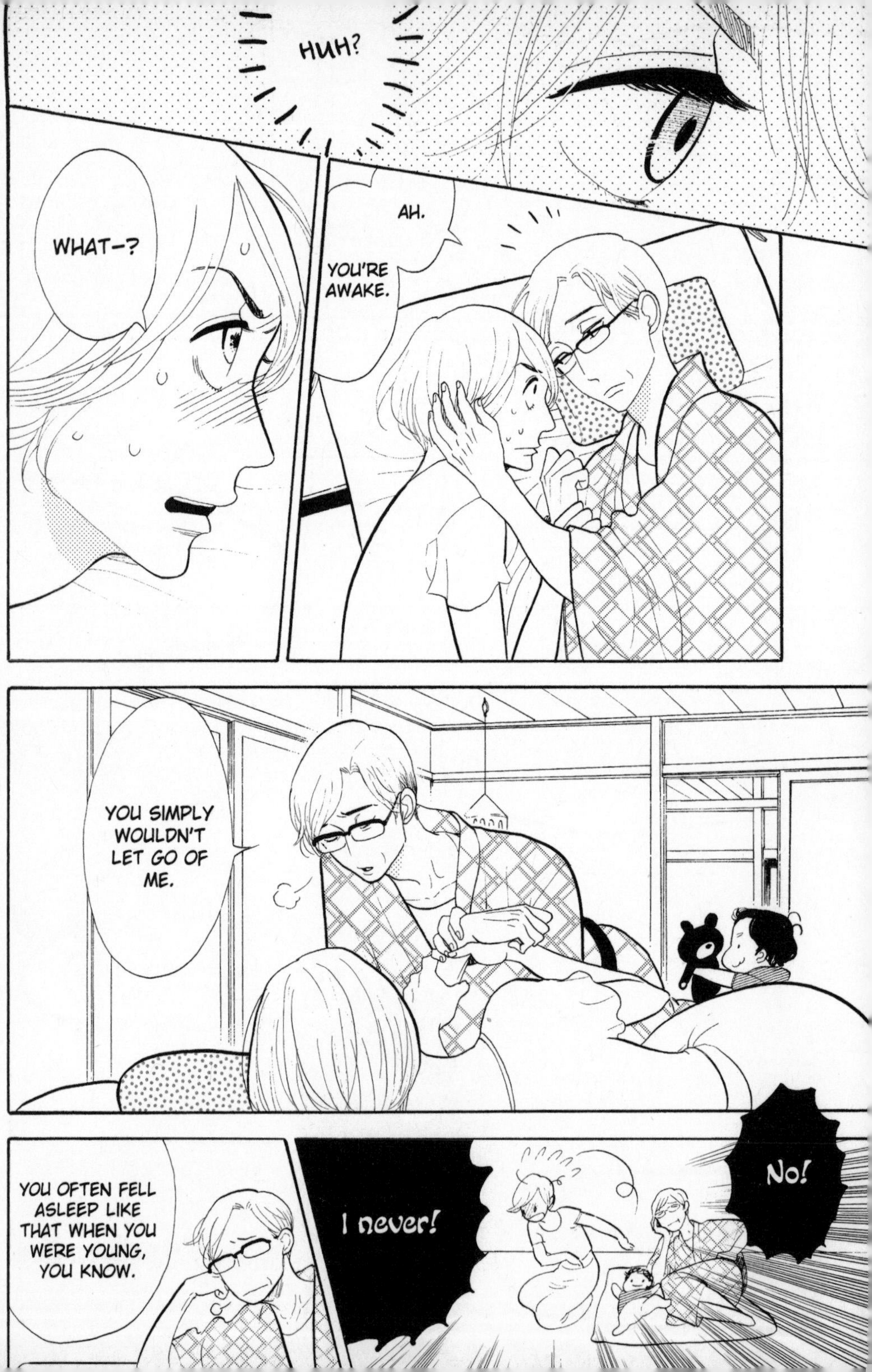
HUH?
AH.
YOU'RE AWAKE.
WHAT-?
YOU SIMPLY WOULDN'T LET GO OF ME.
No!
I never!
YOU OFTEN FELL ASLEEP LIKE THAT WHEN YOU WERE YOUNG, YOU KNOW.

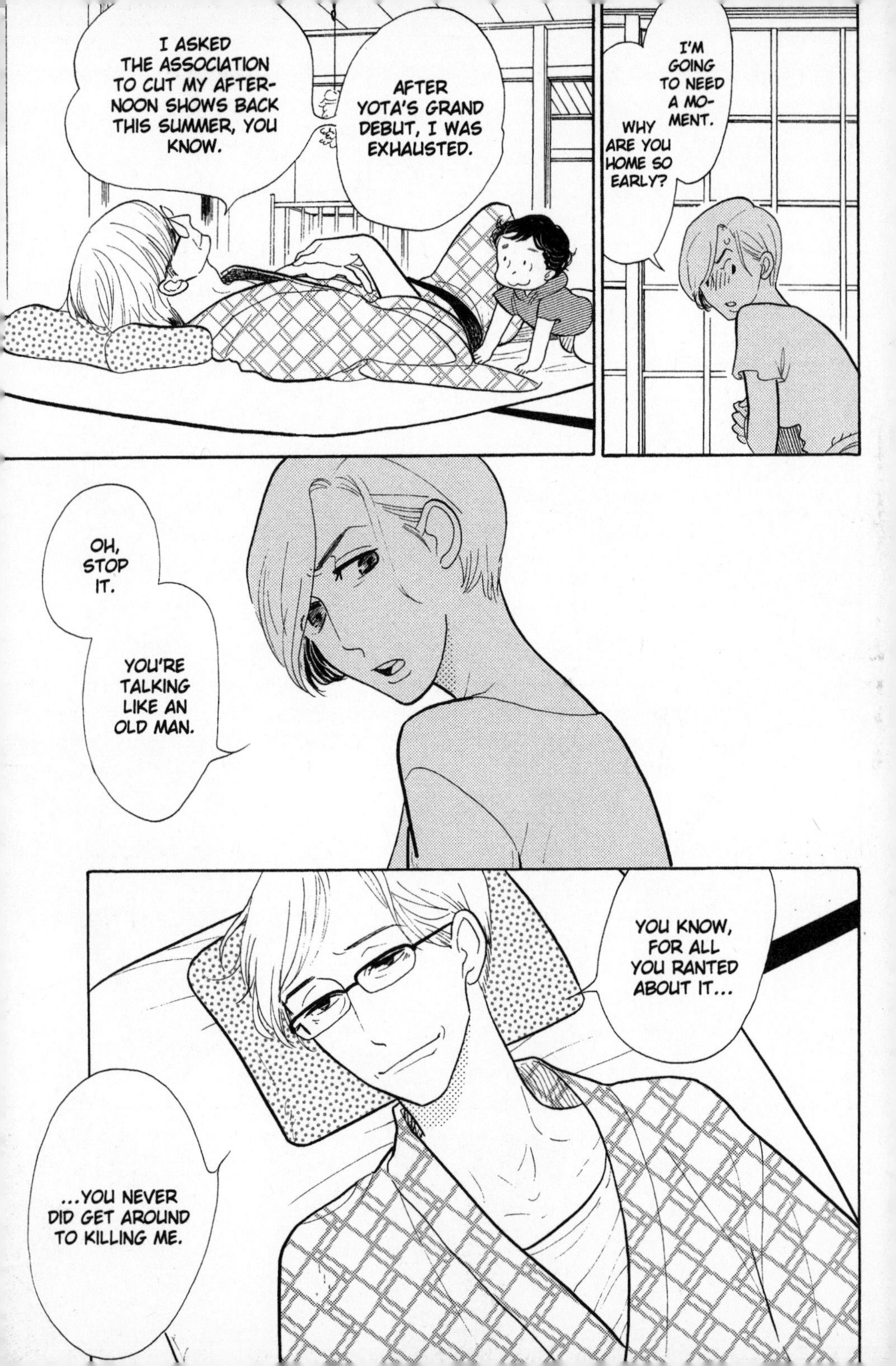
I'M GOING TO NEED A MO-MENT.
WHY ARE YOU HOME SO EARLY?
I ASKED THE ASSOCIATION TO CUT MY AFTER-NOON SHOWS BACK THIS SUMMER, YOU KNOW.
AFTER YOTA'S GRAND DEBUT, I WAS EXHAUSTED.
OH, STOP IT.
YOU'RE TALKING LIKE AN OLD MAN.
YOU KNOW, FOR ALL YOU RANTED ABOUT IT...
...YOU NEVER DID GET AROUND TO KILLING ME.

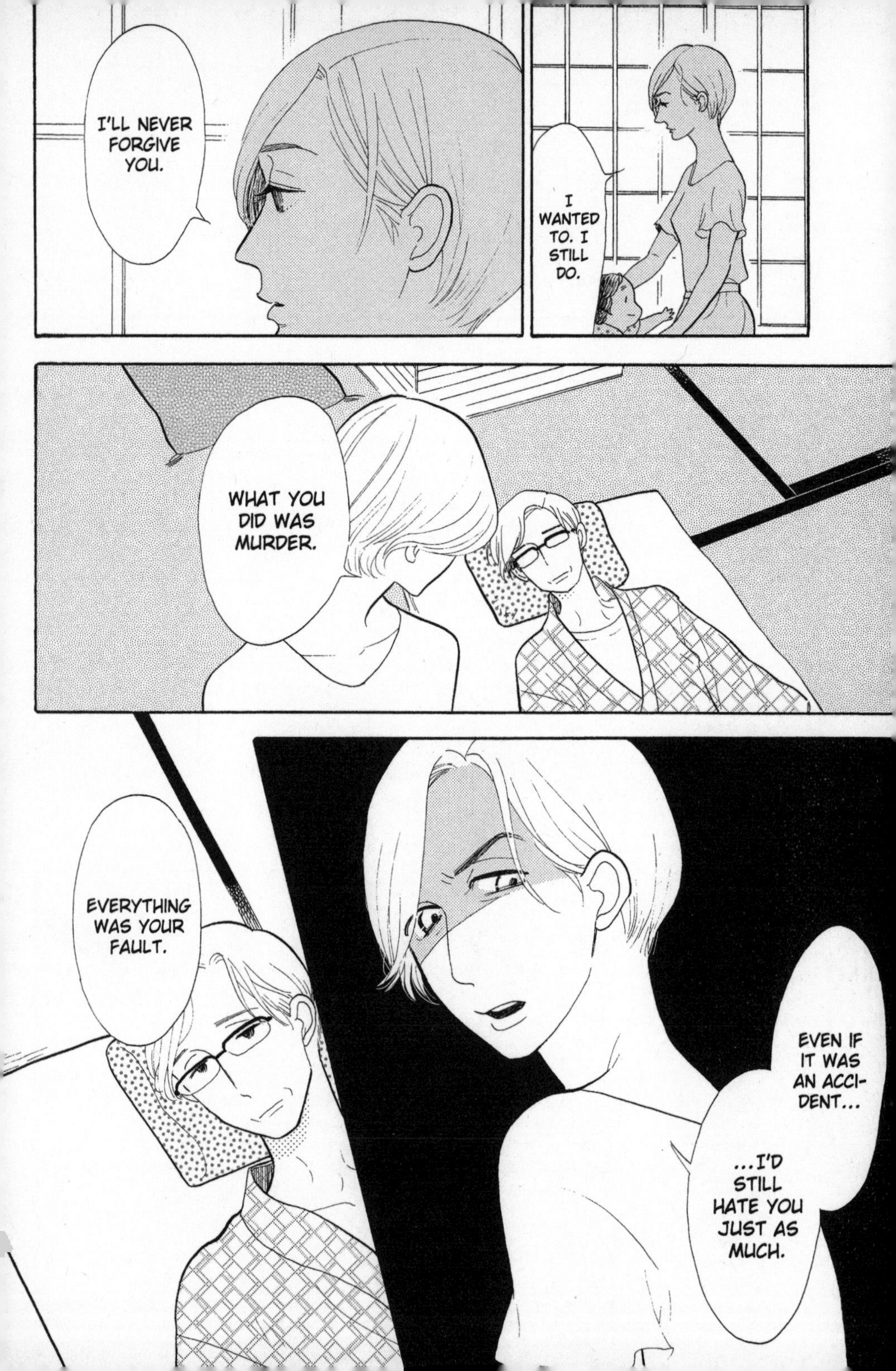
I WANTED TO. I STILL DO.
I'LL NEVER FORGIVE YOU.
WHAT YOU DID WAS MURDER.
EVEN IF IT WAS AN ACCI-DENT...
...I'D STILL HATE YOU JUST AS MUCH.
EVERYTHING WAS YOUR FAULT.

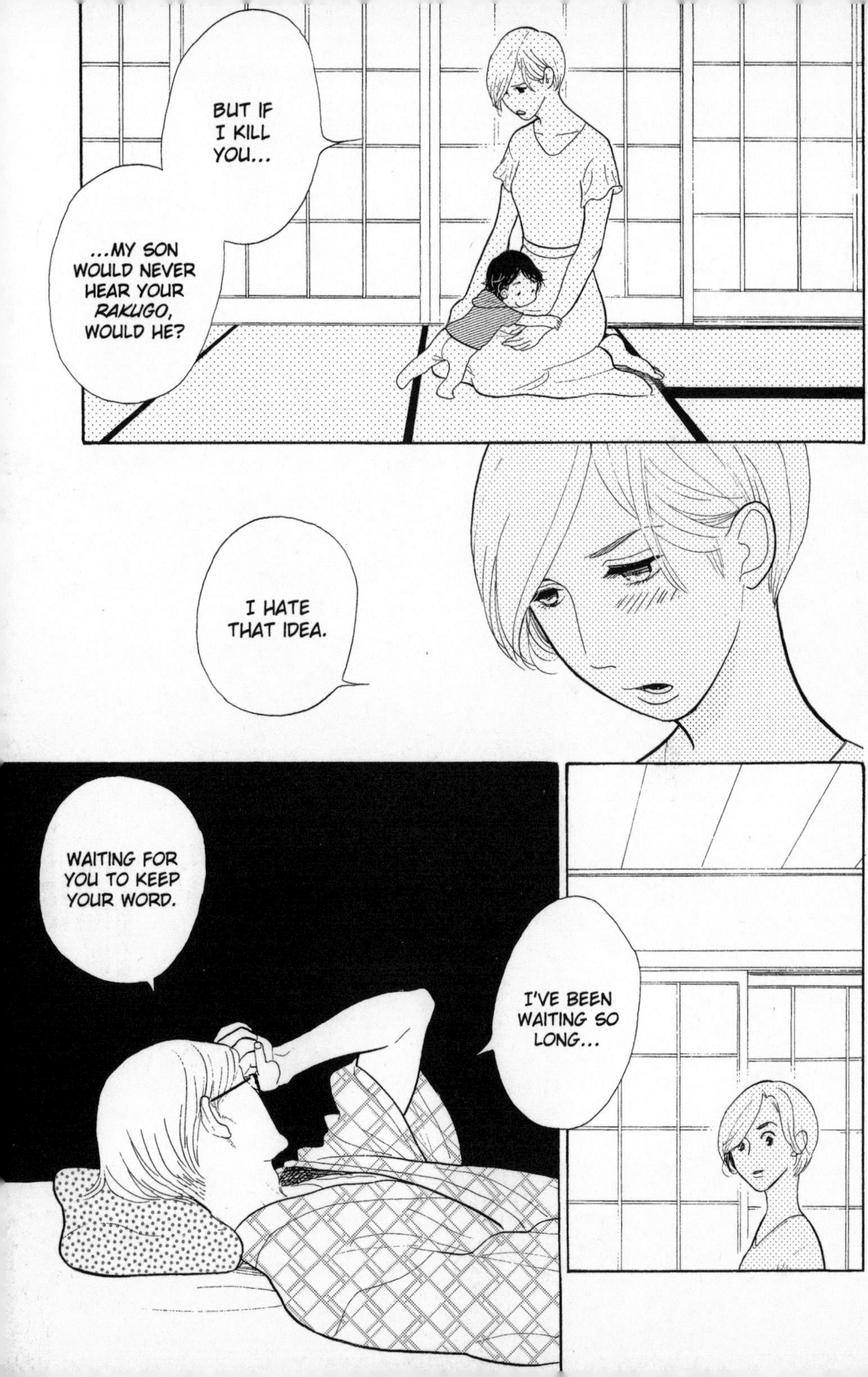
BUT IF I KILL YOU...
...MY SON WOULD NEVER HEAR YOUR *RAKUGO*, WOULD HE?
I HATE THAT IDEA.
I'VE BEEN WAITING SO LONG...
WAITING FOR YOU TO KEEP YOUR WORD.

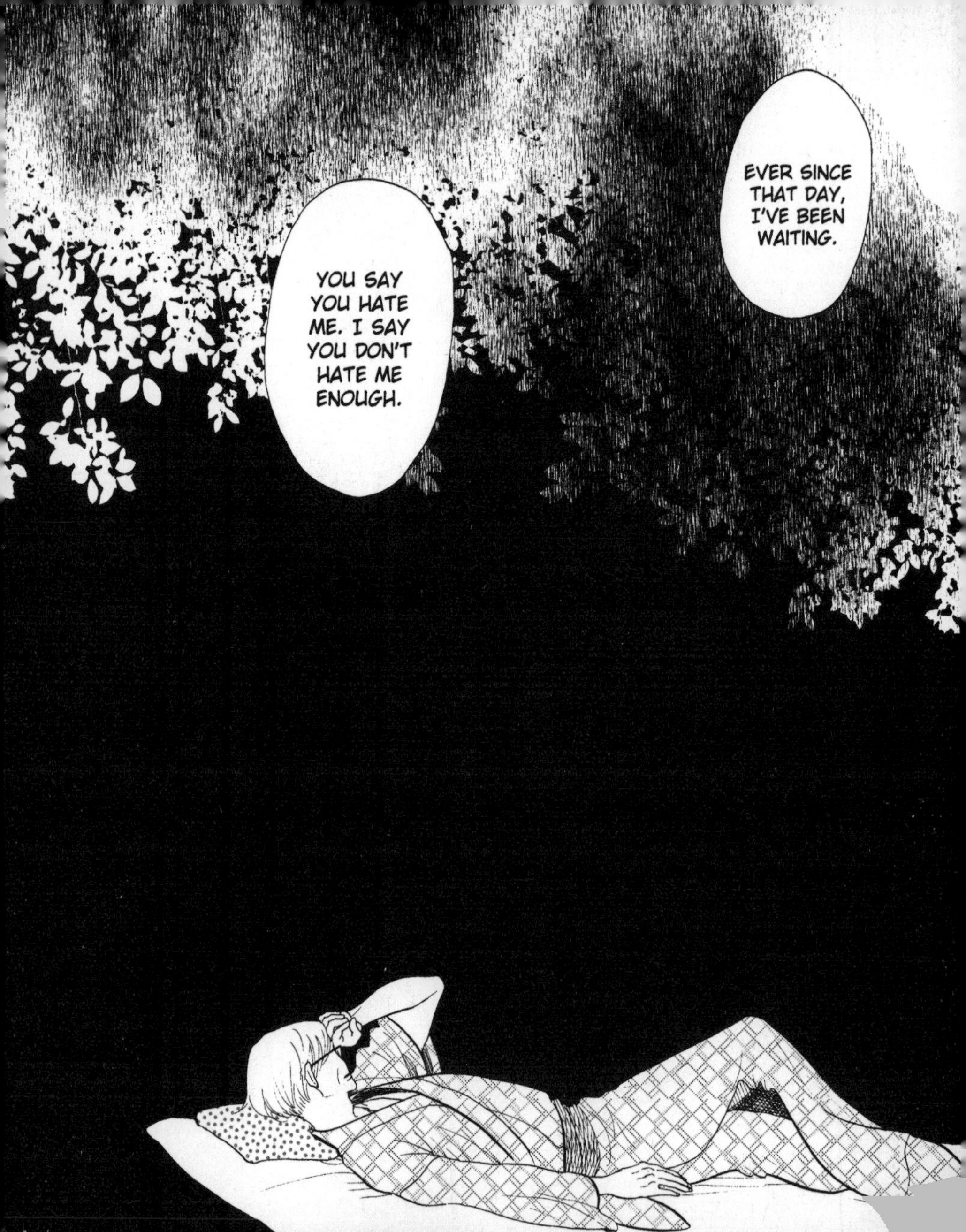
EVER SINCE THAT DAY, I'VE BEEN WAITING.
YOU SAY YOU HATE ME. I SAY YOU DON'T HATE ME ENOUGH.

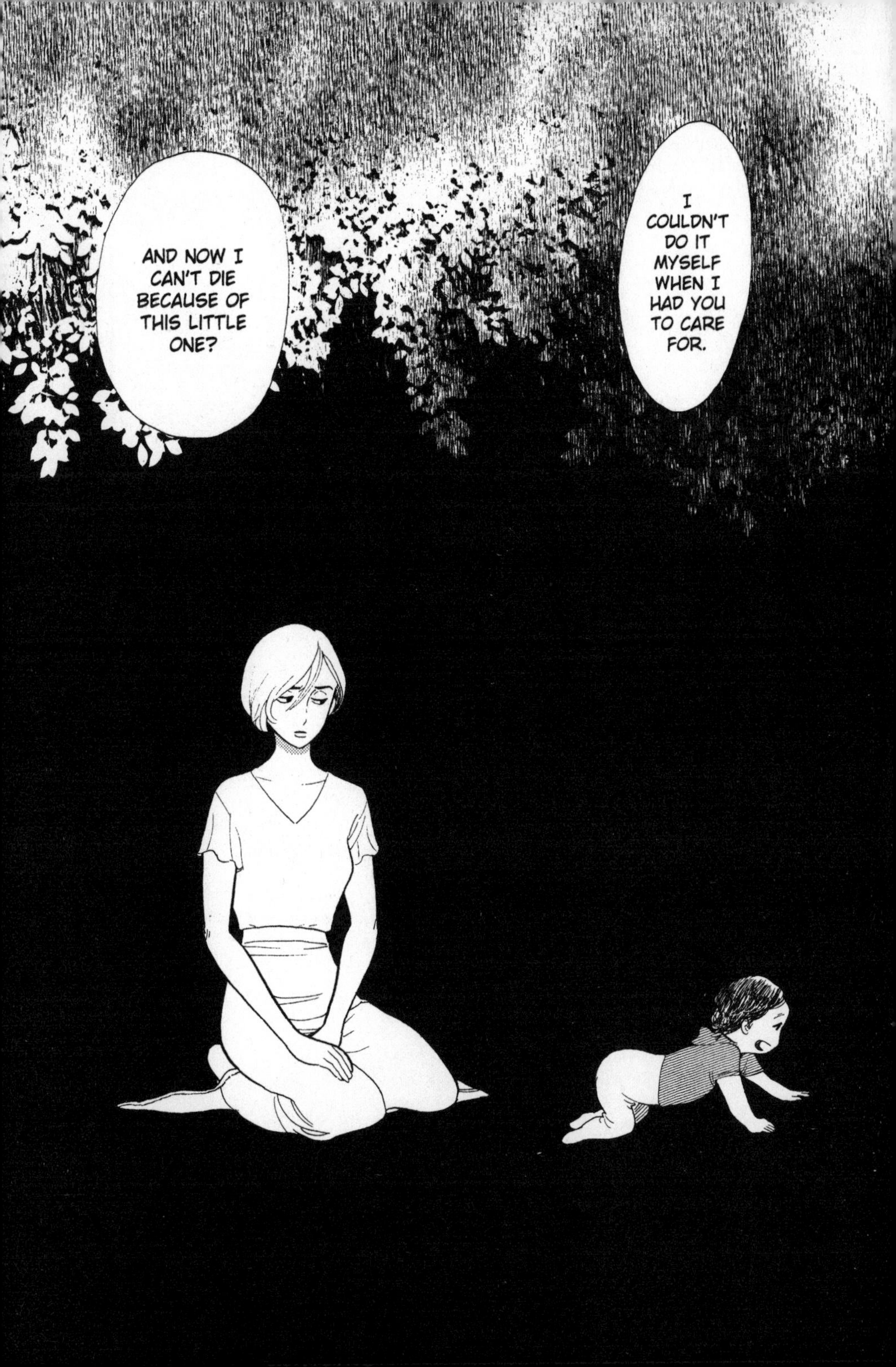
I COULDN'T DO IT MYSELF WHEN I HAD YOU TO CARE FOR.
AND NOW I CAN'T DIE BECAUSE OF THIS LITTLE ONE?

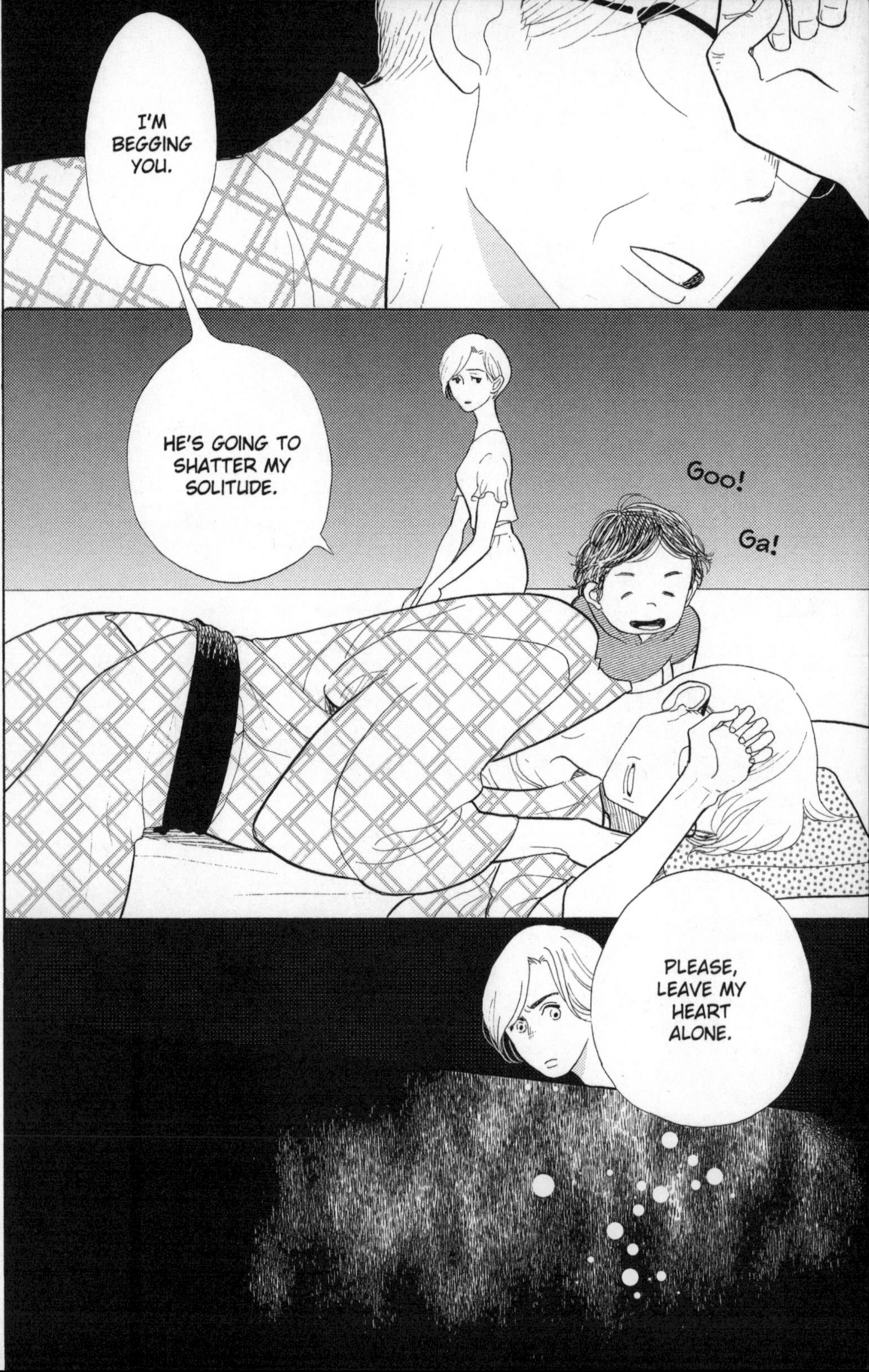
I'M BEGGING YOU.
HE'S GOING TO SHATTER MY SOLITUDE.
Goo!
Ga!
PLEASE, LEAVE MY HEART ALONE.

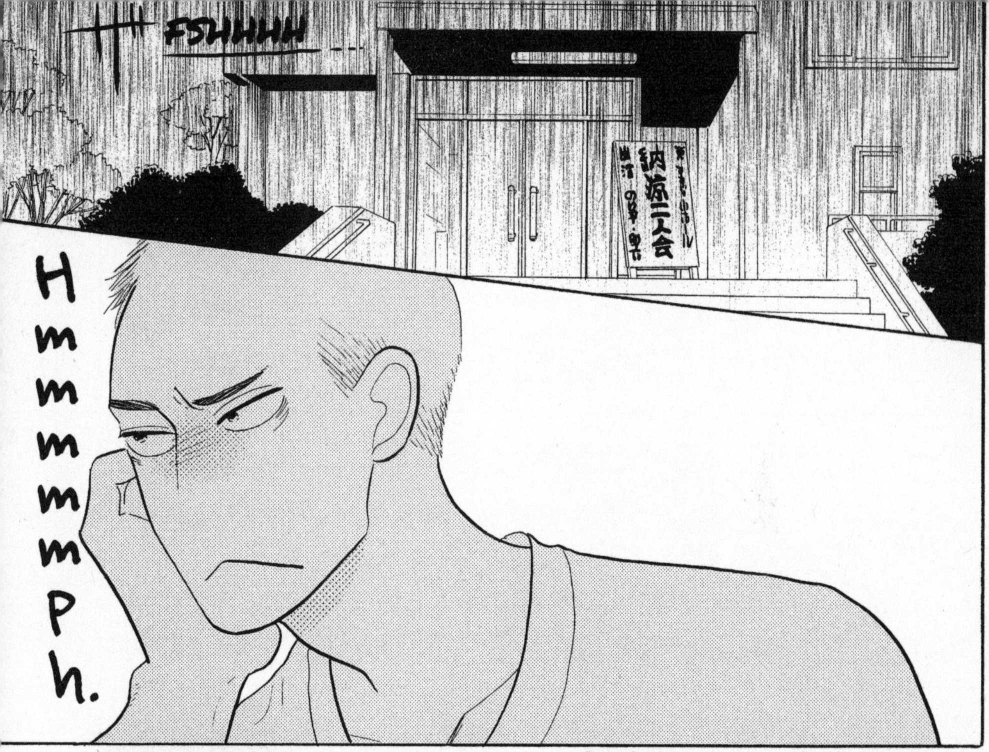
FSHHHH
Hmmmmmmph.

Poster: Special summer program Performing: Norihei, Sukeroku

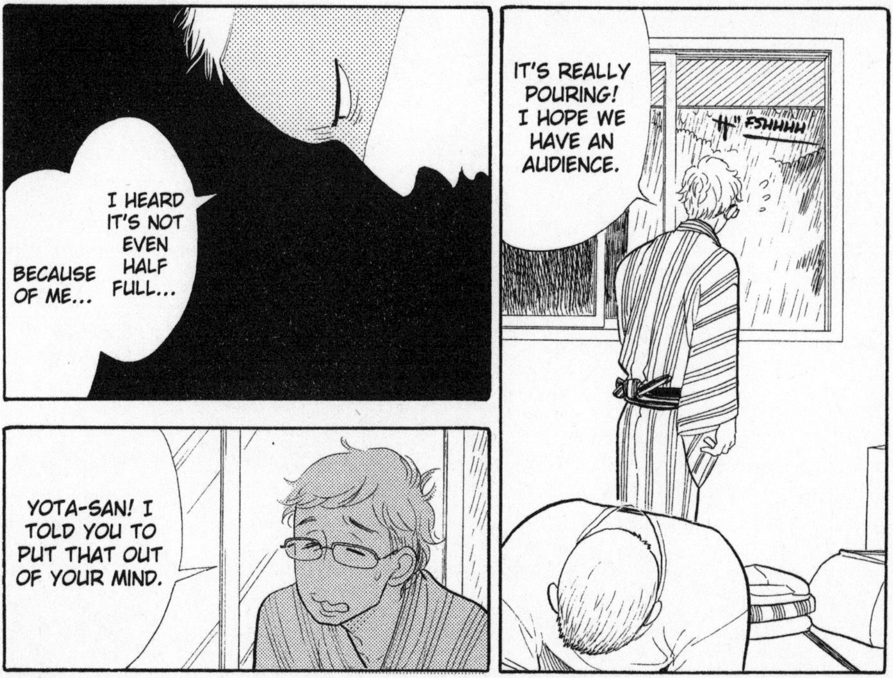
IT'S REALLY POURING! I HOPE WE HAVE AN AUDIENCE.
FSHHHH
I HEARD IT'S NOT EVEN HALF FULL...
BECAUSE OF ME...
YOTA-SAN! I TOLD YOU TO PUT THAT OUT OF YOUR MIND.

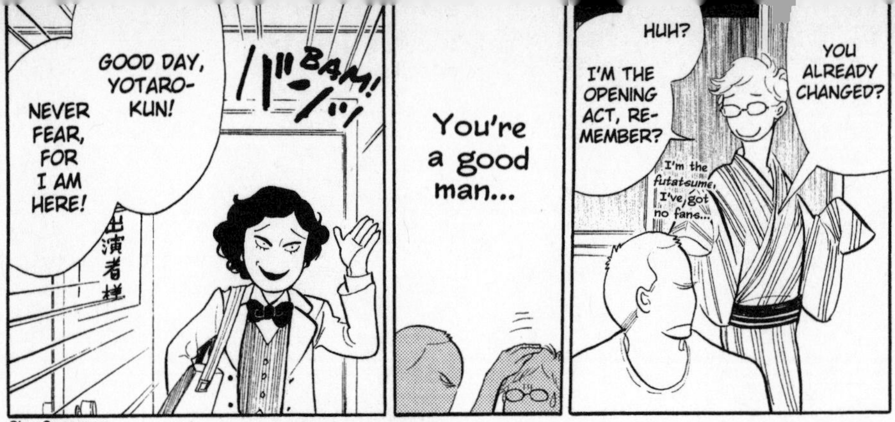
YOU ALREADY CHANGED?
HUH?
I'M THE OPENING ACT, REMEMBER?
I'm the futatsume, I've got no fans...
You're a good man...
BAM!
GOOD DAY, YOTARO-KUN!
NEVER FEAR, FOR I AM HERE!

Sign: Green room

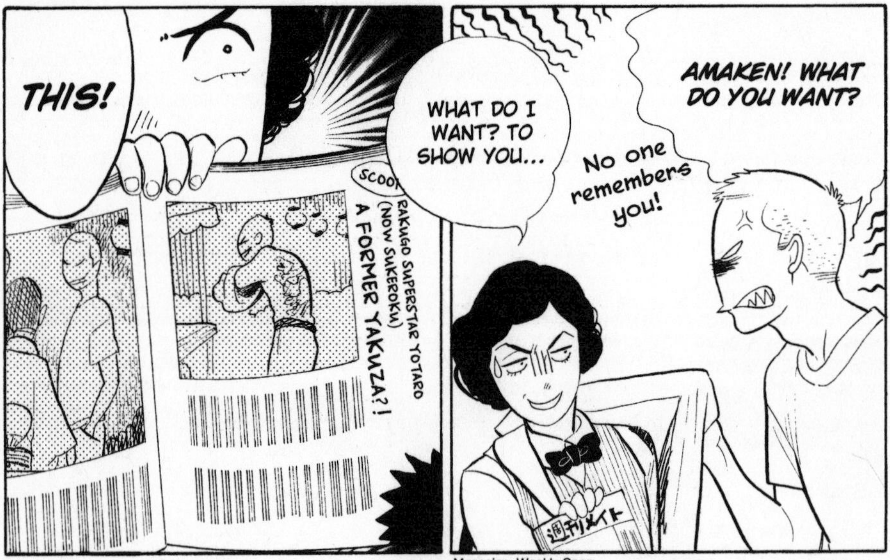
AMAKEN! WHAT DO YOU WANT?
No one remembers you!
WHAT DO I WANT? TO SHOW YOU...
SCOOP
RAKUGO SUPERSTAR YOTARO (NOW SUKEROKU) A FORMER YAKUZA?!
THIS!

Magazine: Weekly Snap

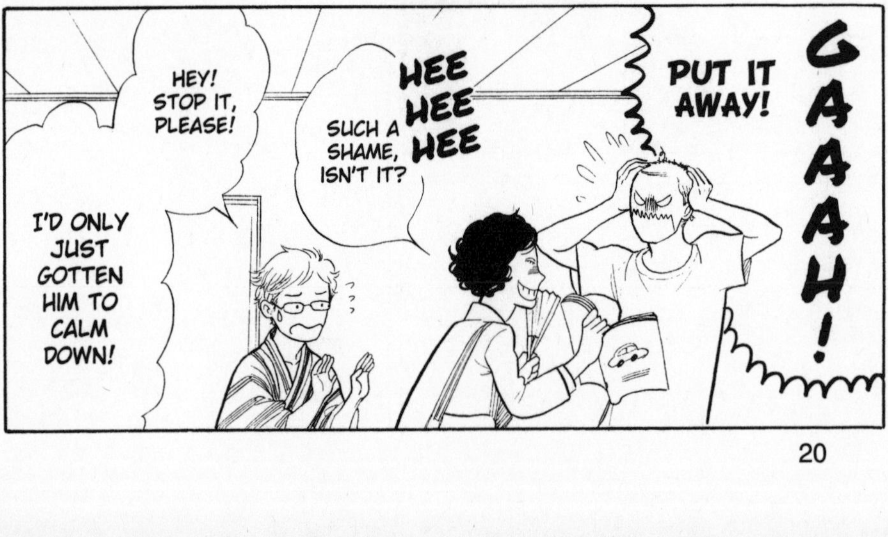
GAAAH!
PUT IT AWAY!
HEE HEE HEE
SUCH A SHAME, ISN'T IT?
HEY! STOP IT, PLEASE!
I'D ONLY JUST GOTTEN HIM TO CALM DOWN!

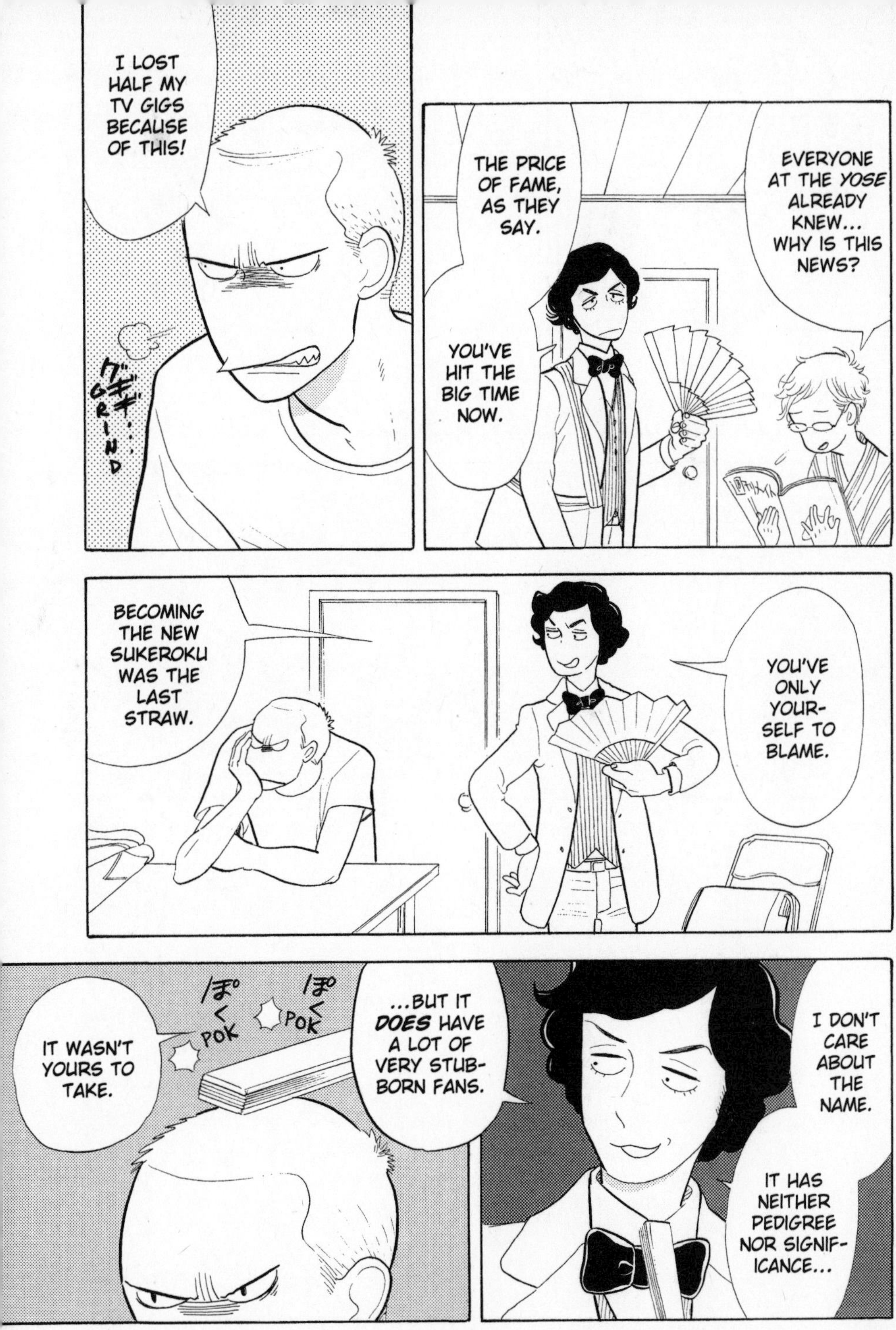
EVERYONE AT THE *YOSE* ALREADY KNEW... WHY IS THIS NEWS?
THE PRICE OF FAME, AS THEY SAY.
YOU'VE HIT THE BIG TIME NOW.
I LOST HALF MY TV GIGS BECAUSE OF THIS!
GRIND
YOU'VE ONLY YOURSELF TO BLAME.
BECOMING THE NEW SUKEROKU WAS THE LAST STRAW.
I DON'T CARE ABOUT THE NAME.
IT HAS NEITHER PEDIGREE NOR SIGNIFICANCE...
...BUT IT **DOES** HAVE A LOT OF VERY STUBBORN FANS.
ぽく POK
ぽく POK
IT WASN'T YOURS TO TAKE.

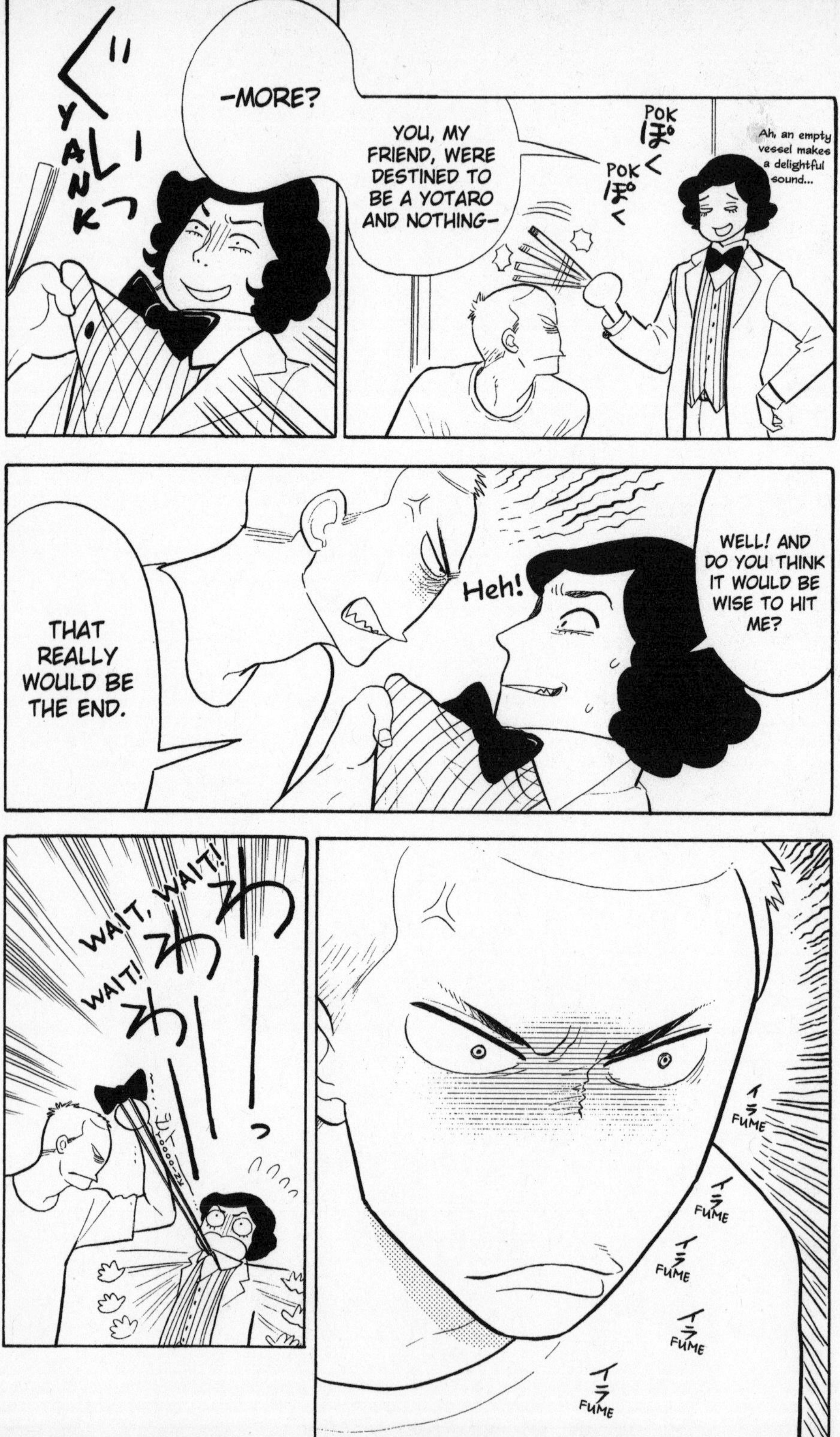

POK ぽく
POK ぽく
Ah, an empty vessel makes a delightful sound...
YOU, MY FRIEND, WERE DESTINED TO BE A YOTARO AND NOTHING-
-MORE?
YANK ぐいっ
WELL! AND DO YOU THINK IT WOULD BE WISE TO HIT ME?
Heh!
THAT REALLY WOULD BE THE END.
イラ FUME
イラ FUME
イラ FUME
イラ FUME
イラ FUME
WAIT, WAIT! WAIT!
わわわーっ

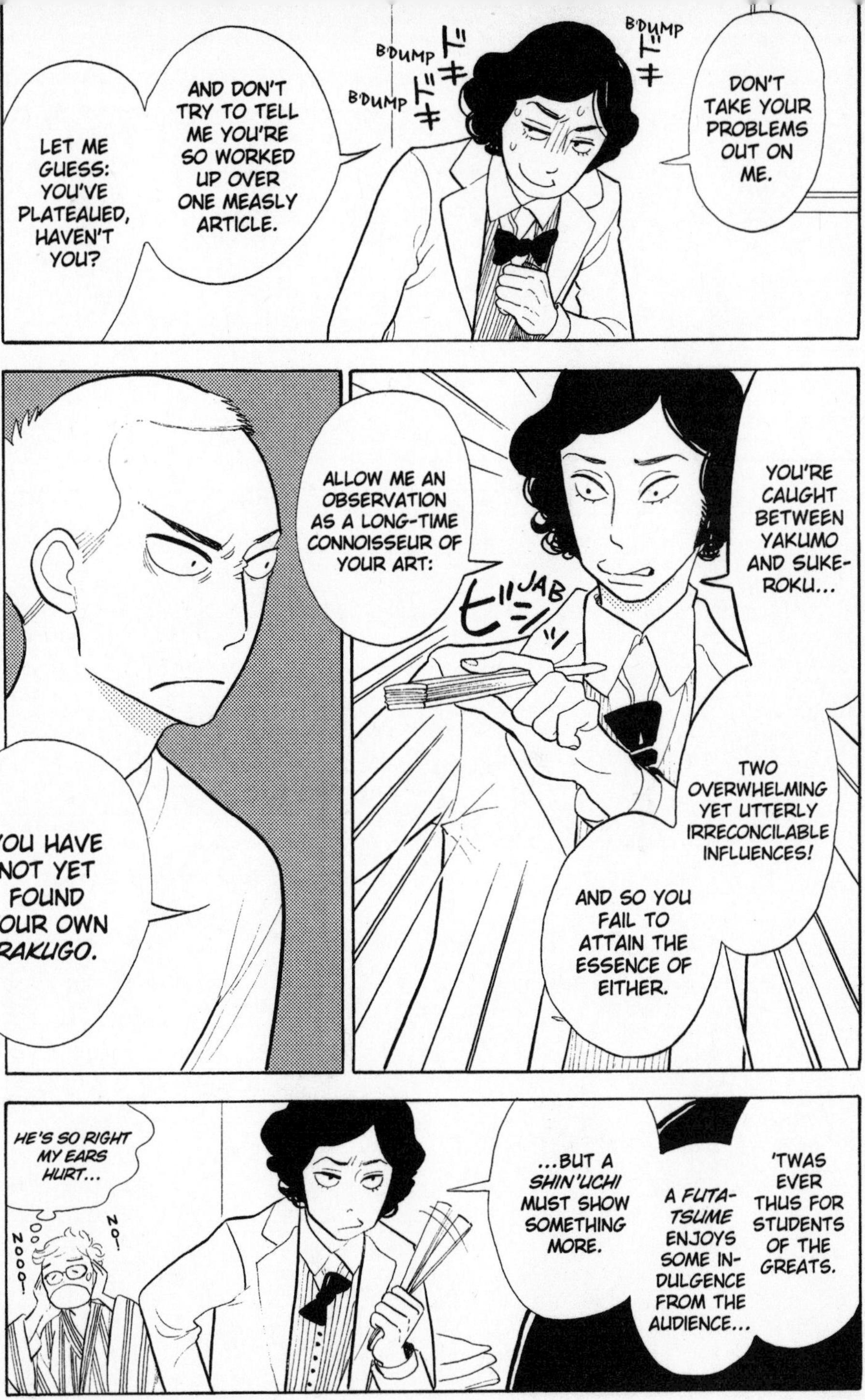
B'DUMP
B'DUMP
B'DUMP
DON'T TAKE YOUR PROBLEMS OUT ON ME.
AND DON'T TRY TO TELL ME YOU'RE SO WORKED UP OVER ONE MEASLY ARTICLE.
LET ME GUESS: YOU'VE PLATEAUED, HAVEN'T YOU?
ALLOW ME AN OBSERVATION AS A LONG-TIME CONNOISSEUR OF YOUR ART:
YOU'RE CAUGHT BETWEEN YAKUMO AND SUKE-ROKU...
JAB
TWO OVERWHELMING YET UTTERLY IRRECONCILABLE INFLUENCES!
AND SO YOU FAIL TO ATTAIN THE ESSENCE OF EITHER.
YOU HAVE NOT YET FOUND YOUR OWN *RAKUGO*.
'TWAS EVER THUS FOR STUDENTS OF THE GREATS.
A *FUTATSUME* ENJOYS SOME INDULGENCE FROM THE AUDIENCE...
...BUT A *SHIN'UCHI* MUST SHOW SOMETHING MORE.
HE'S SO RIGHT MY EARS HURT...
NO!
NOOO!

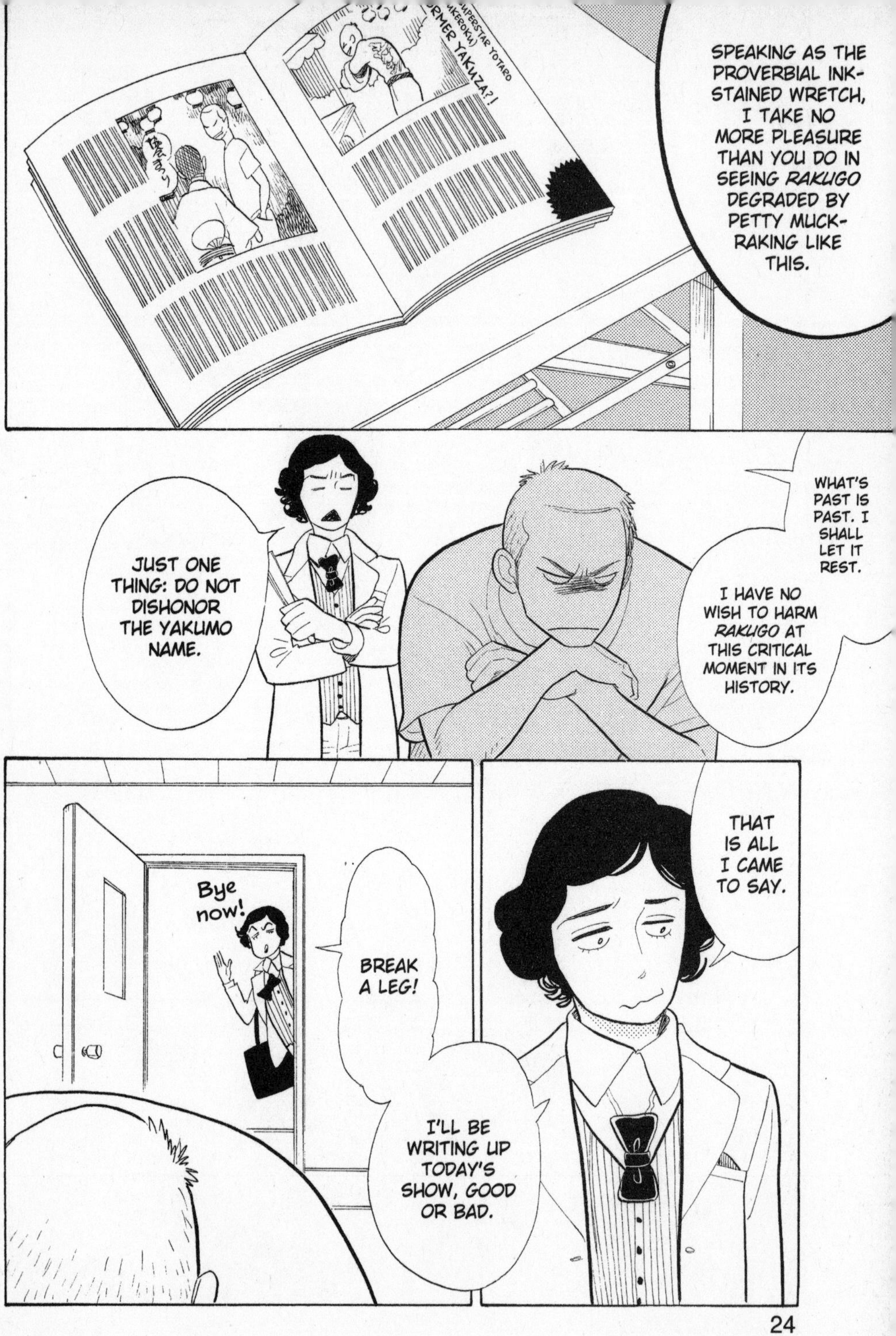
SUPERSTAR YOTARO
SPEAKING AS THE PROVERBIAL INK-STAINED WRETCH, I TAKE NO MORE PLEASURE THAN YOU DO IN SEEING *RAKUGO* DEGRADED BY PETTY MUCK-RAKING LIKE THIS.
WHAT'S PAST IS PAST. I SHALL LET IT REST.
I HAVE NO WISH TO HARM *RAKUGO* AT THIS CRITICAL MOMENT IN ITS HISTORY.
JUST ONE THING: DO NOT DISHONOR THE YAKUMO NAME.
THAT IS ALL I CAME TO SAY.
I'LL BE WRITING UP TODAY'S SHOW, GOOD OR BAD.
BREAK A LEG!
Bye now!

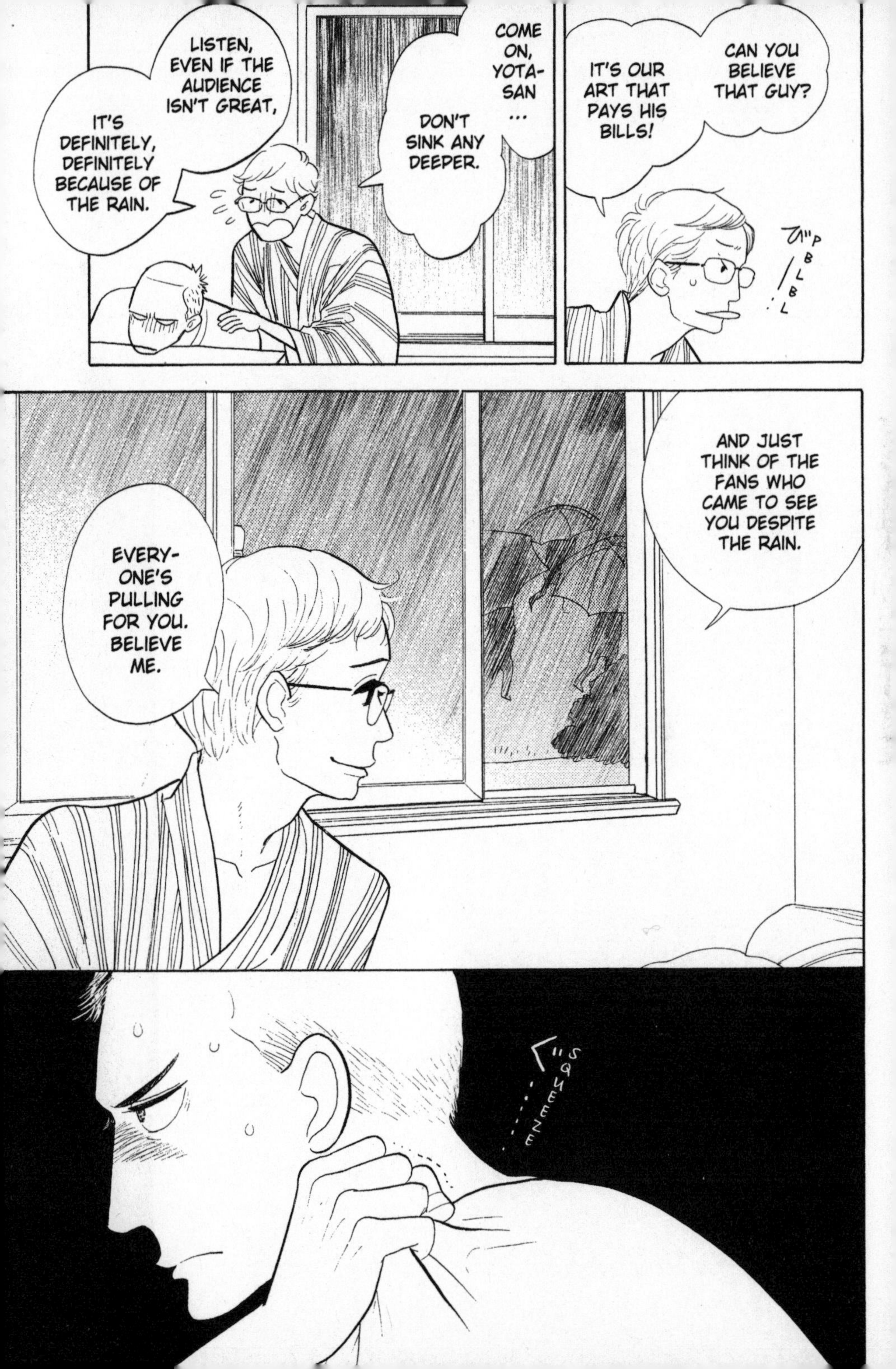
CAN YOU BELIEVE THAT GUY?
IT'S OUR ART THAT PAYS HIS BILLS!
PBLBL
COME ON, YOTA-SAN...
DON'T SINK ANY DEEPER.
LISTEN, EVEN IF THE AUDIENCE ISN'T GREAT,
IT'S DEFINITELY, DEFINITELY BECAUSE OF THE RAIN.
AND JUST THINK OF THE FANS WHO CAME TO SEE YOU DESPITE THE RAIN.
EVERY-ONE'S PULLING FOR YOU. BELIEVE ME.
SQUEEZE...

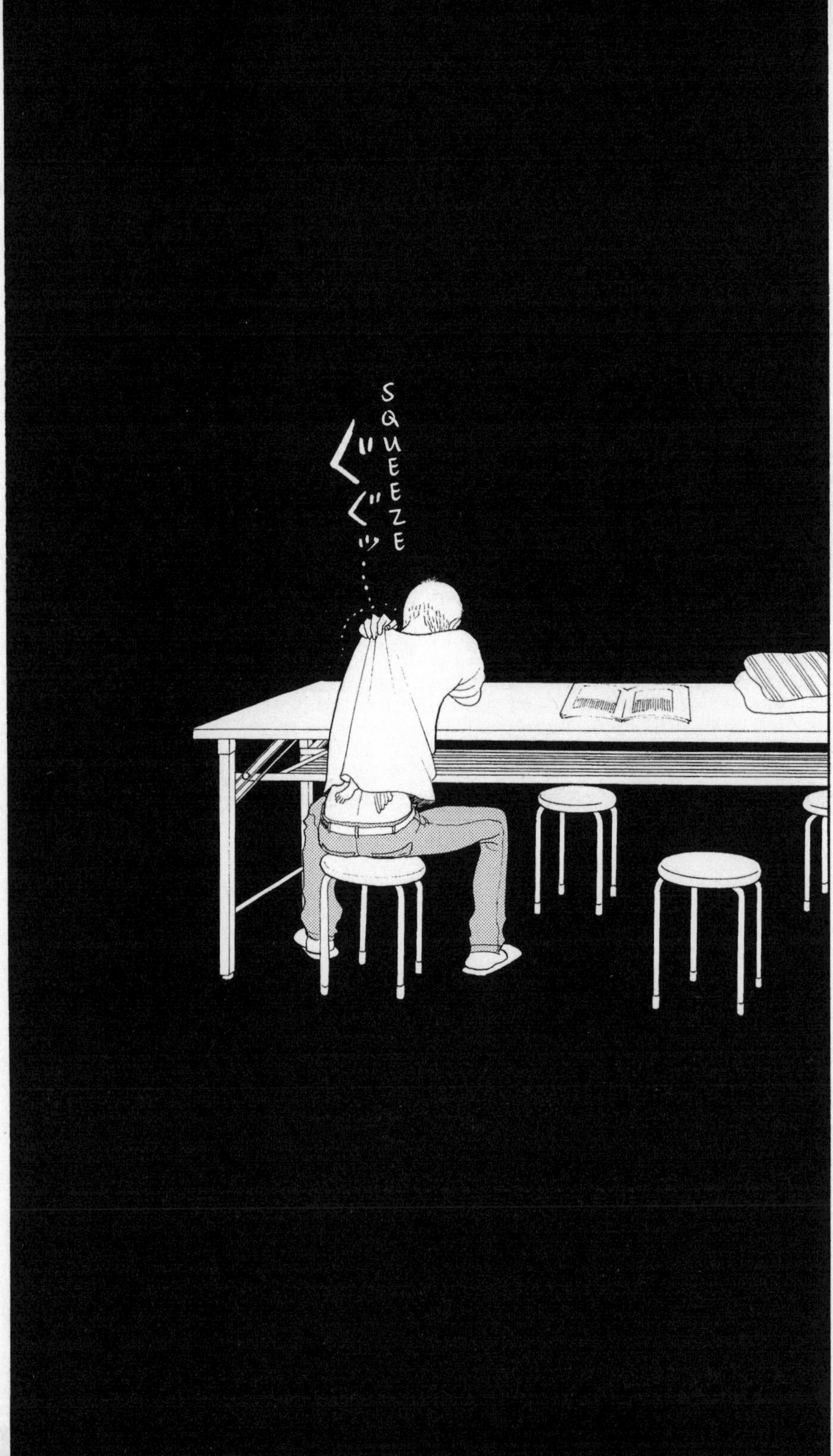
SQUEEZE
ぐぐッ…

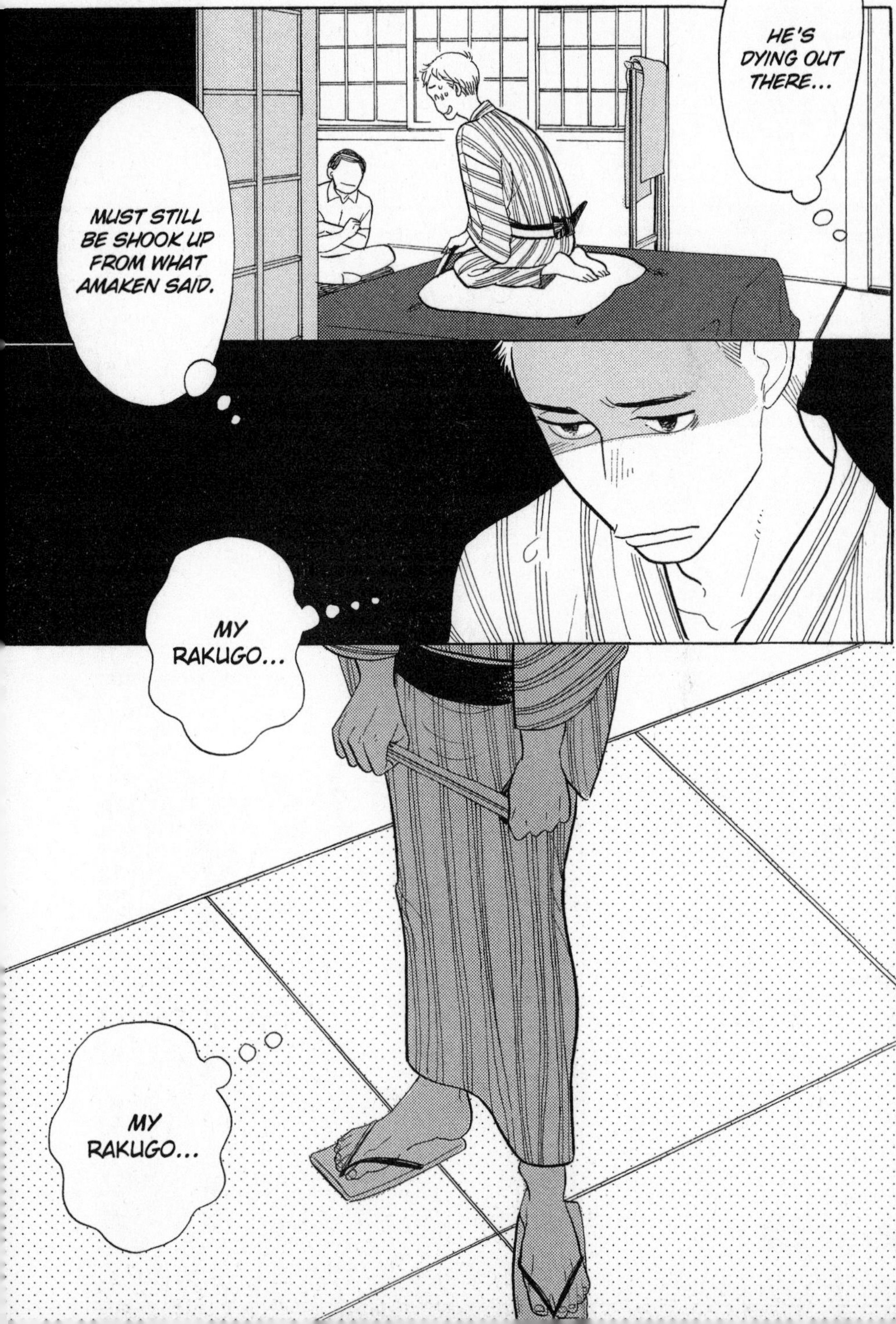
HE'S DYING OUT THERE...
MUST STILL BE SHOOK UP FROM WHAT AMAKEN SAID.
MY RAKUGO...
MY RAKUGO...

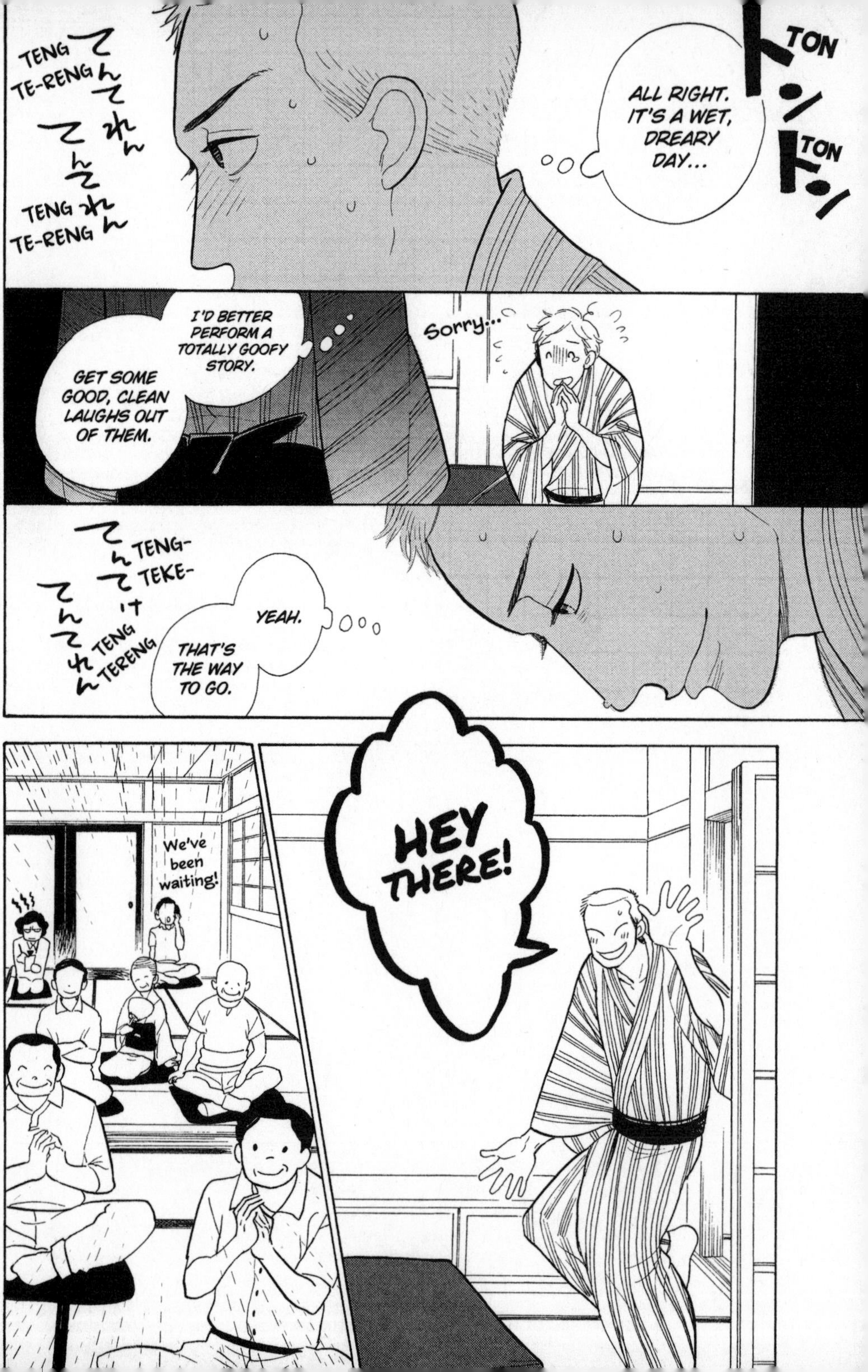

トン TON
トン TON
ALL RIGHT. IT'S A WET, DREARY DAY...
てんてれん TENG TE-RENG
てんてれん TENG TE-RENG
Sorry...
I'D BETTER PERFORM A TOTALLY GOOFY STORY.
GET SOME GOOD, CLEAN LAUGHS OUT OF THEM.
YEAH.
THAT'S THE WAY TO GO.
てんてけ TENG-TEKE-
てんてれん TENG TERENG
HEY THERE!
We've been waiting!

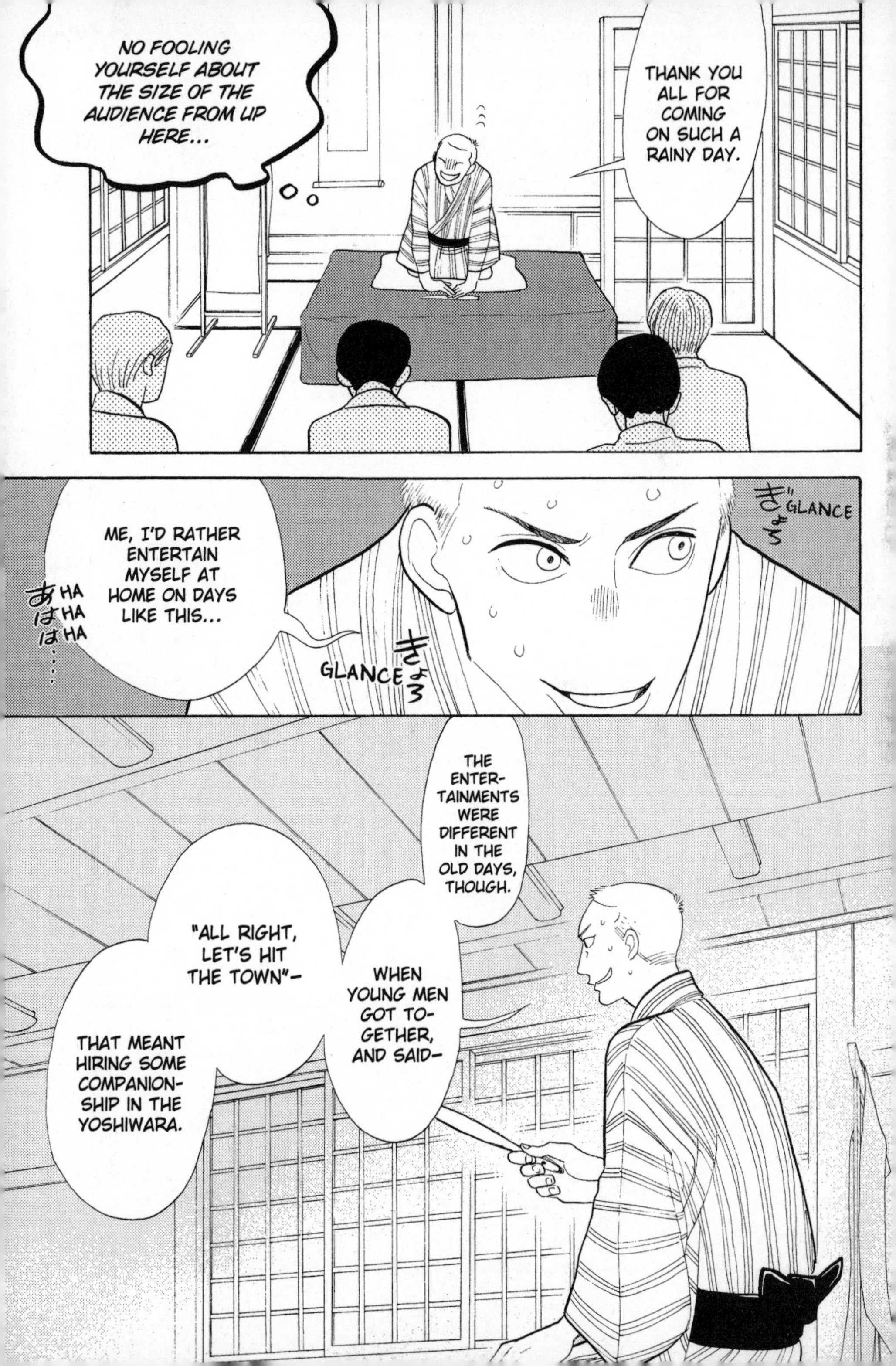
THANK YOU ALL FOR COMING ON SUCH A RAINY DAY.
NO FOOLING YOURSELF ABOUT THE SIZE OF THE AUDIENCE FROM UP HERE...
ぎょろ GLANCE
ME, I'D RATHER ENTERTAIN MYSELF AT HOME ON DAYS LIKE THIS...
GLANCE きょろ
あはは… HA HA HA
THE ENTER-TAINMENTS WERE DIFFERENT IN THE OLD DAYS, THOUGH.
WHEN YOUNG MEN GOT TO-GETHER, AND SAID-
"ALL RIGHT, LET'S HIT THE TOWN"-
THAT MEANT HIRING SOME COMPANION-SHIP IN THE YOSHIWARA.

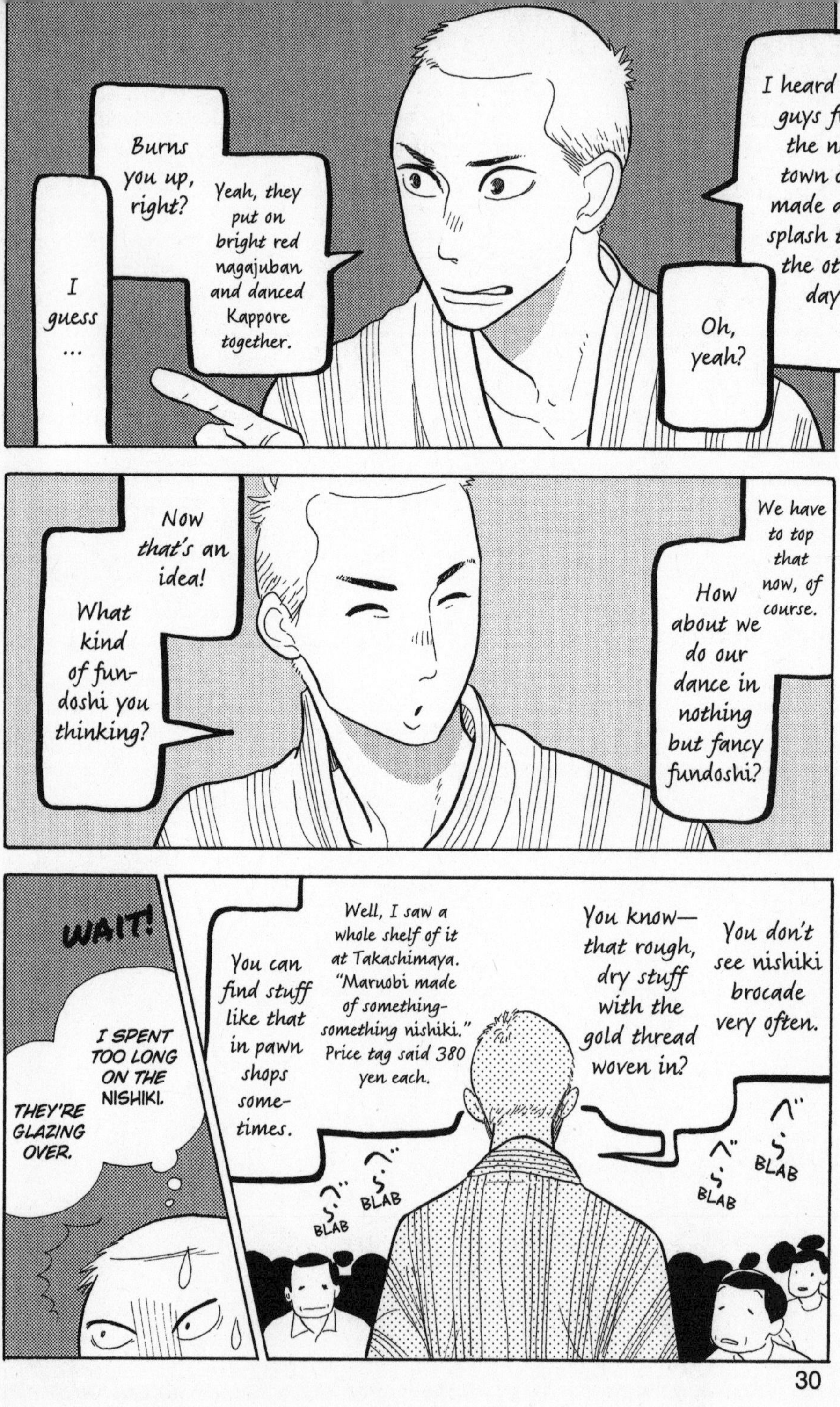
I heard some guys from the next town over made a big splash there the other day.
Oh, yeah?
Yeah, they put on bright red nagajuban and danced Kappore together.
Burns you up, right?
I guess ...
We have to top that now, of course.
How about we do our dance in nothing but fancy fundoshi?
Now that's an idea!
What kind of fun-doshi you thinking?
You don't see nishiki brocade very often.
You know— that rough, dry stuff with the gold thread woven in?
Well, I saw a whole shelf of it at Takashimaya. "Maruobi made of something-something nishiki." Price tag said 380 yen each.
You can find stuff like that in pawn shops some-times.
BLAB
BLAB
BLAB
BLAB
WAIT!
I SPENT TOO LONG ON THE NISHIKI.
THEY'RE GLAZING OVER.

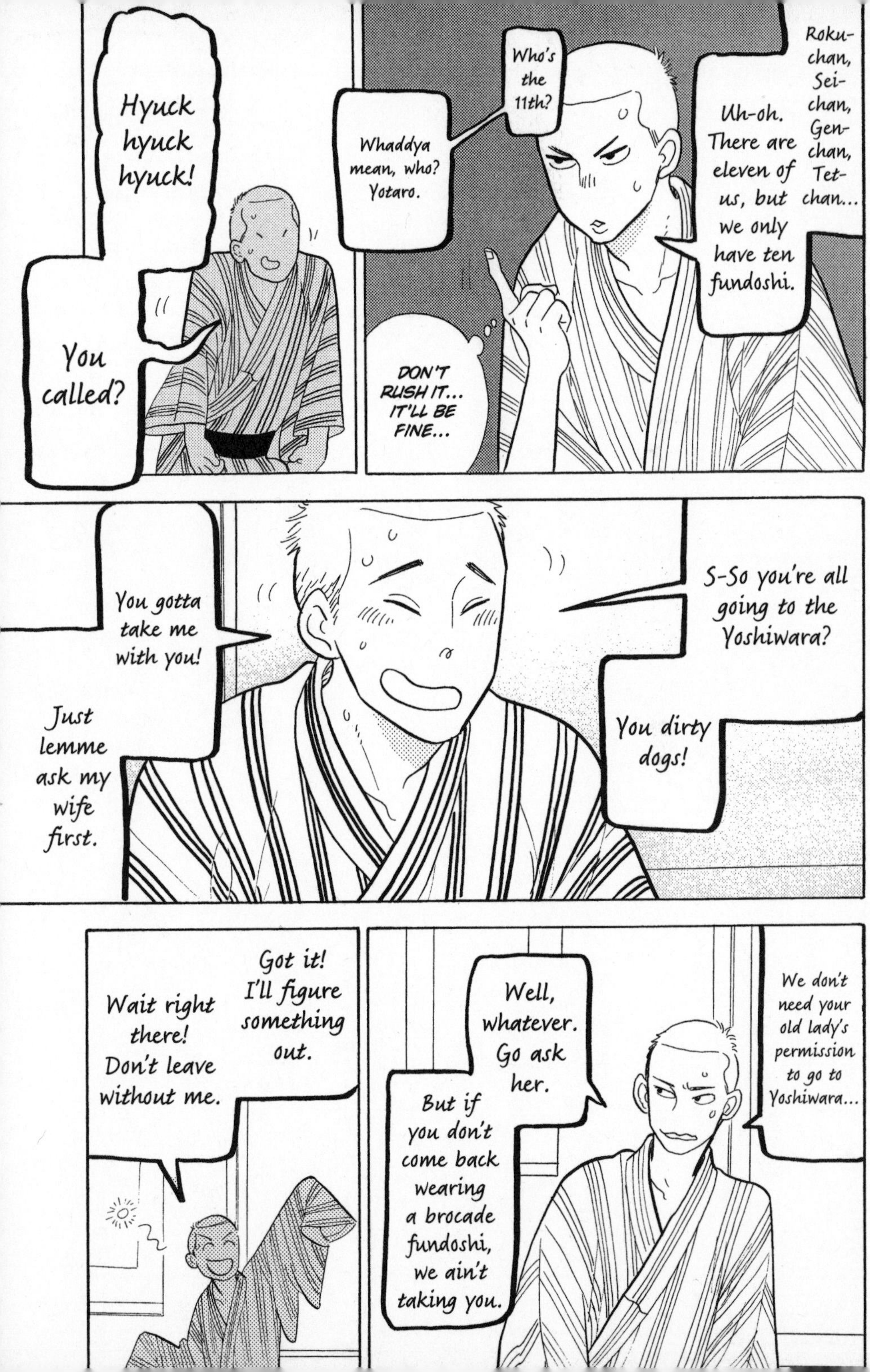
Roku-chan, Sei-chan, Gen-chan, Tet-chan...
Uh-oh. There are eleven of us, but we only have ten fundoshi.
Who's the 11th?
Whaddya mean, who? Yotaro.
DON'T RUSH IT... IT'LL BE FINE...
Hyuck hyuck hyuck!
You called?
S-So you're all going to the Yoshiwara?
You dirty dogs!
You gotta take me with you!
Just lemme ask my wife first.
We don't need your old lady's permission to go to Yoshiwara...
Well, whatever. Go ask her.
But if you don't come back wearing a brocade fundoshi, we ain't taking you.
Got it! I'll figure something out.
Wait right there! Don't leave without me.

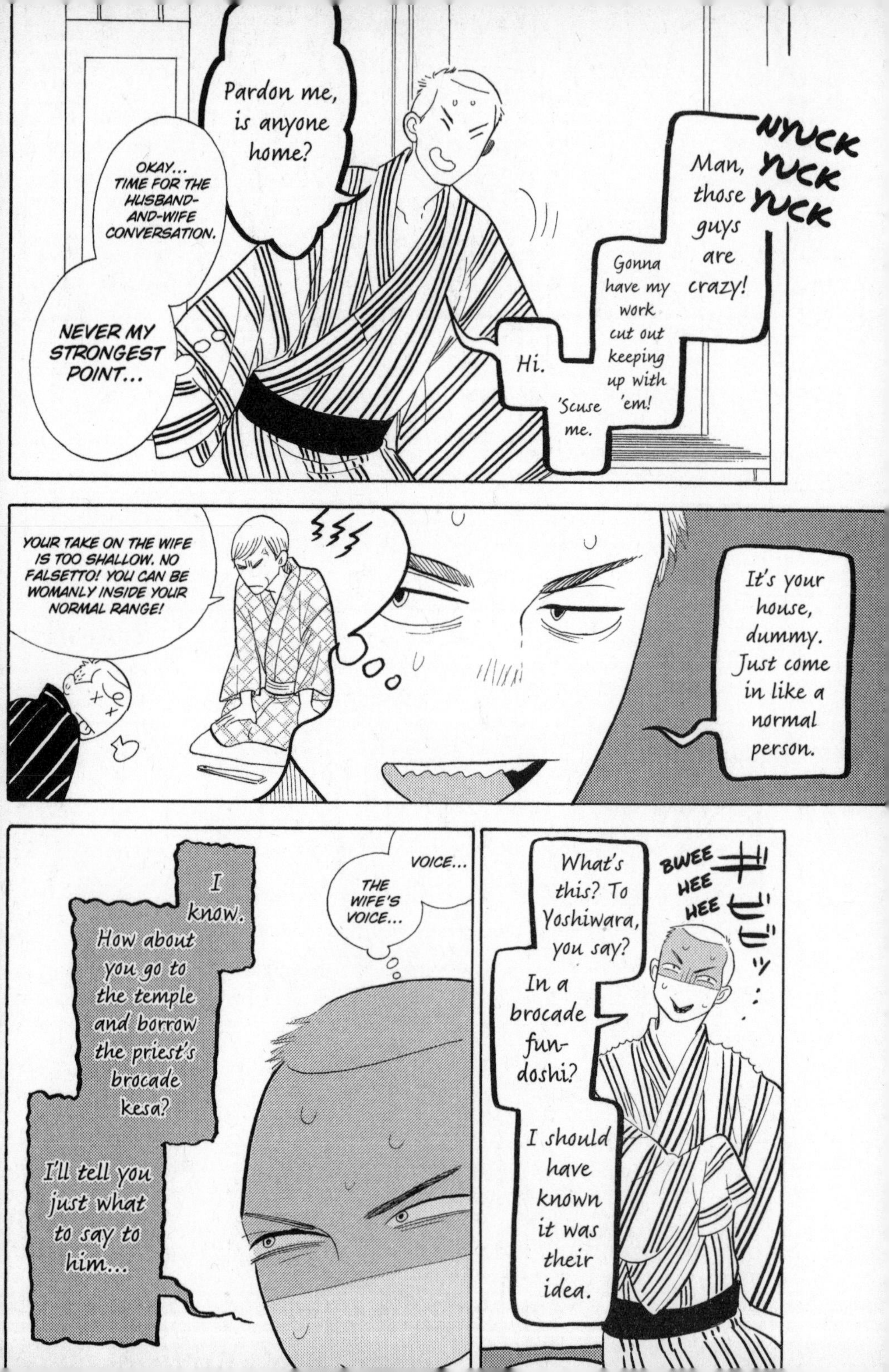
NYUCK YUCK YUCK
Man, those guys are crazy!
Gonna have my work cut out keeping up with 'em!
Hi. 'Scuse me.
Pardon me, is anyone home?
OKAY... TIME FOR THE HUSBAND-AND-WIFE CONVERSATION.
NEVER MY STRONGEST POINT...
It's your house, dummy. Just come in like a normal person.
YOUR TAKE ON THE WIFE IS TOO SHALLOW. NO FALSETTO! YOU CAN BE WOMANLY INSIDE YOUR NORMAL RANGE!
BWEE HEE HEE
What's this? To Yoshiwara, you say?
In a brocade fun-doshi?
I should have known it was their idea.
VOICE...
THE WIFE'S VOICE...
I know. How about you go to the temple and borrow the priest's brocade kesa?
I'll tell you just what to say to him...

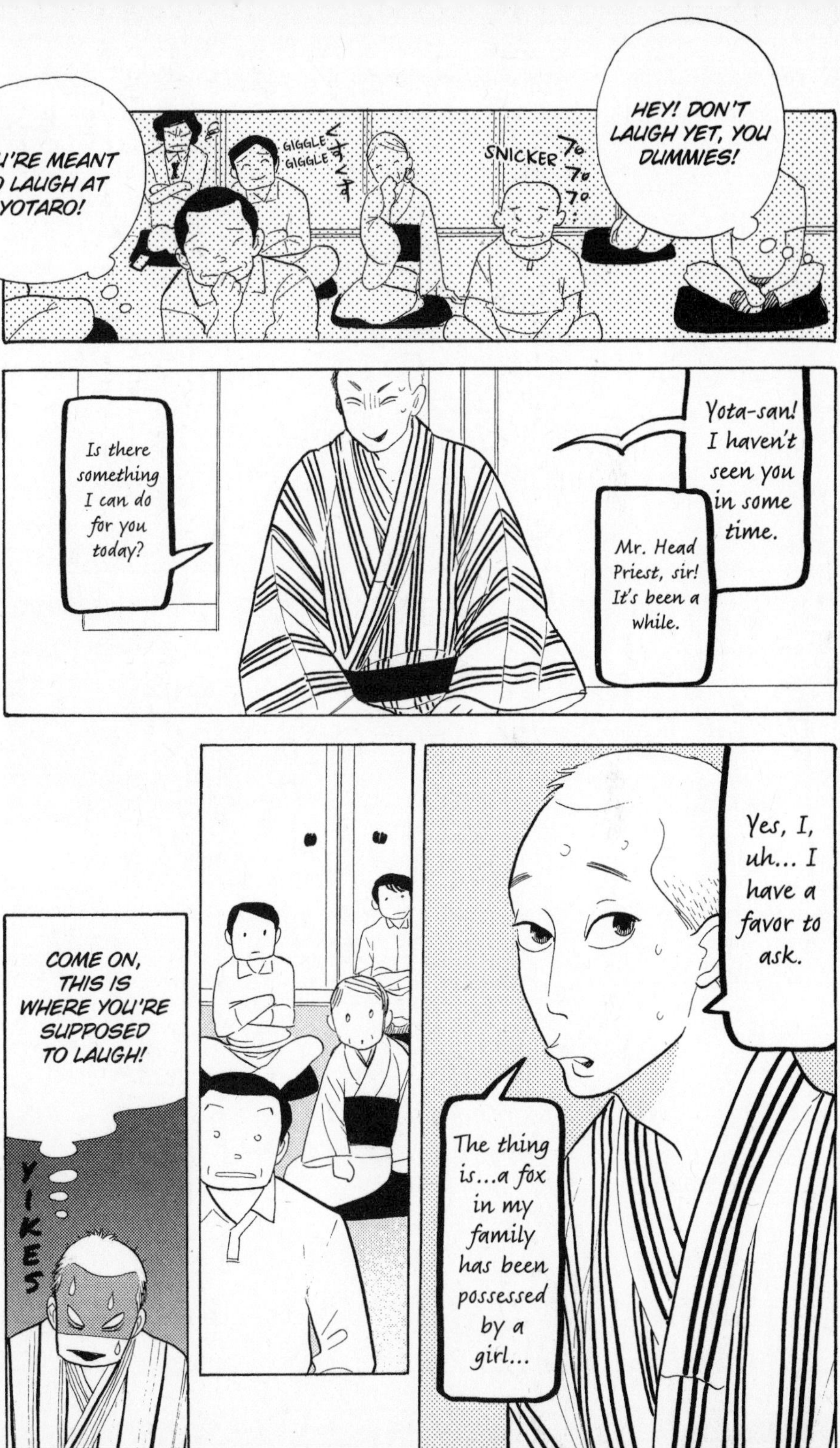
HEY! DON'T LAUGH YET, YOU DUMMIES!
SNICKER
GIGGLE GIGGLE
くすくす
YOU'RE MEANT TO LAUGH AT YOTARO!
Yota-san! I haven't seen you in some time.
Mr. Head Priest, sir! It's been a while.
Is there something I can do for you today?
Yes, I, uh... I have a favor to ask.
The thing is...a fox in my family has been possessed by a girl...
COME ON, THIS IS WHERE YOU'RE SUPPOSED TO LAUGH!
YIKES

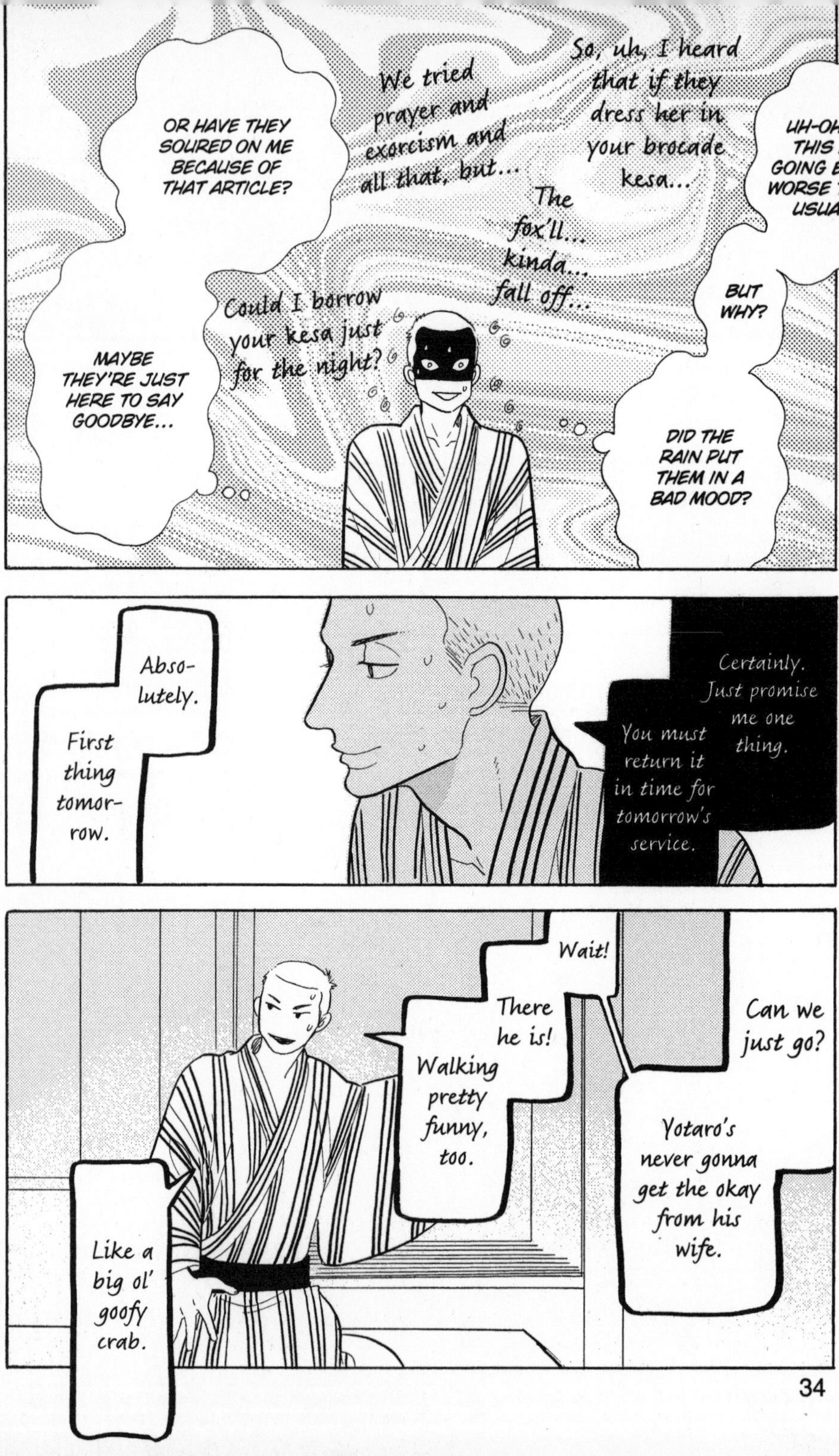
UH-OH... THIS IS GOING EVEN WORSE THAN USUAL.
So, uh, I heard that if they dress her in your brocade kesa...
We tried prayer and exorcism and all that, but...
The fox'll... kinda... fall off...
Could I borrow your kesa just for the night?
OR HAVE THEY SOURED ON ME BECAUSE OF THAT ARTICLE?
BUT WHY?
DID THE RAIN PUT THEM IN A BAD MOOD?
MAYBE THEY'RE JUST HERE TO SAY GOODBYE...
Certainly. Just promise me one thing.
You must return it in time for tomorrow's service.
Abso-lutely.
First thing tomor-row.
Can we just go?
Yotaro's never gonna get the okay from his wife.
Wait!
There he is!
Walking pretty funny, too.
Like a big ol' goofy crab.

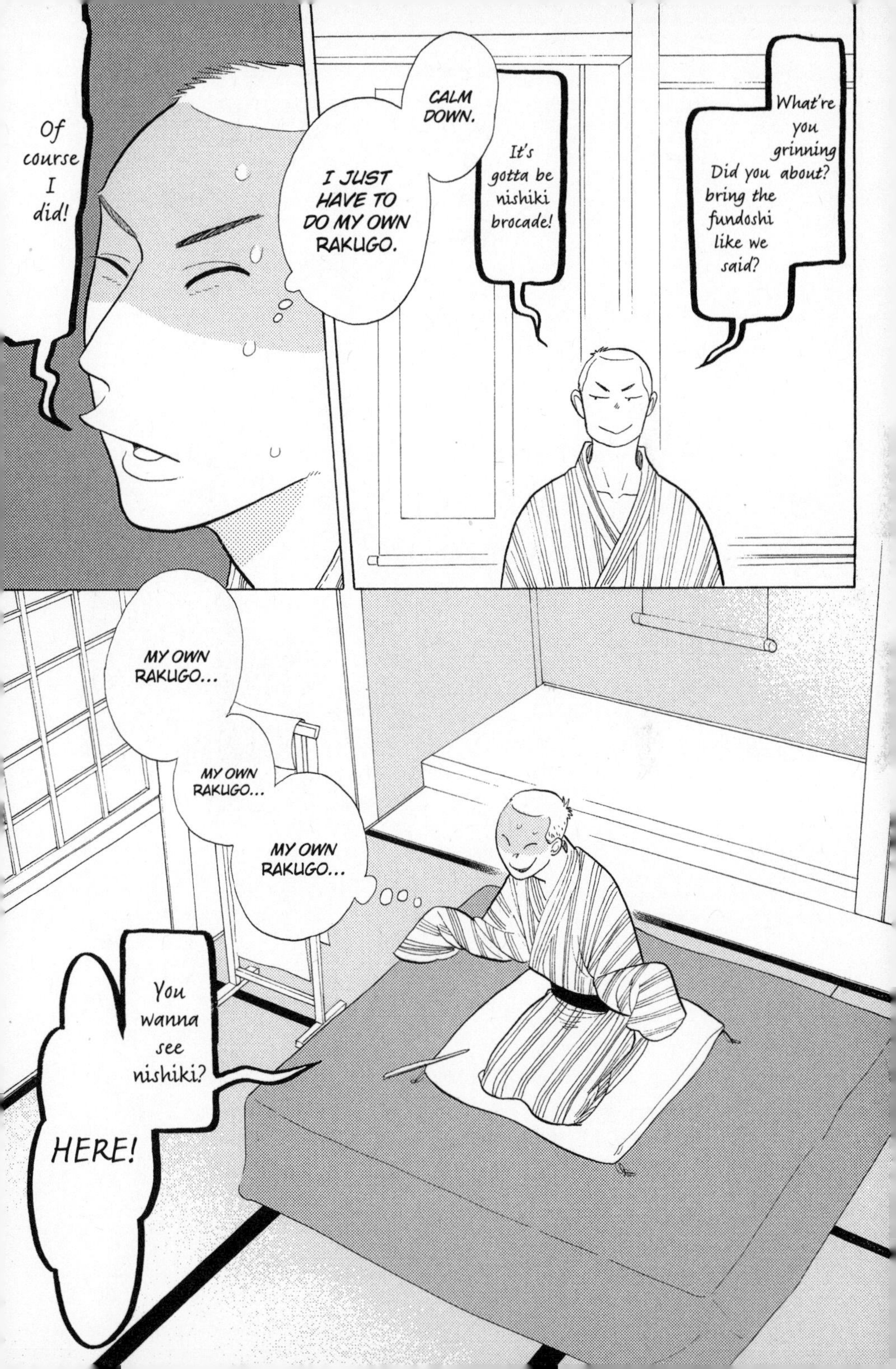

What're you grinning about?
Did you bring the fundoshi like we said?
It's gotta be nishiki brocade!
CALM DOWN.
I JUST HAVE TO DO MY OWN RAKUGO.
Of course I did!
MY OWN RAKUGO...
MY OWN RAKUGO...
MY OWN RAKUGO...
You wanna see nishiki?
HERE!

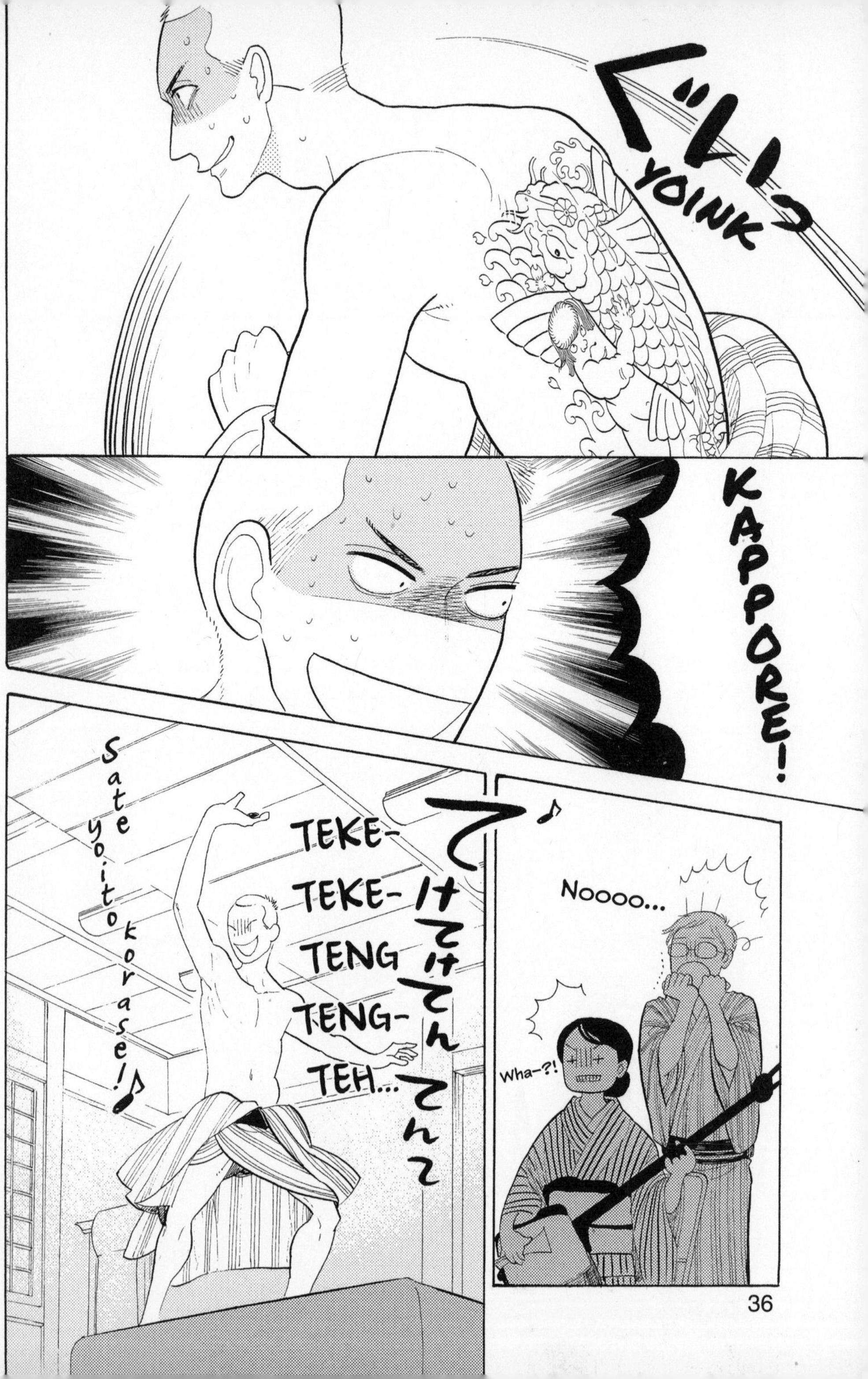
ぐいっ
YOINK
KAPPORE!
Noooo...
Wha-?!
TEKE-TEKE-TENG TENG-TEH...
てけてけてんてん
Sate yo-ito korase!♪

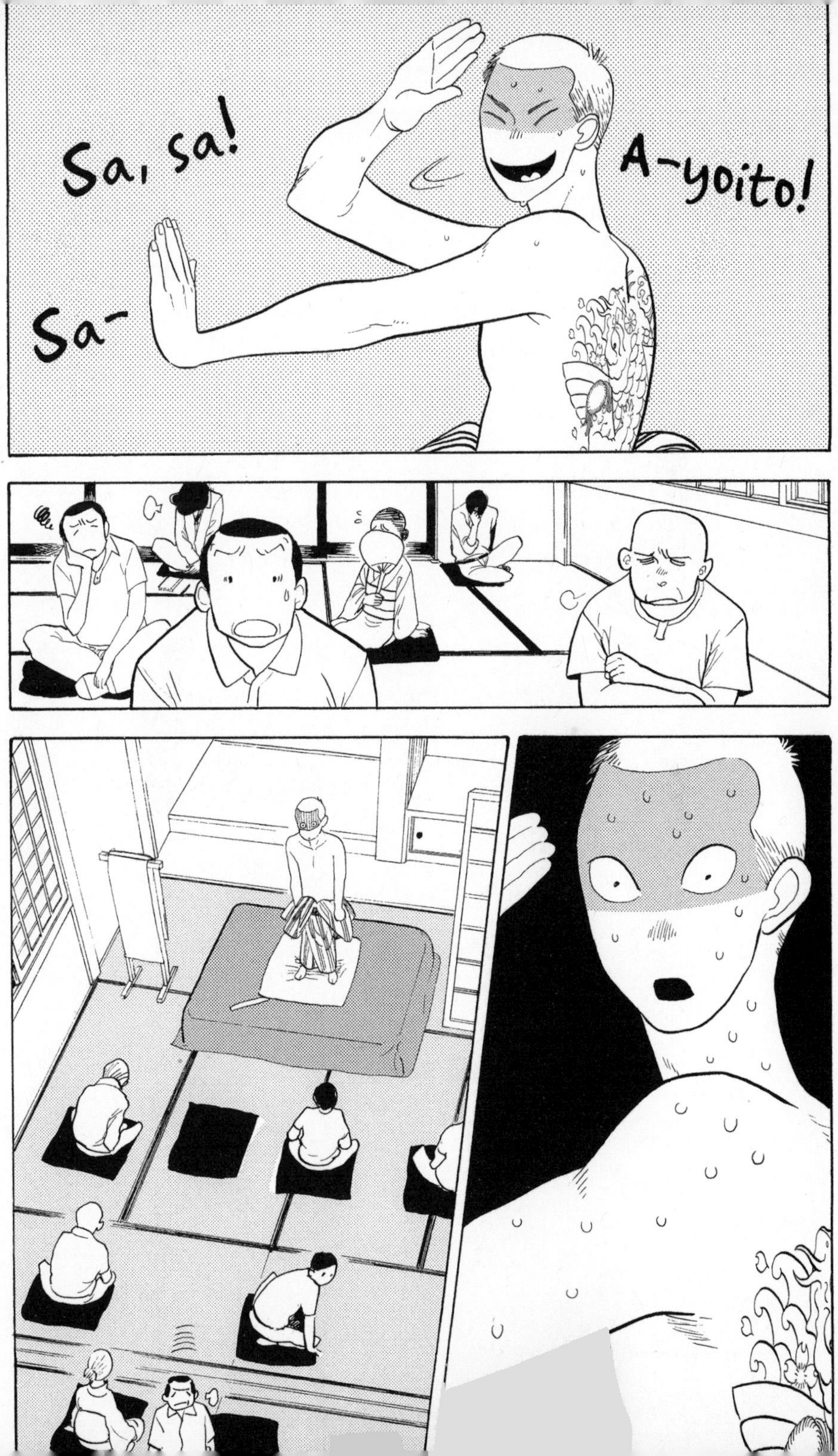
A-yoito!
Sa, sa!
Sa-

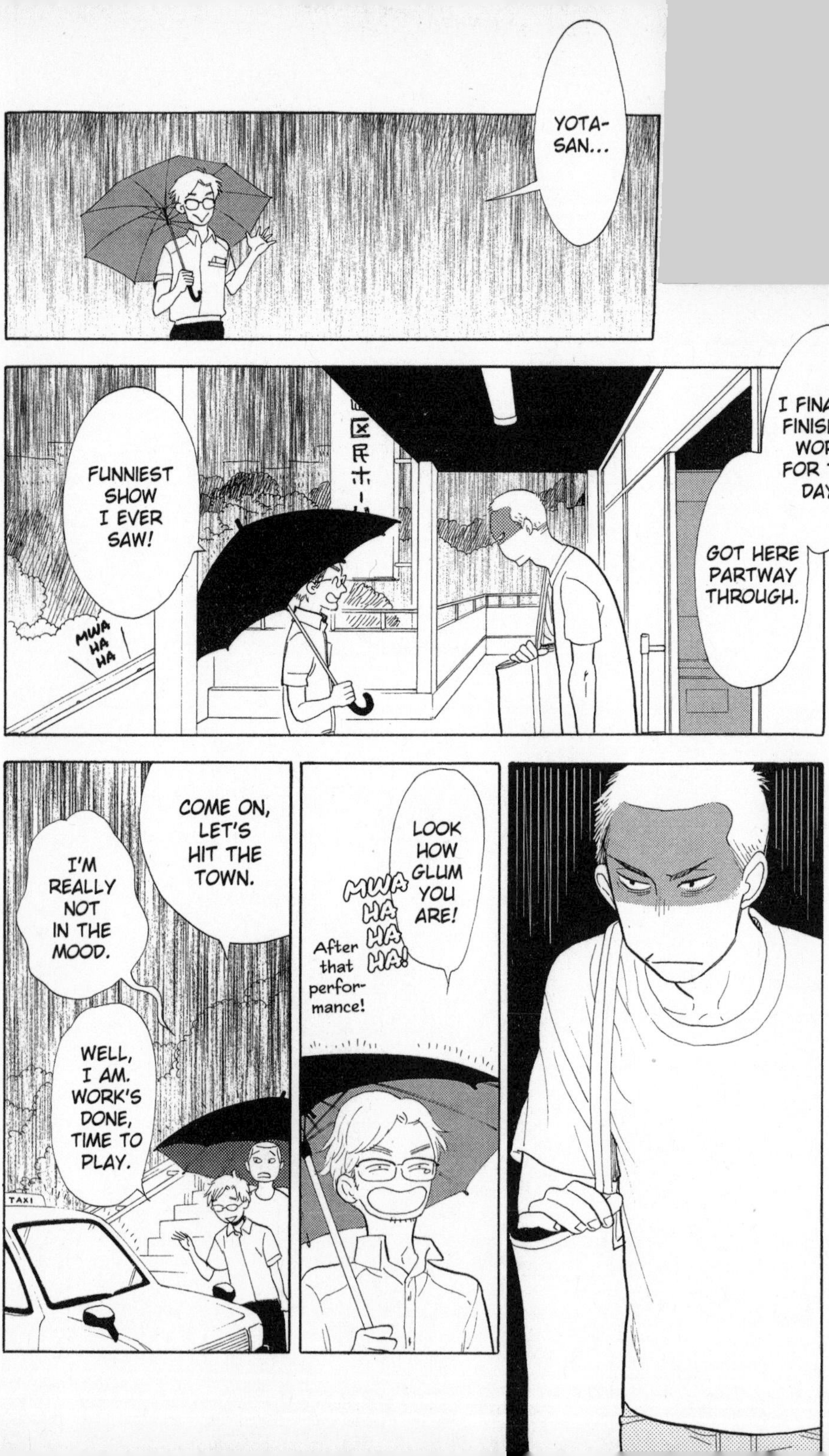
YOTA-SAN...
I FINALLY FINISHED WORK FOR THE DAY.
GOT HERE PARTWAY THROUGH.
FUNNIEST SHOW I EVER SAW!
MWA HA HA
LOOK HOW GLUM YOU ARE!
MWA HA HA HA!
After that performance!
COME ON, LET'S HIT THE TOWN.
I'M REALLY NOT IN THE MOOD.
WELL, I AM. WORK'S DONE, TIME TO PLAY.
TAXI

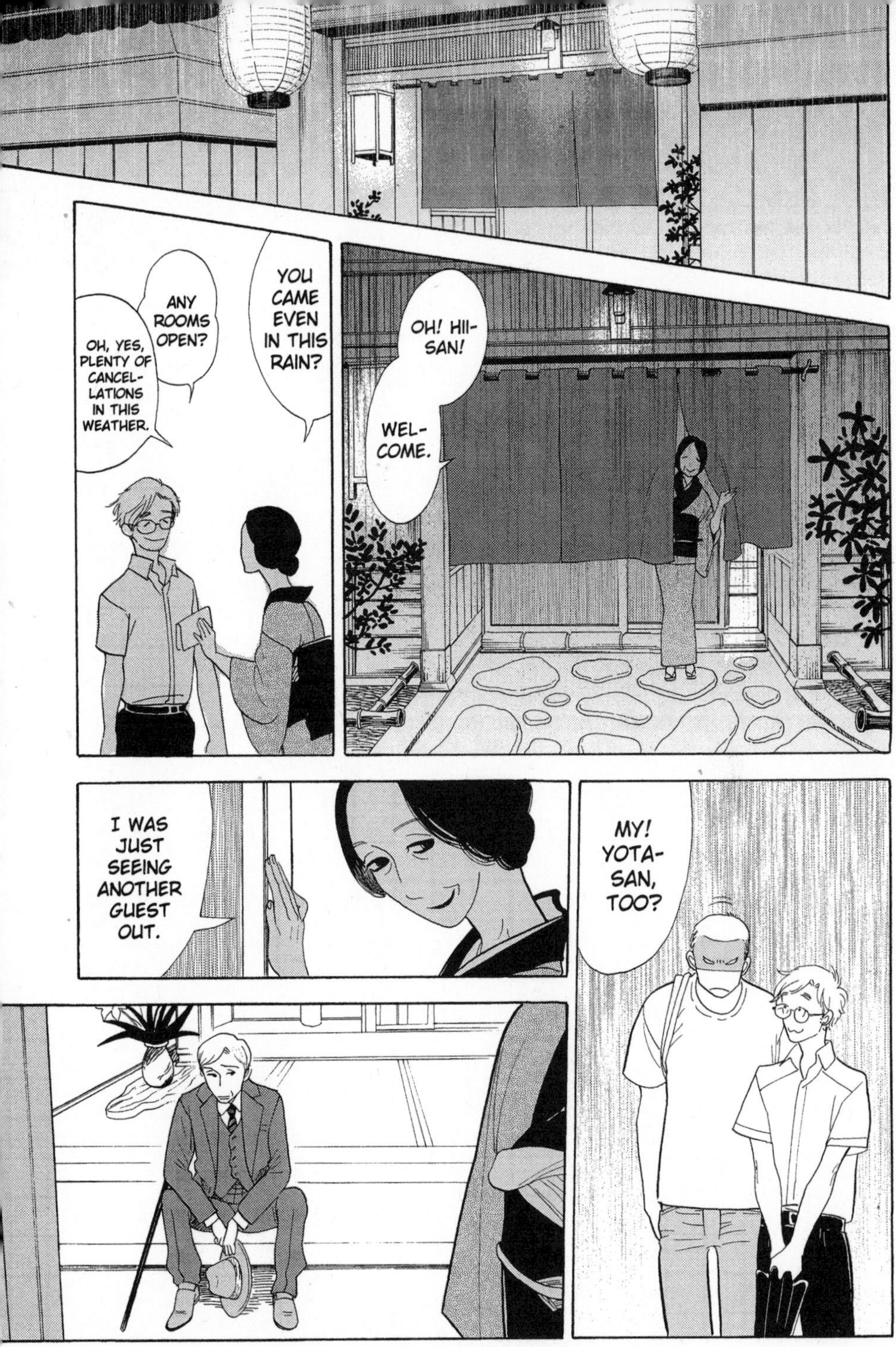
OH! HII-SAN!
WELCOME.
YOU CAME EVEN IN THIS RAIN?
ANY ROOMS OPEN?
OH, YES, PLENTY OF CANCEL-LATIONS IN THIS WEATHER.
MY! YOTA-SAN, TOO?
I WAS JUST SEEING ANOTHER GUEST OUT.

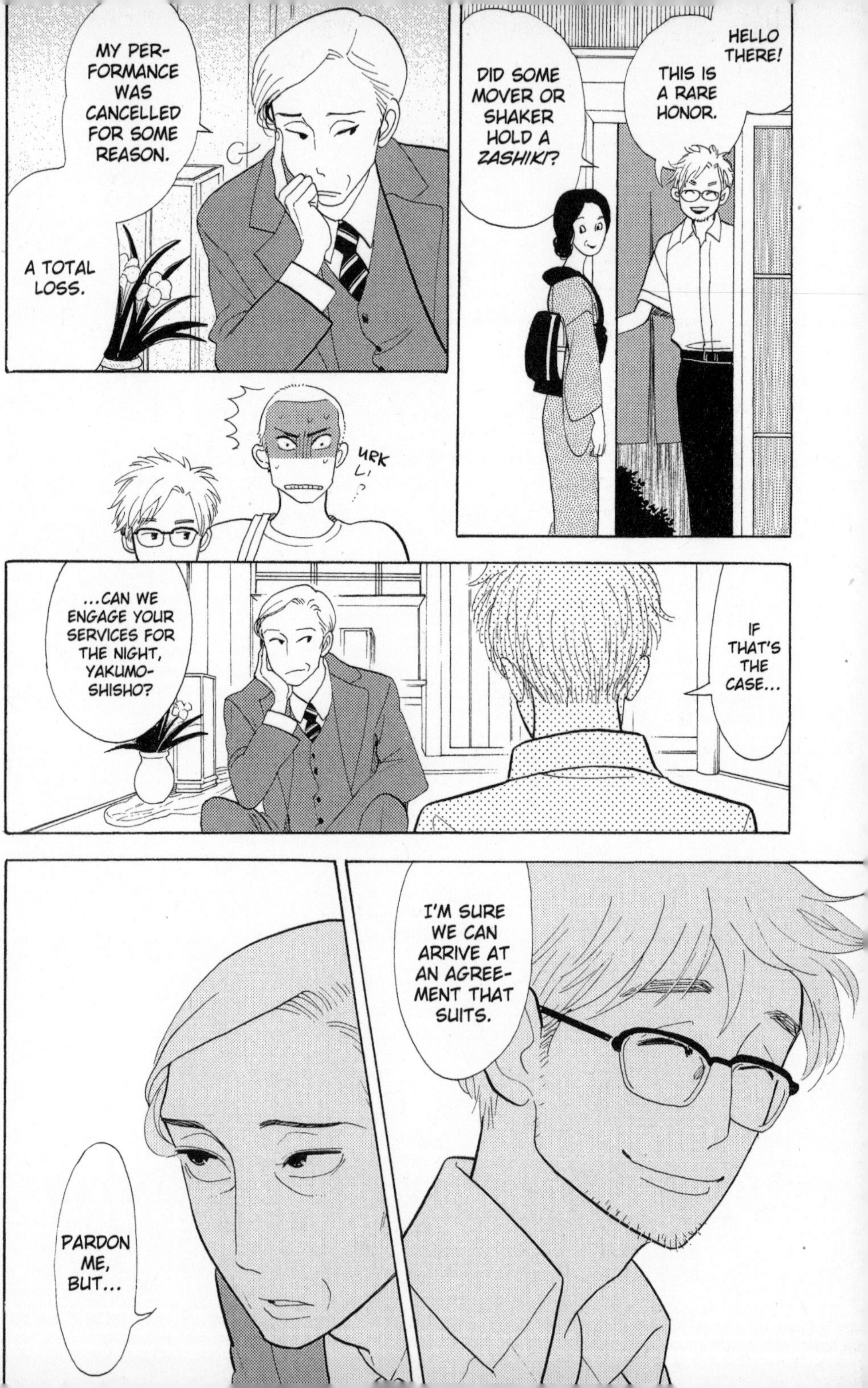
HELLO THERE!
THIS IS A RARE HONOR.
DID SOME MOVER OR SHAKER HOLD A *ZASHIKI*?
MY PERFORMANCE WAS CANCELLED FOR SOME REASON.
A TOTAL LOSS.
URK
IF THAT'S THE CASE...
...CAN WE ENGAGE YOUR SERVICES FOR THE NIGHT, YAKUMO-SHISHO?
I'M SURE WE CAN ARRIVE AT AN AGREEMENT THAT SUITS.
PARDON ME, BUT...

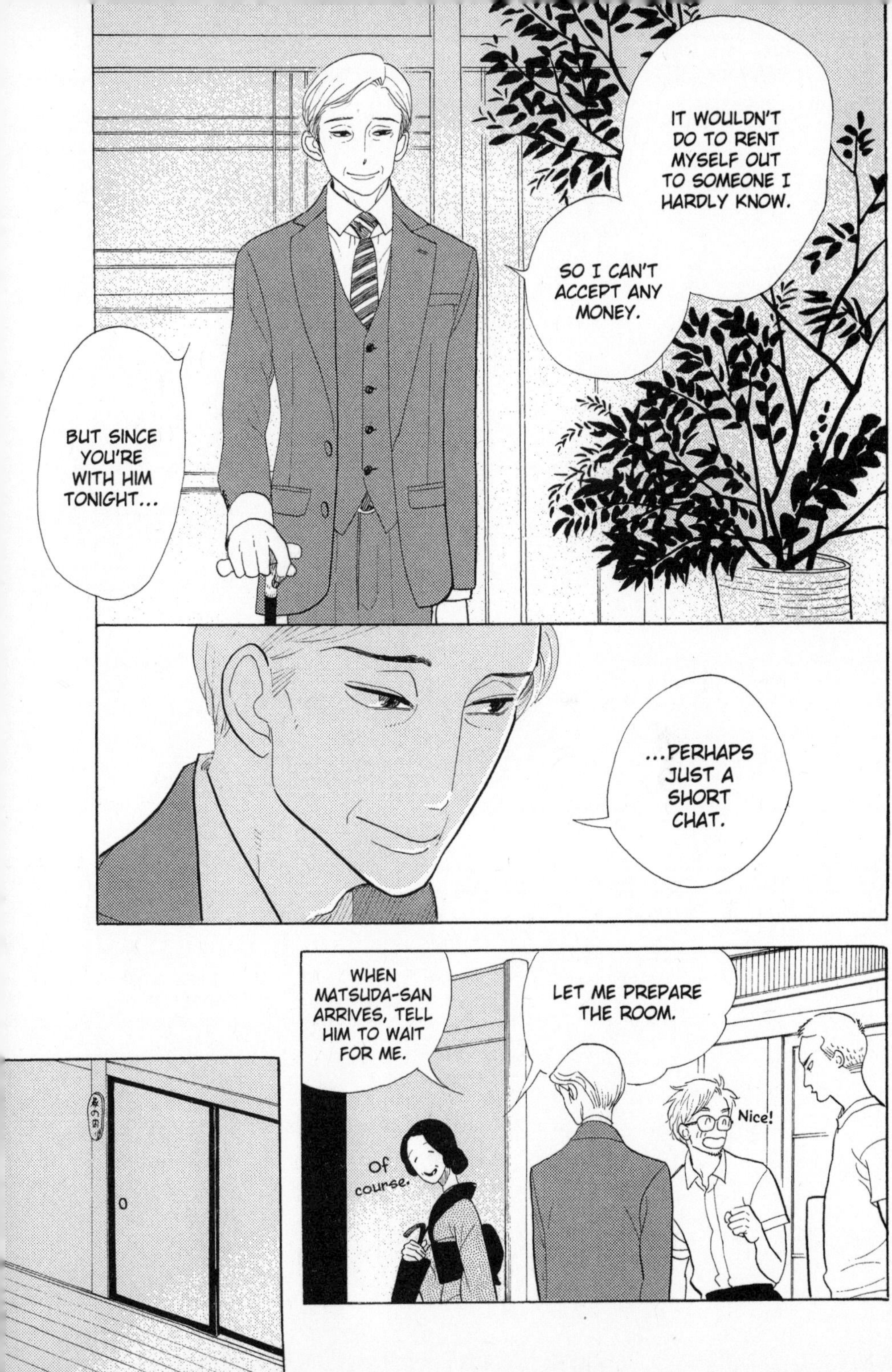
IT WOULDN'T DO TO RENT MYSELF OUT TO SOMEONE I HARDLY KNOW.
SO I CAN'T ACCEPT ANY MONEY.
BUT SINCE YOU'RE WITH HIM TONIGHT...
...PERHAPS JUST A SHORT CHAT.
Nice!
LET ME PREPARE THE ROOM.
WHEN MATSUDA-SAN ARRIVES, TELL HIM TO WAIT FOR ME.
Of course.

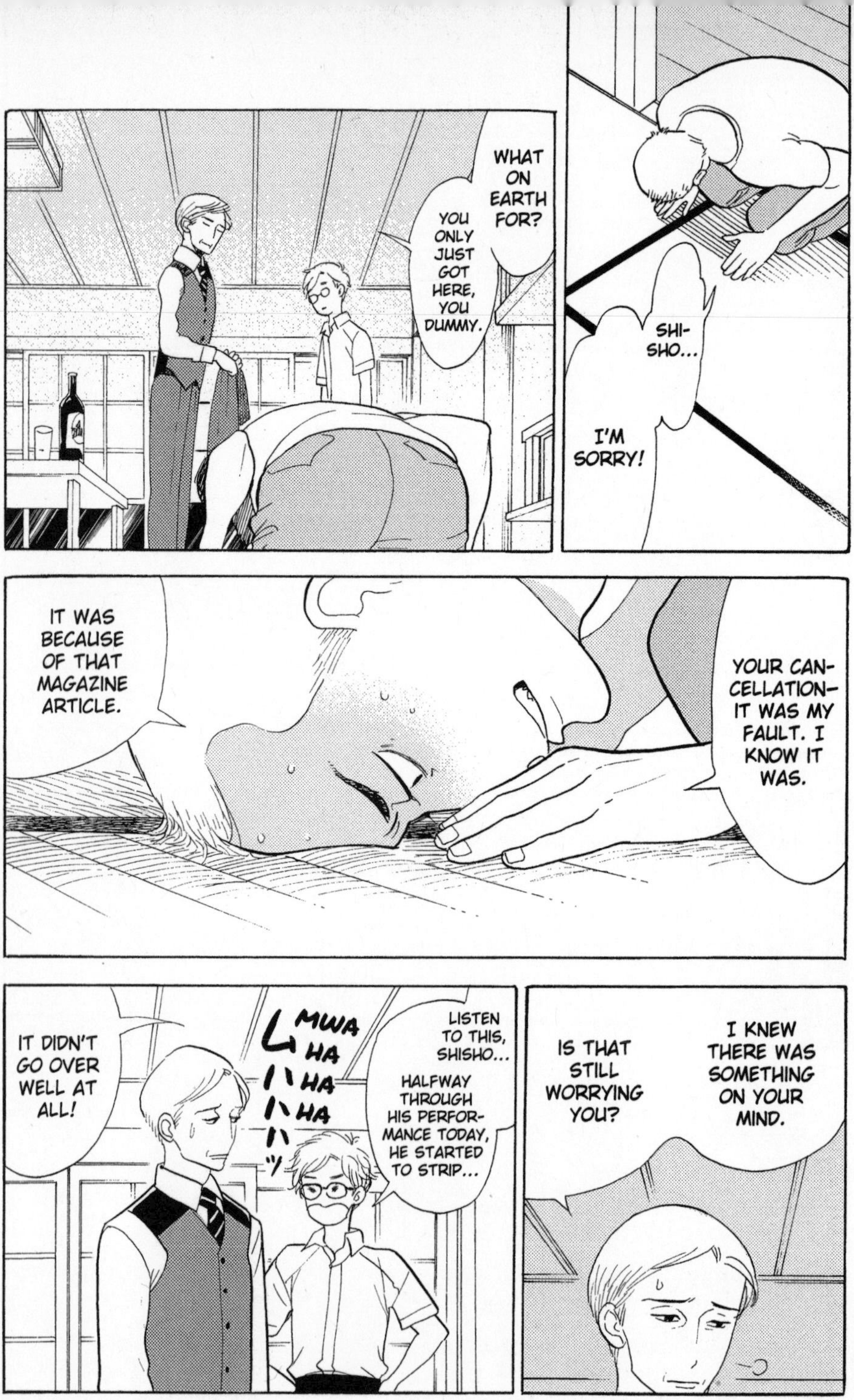
SHI-SHO...
I'M SORRY!
WHAT ON EARTH FOR?
YOU ONLY JUST GOT HERE, YOU DUMMY.
YOUR CAN-CELLATION— IT WAS MY FAULT. I KNOW IT WAS.
IT WAS BECAUSE OF THAT MAGAZINE ARTICLE.
I KNEW THERE WAS SOMETHING ON YOUR MIND.
IS THAT STILL WORRYING YOU?
LISTEN TO THIS, SHISHO...
HALFWAY THROUGH HIS PERFOR-MANCE TODAY, HE STARTED TO STRIP...
MWA HA HA HA
IT DIDN'T GO OVER WELL AT ALL!

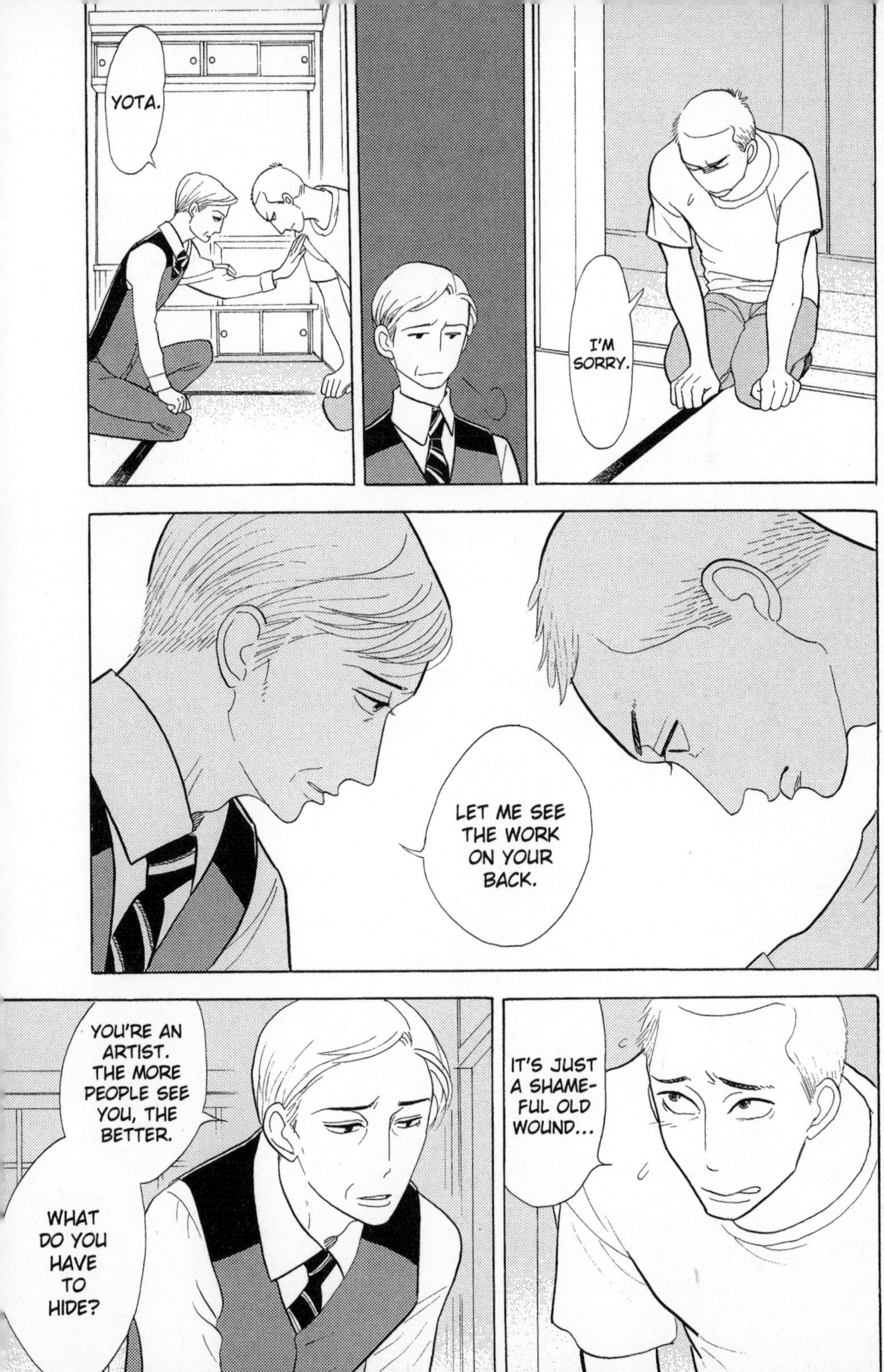
I'M SORRY.
YOTA.
LET ME SEE THE WORK ON YOUR BACK.
IT'S JUST A SHAME-FUL OLD WOUND...
YOU'RE AN ARTIST. THE MORE PEOPLE SEE YOU, THE BETTER.
WHAT DO YOU HAVE TO HIDE?

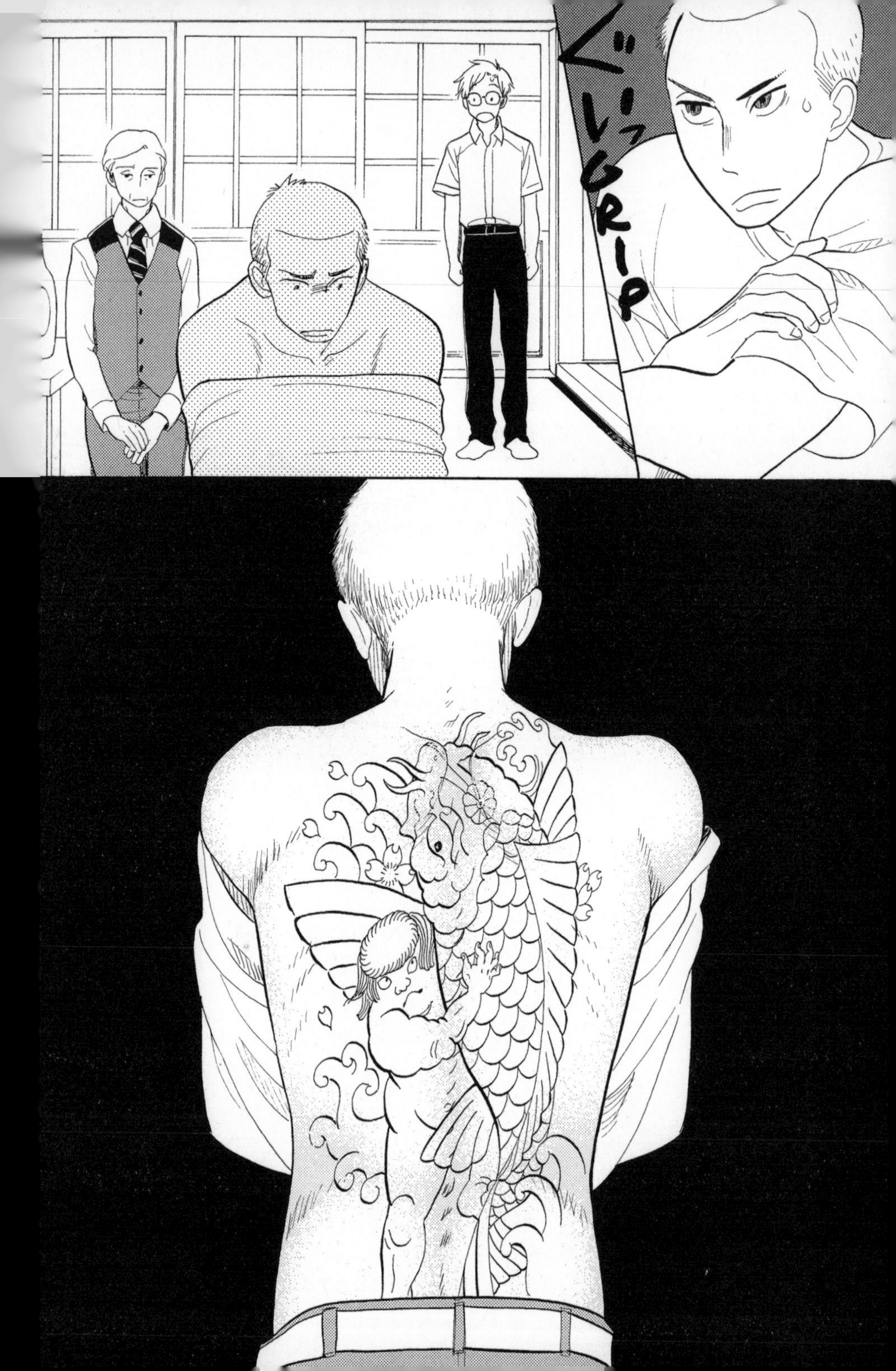
ぐいっ
GRIP

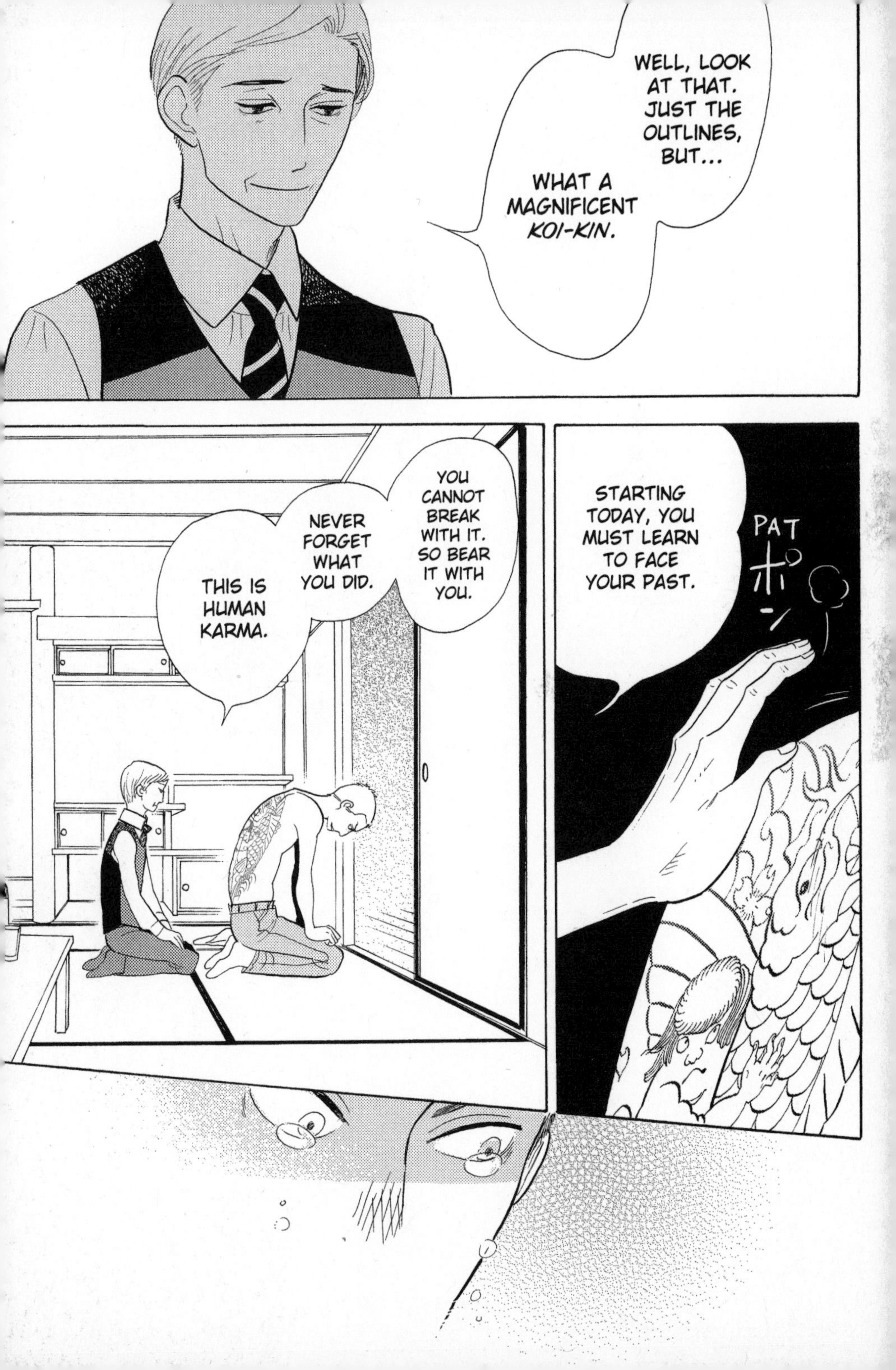
WELL, LOOK AT THAT. JUST THE OUTLINES, BUT...
WHAT A MAGNIFICENT *KOI-KIN*.
STARTING TODAY, YOU MUST LEARN TO FACE YOUR PAST.
PAT
YOU CANNOT BREAK WITH IT. SO BEAR IT WITH YOU.
NEVER FORGET WHAT YOU DID.
THIS IS HUMAN KARMA.

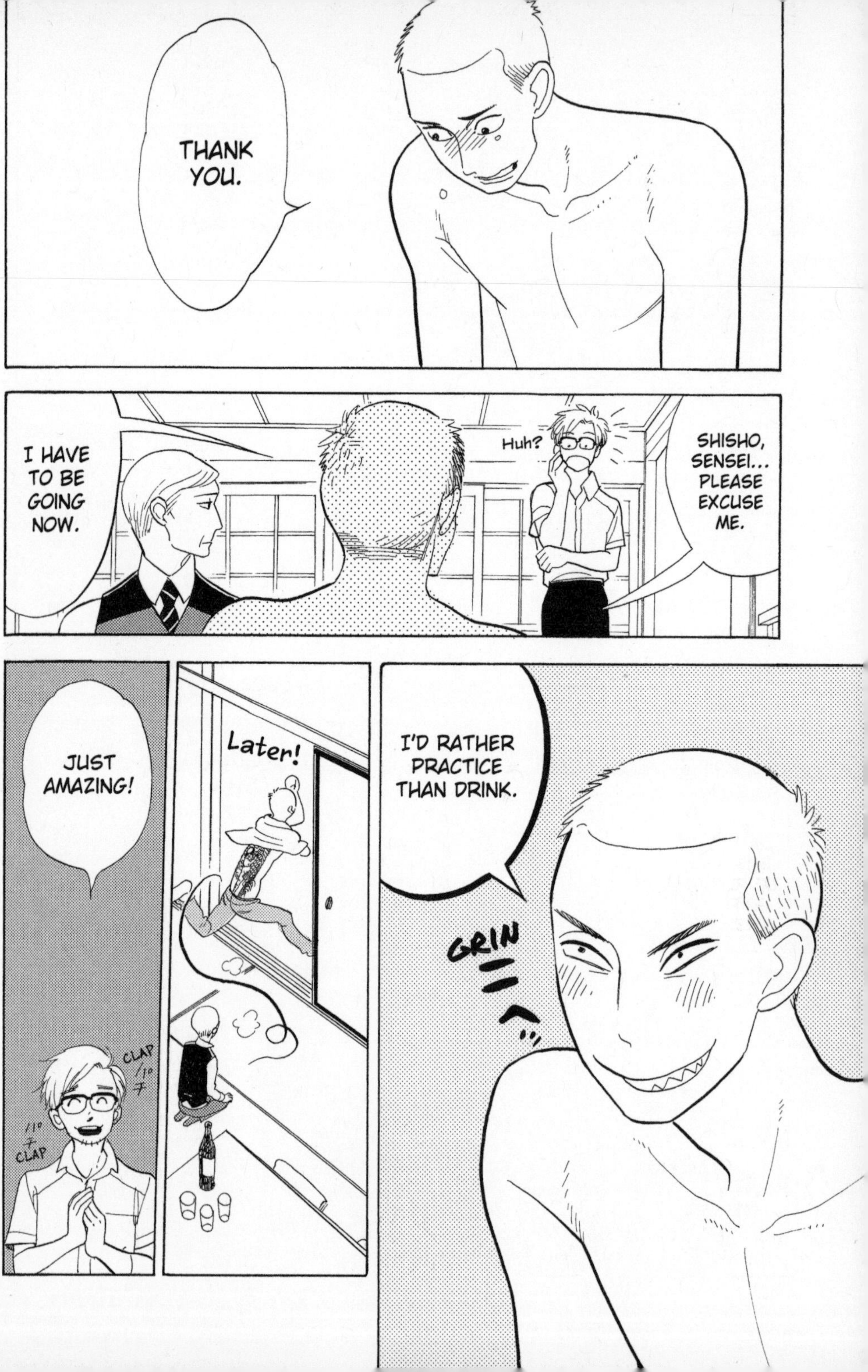
THANK YOU.
SHISHO, SENSEI... PLEASE EXCUSE ME.
Huh?
I HAVE TO BE GOING NOW.
I'D RATHER PRACTICE THAN DRINK.
GRIN
Later!
JUST AMAZING!
CLAP
CLAP

WANT-TO-LEAVE AURA
COME ON. I KNOW TWO GUYS ISN'T THE BEST PARTY, BUT...
JUST ONE DRINK?
I WITNESSED SOMETHING VERY SPECIAL TONIGHT.
THE BONDS OF LOVE BETWEEN MASTER AND APPRENTICE.
TOK トク
TOK トク
IT'S BEEN SOME TIME SINCE WE MET.
I NEVER IMAGINED THAT SCHOOL-BOY MIGHT GROW INTO SUCH A FINE PATRON OF THE ARTS.
TOK トク
TOK トク
TOK トク
YOU REMEMBER ME!
HUH!
IT WAS THE DAY MY SHISHO COLLAPSED AT OUR FATHER-AND-SON PERFORMANCE.
I RE-MEMBER IT WELL.
I'M IN THE BUSINESS OF REMEM-BERING, AFTER ALL.

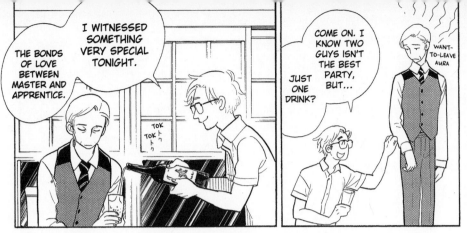

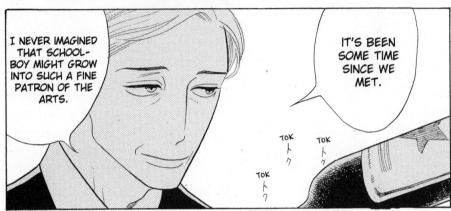

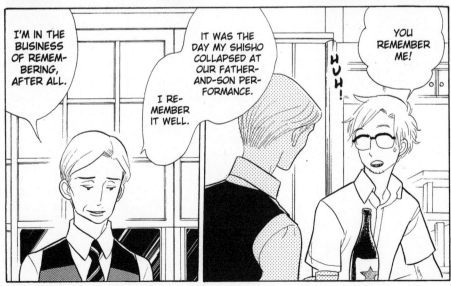

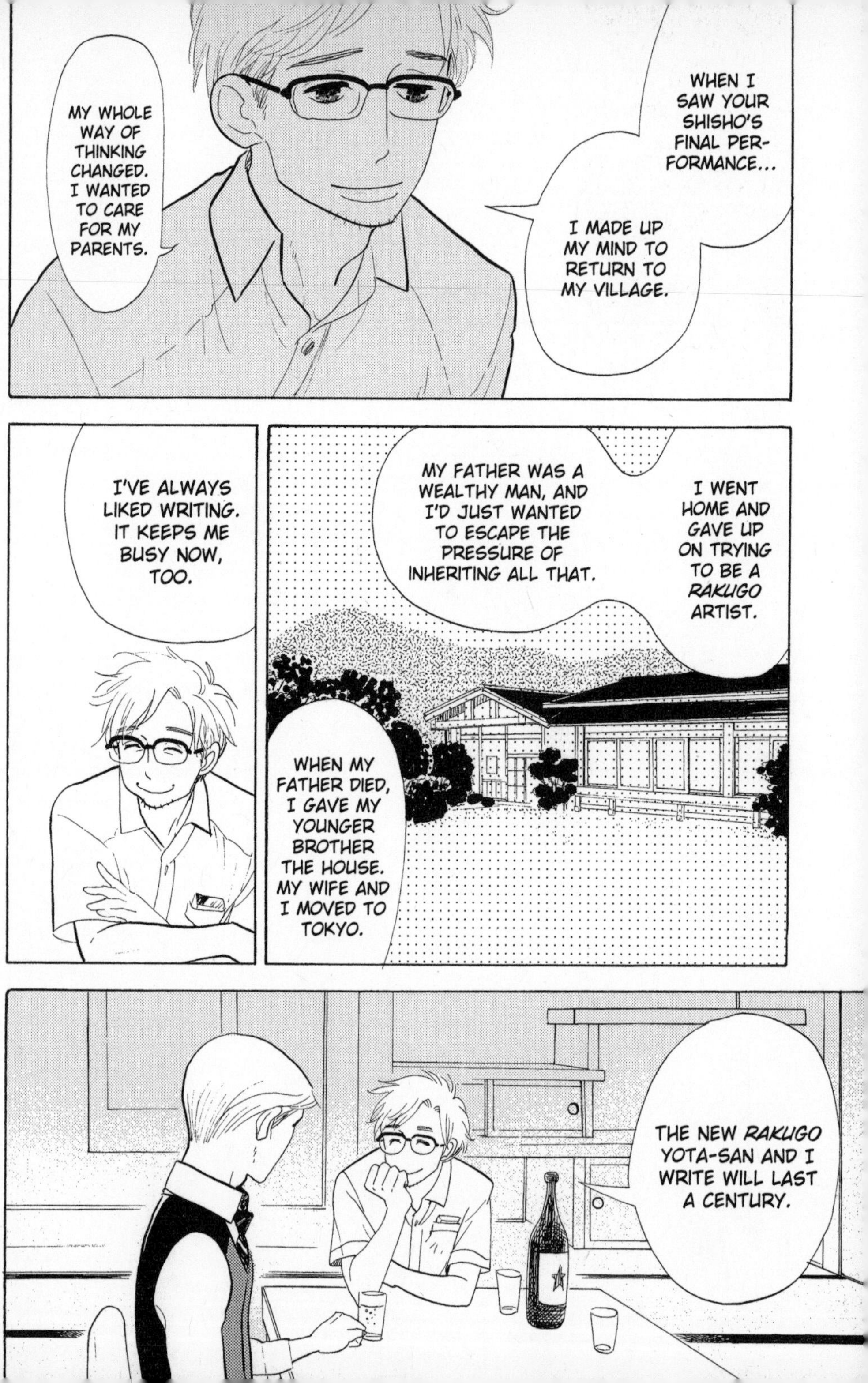
WHEN I SAW YOUR SHISHO'S FINAL PERFORMANCE...
I MADE UP MY MIND TO RETURN TO MY VILLAGE.
MY WHOLE WAY OF THINKING CHANGED. I WANTED TO CARE FOR MY PARENTS.
I WENT HOME AND GAVE UP ON TRYING TO BE A *RAKUGO* ARTIST.
MY FATHER WAS A WEALTHY MAN, AND I'D JUST WANTED TO ESCAPE THE PRESSURE OF INHERITING ALL THAT.
WHEN MY FATHER DIED, I GAVE MY YOUNGER BROTHER THE HOUSE. MY WIFE AND I MOVED TO TOKYO.
I'VE ALWAYS LIKED WRITING. IT KEEPS ME BUSY NOW, TOO.
THE NEW *RAKUGO* YOTA-SAN AND I WRITE WILL LAST A CENTURY.

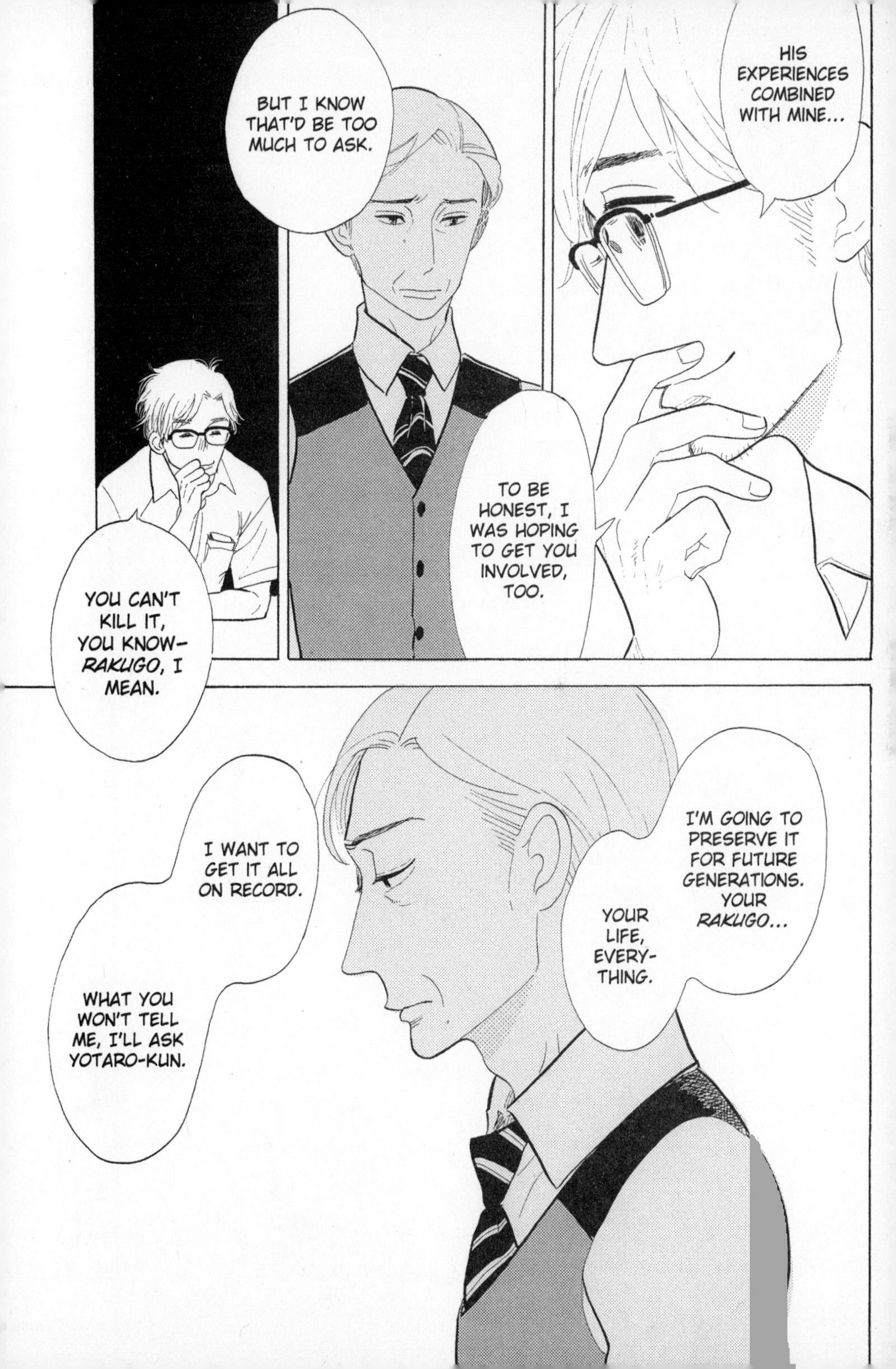
HIS EXPERIENCES COMBINED WITH MINE...
TO BE HONEST, I WAS HOPING TO GET YOU INVOLVED, TOO.
BUT I KNOW THAT'D BE TOO MUCH TO ASK.
YOU CAN'T KILL IT, YOU KNOW— *RAKUGO*, I MEAN.
I'M GOING TO PRESERVE IT FOR FUTURE GENERATIONS. YOUR *RAKUGO*...
YOUR LIFE, EVERY-THING.
I WANT TO GET IT ALL ON RECORD.
WHAT YOU WON'T TELL ME, I'LL ASK YOTARO-KUN.

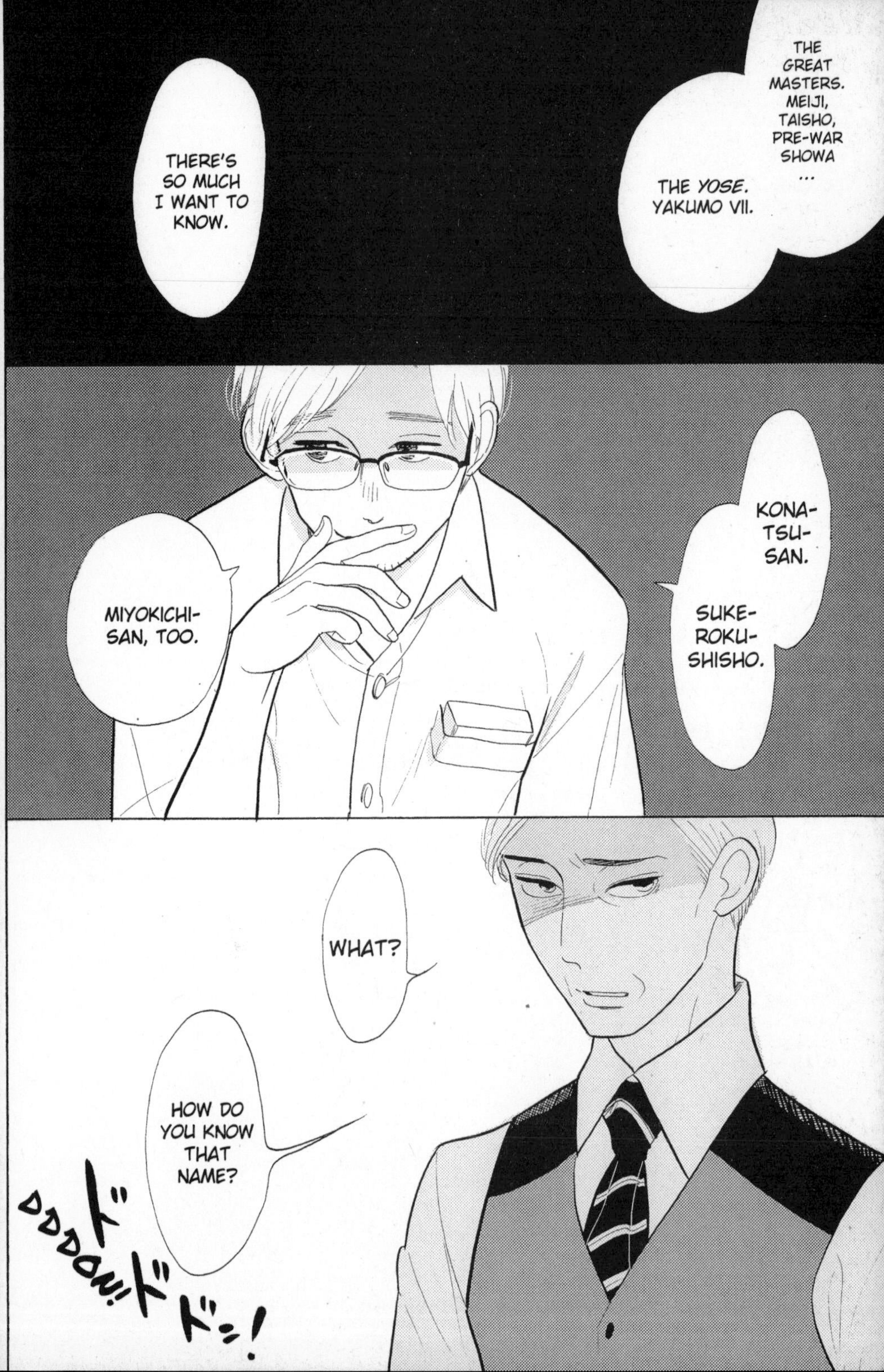
THE GREAT MASTERS. MEIJI, TAISHO, PRE-WAR SHOWA ...
THE YOSE. YAKUMO VII.
THERE'S SO MUCH I WANT TO KNOW.
KONATSU-SAN.
SUKEROKU-SHISHO.
MIYOKICHI-SAN, TOO.
WHAT?
HOW DO YOU KNOW THAT NAME?
DDDON!

DESCENDING STORIES SHOWA GENROKU RAKUGO SHINJU

HARUKO KUMOTA

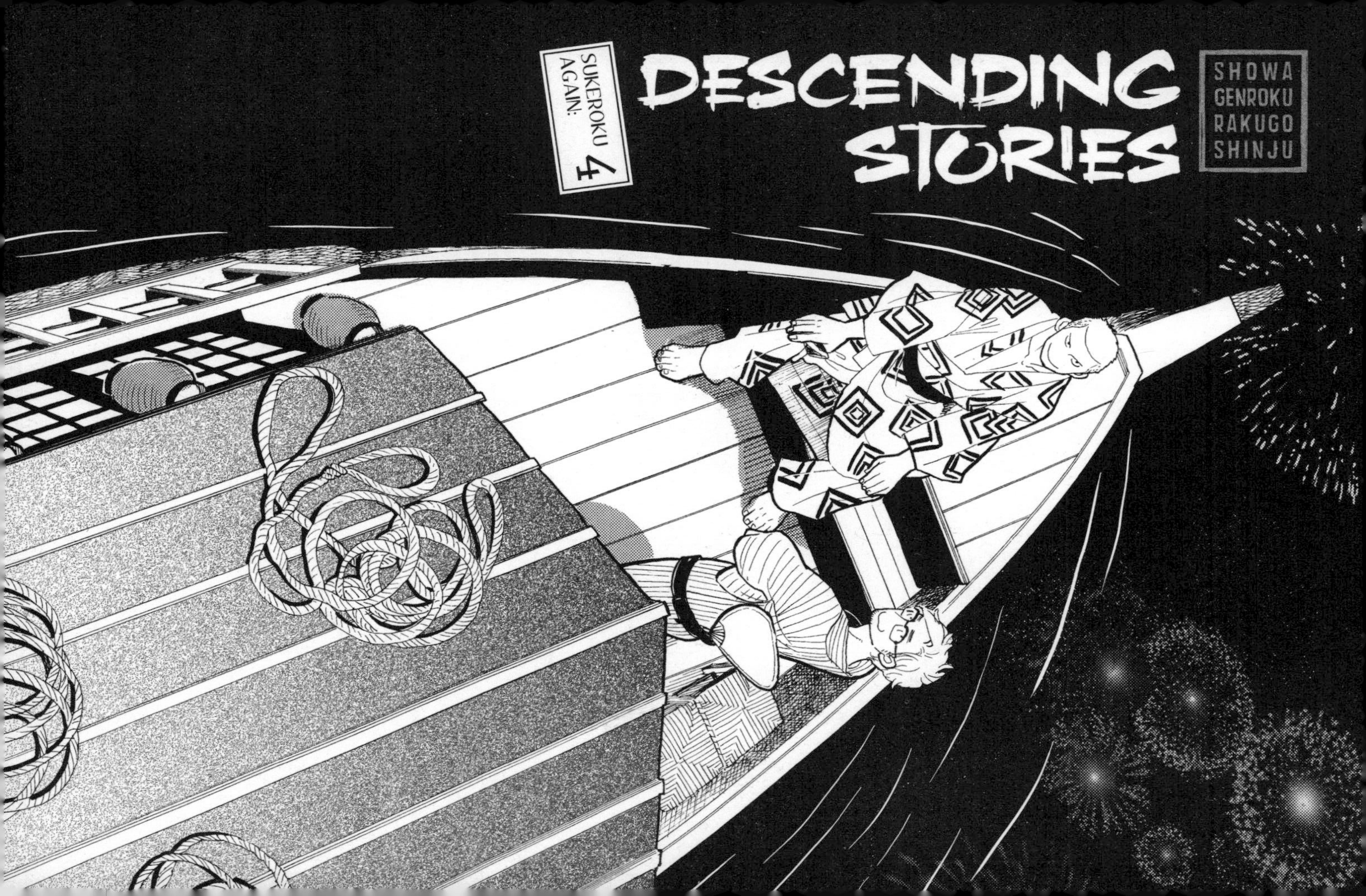
SHOWA GENROKU RAKUGO SHINJU
DESCENDING STORIES
SUKEROKU AGAIN: 4

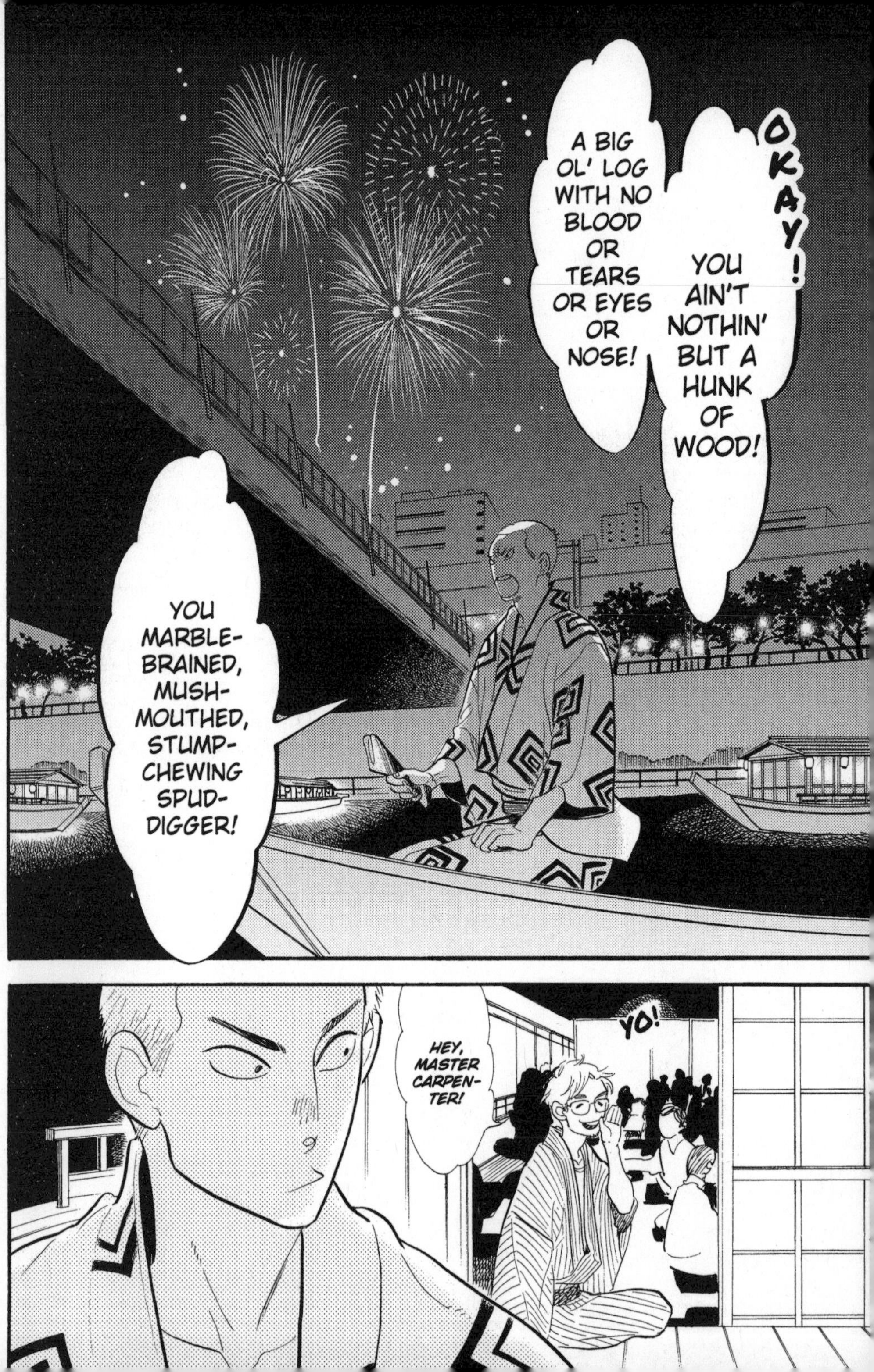
OKAY!
YOU AIN'T NOTHIN' BUT A HUNK OF WOOD!
A BIG OL' LOG WITH NO BLOOD OR TEARS OR EYES OR NOSE!
YOU MARBLE-BRAINED, MUSH-MOUTHED, STUMP-CHEWING SPUD-DIGGER!
YO!
HEY, MASTER CARPENTER!

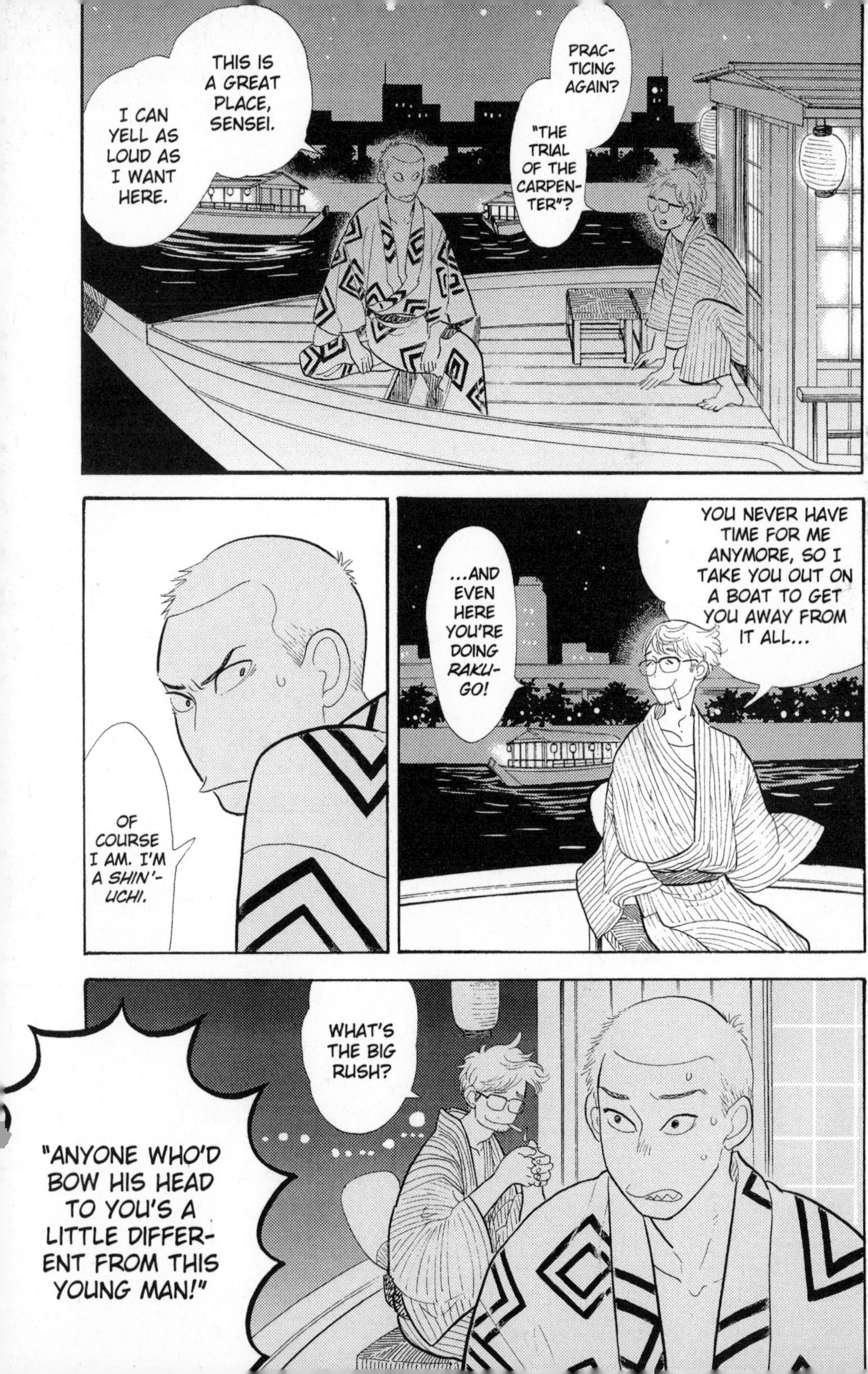
PRAC-TICING AGAIN?
"THE TRIAL OF THE CARPEN-TER"?
THIS IS A GREAT PLACE, SENSEI.
I CAN YELL AS LOUD AS I WANT HERE.
YOU NEVER HAVE TIME FOR ME ANYMORE, SO I TAKE YOU OUT ON A BOAT TO GET YOU AWAY FROM IT ALL...
...AND EVEN HERE YOU'RE DOING *RAKU-GO*!
OF COURSE I AM. I'M A *SHIN'-UCHI*.
WHAT'S THE BIG RUSH?
"ANYONE WHO'D BOW HIS HEAD TO YOU'S A LITTLE DIFFER-ENT FROM THIS YOUNG MAN!"

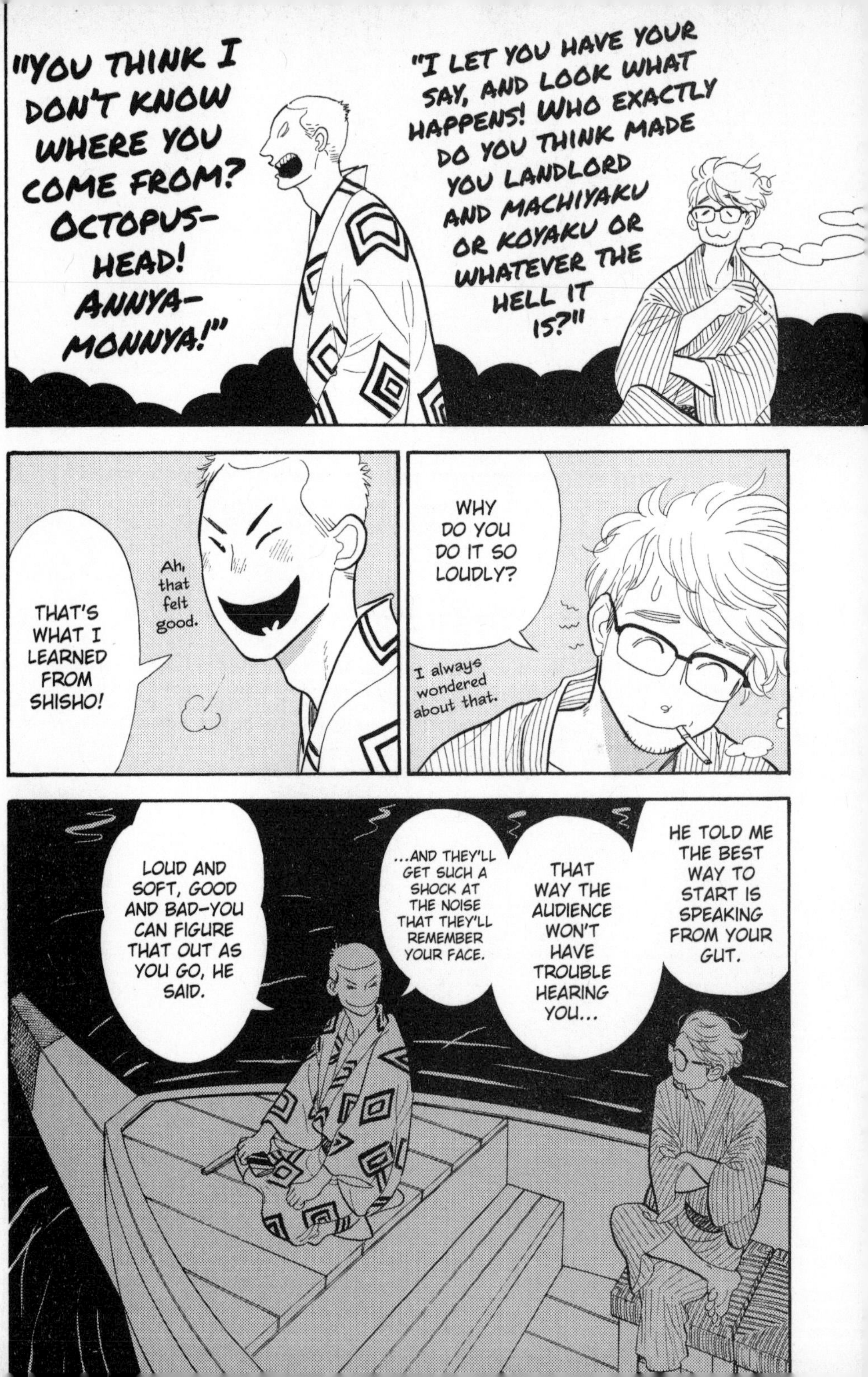
"I LET YOU HAVE YOUR SAY, AND LOOK WHAT HAPPENS! WHO EXACTLY DO YOU THINK MADE YOU LANDLORD AND MACHIYAKU OR KOYAKU OR WHATEVER THE HELL IT IS?"
"YOU THINK I DON'T KNOW WHERE YOU COME FROM? OCTOPUS-HEAD! ANNYA-MONNYA!"
WHY DO YOU DO IT SO LOUDLY?
I always wondered about that.
Ah, that felt good.
THAT'S WHAT I LEARNED FROM SHISHO!
HE TOLD ME THE BEST WAY TO START IS SPEAKING FROM YOUR GUT.
THAT WAY THE AUDIENCE WON'T HAVE TROUBLE HEARING YOU...
...AND THEY'LL GET SUCH A SHOCK AT THE NOISE THAT THEY'LL REMEMBER YOUR FACE.
LOUD AND SOFT, GOOD AND BAD—YOU CAN FIGURE THAT OUT AS YOU GO, HE SAID.

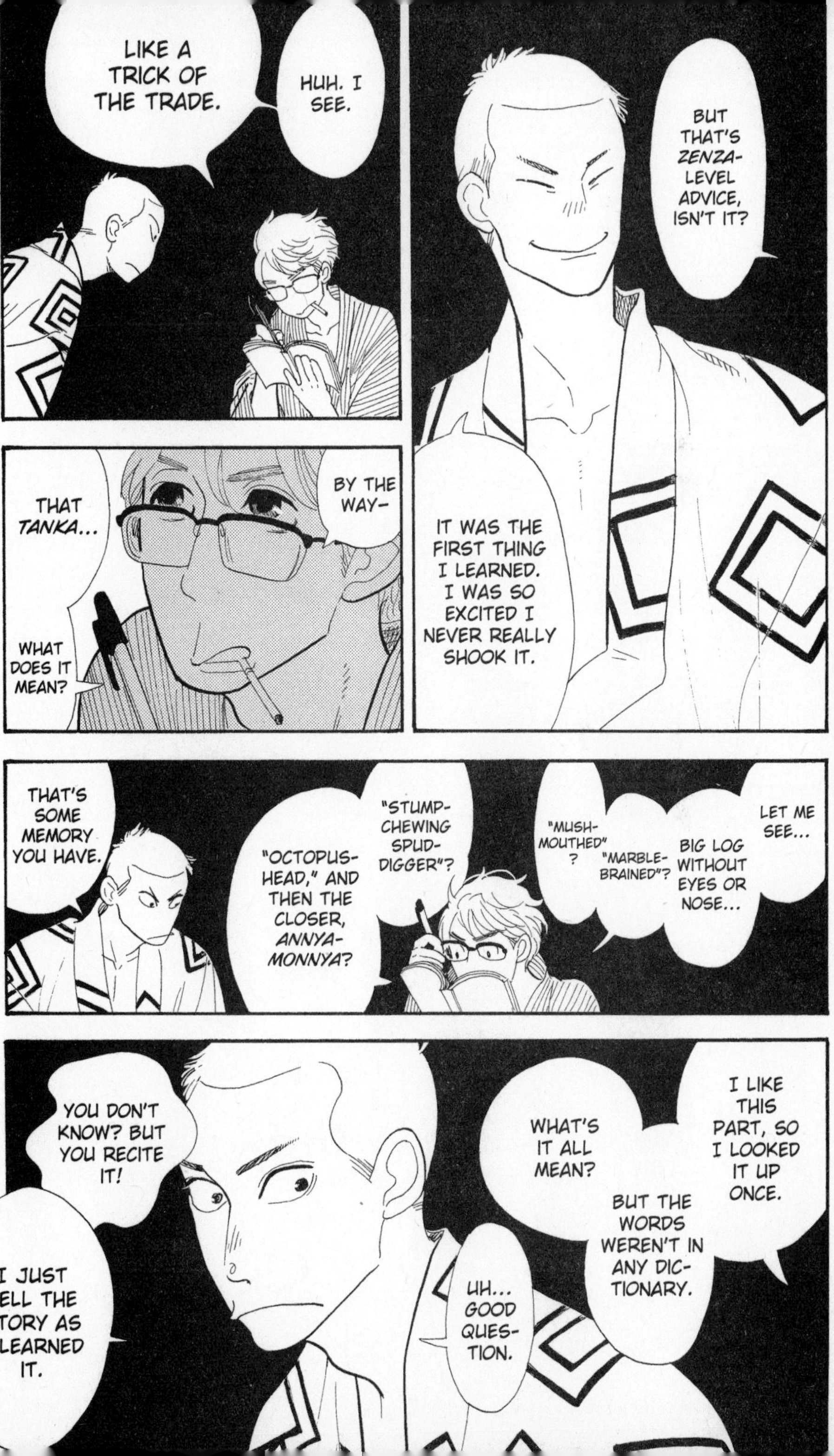
BUT THAT'S *ZENZA*-LEVEL ADVICE, ISN'T IT?
IT WAS THE FIRST THING I LEARNED. I WAS SO EXCITED I NEVER REALLY SHOOK IT.
LIKE A TRICK OF THE TRADE.
HUH. I SEE.
BY THE WAY—
THAT *TANKA*...
WHAT DOES IT MEAN?
LET ME SEE...
BIG LOG WITHOUT EYES OR NOSE...
"MARBLE-BRAINED"?
"MUSH-MOUTHED"?
"STUMP-CHEWING SPUD-DIGGER"?
"OCTOPUS-HEAD," AND THEN THE CLOSER, *ANNYA-MONNYA*?
THAT'S SOME MEMORY YOU HAVE.
I LIKE THIS PART, SO I LOOKED IT UP ONCE.
WHAT'S IT ALL MEAN?
BUT THE WORDS WEREN'T IN ANY DICTIONARY.
UH... GOOD QUESTION.
YOU DON'T KNOW? BUT YOU RECITE IT!
I JUST TELL THE STORY AS I LEARNED IT.

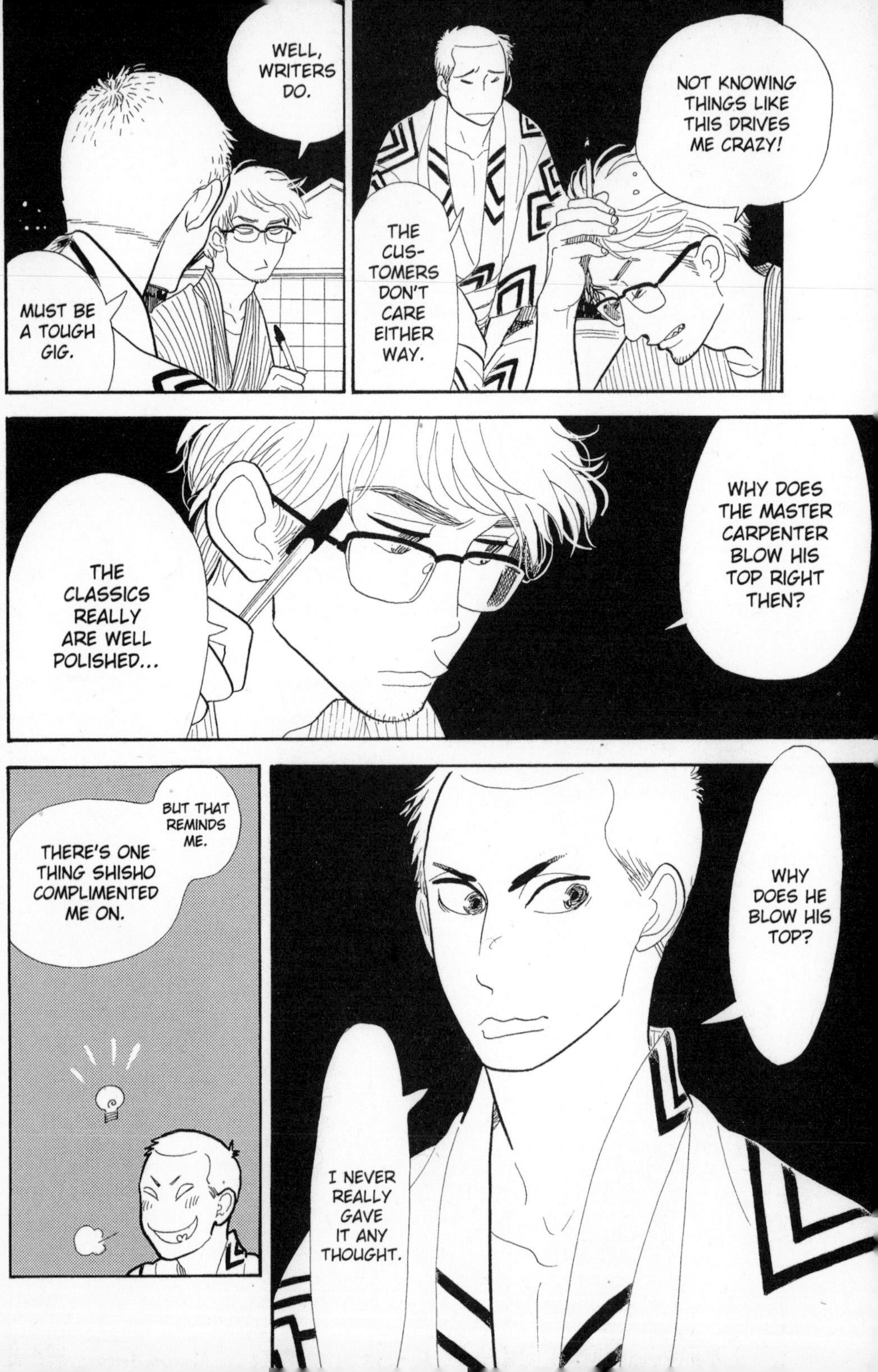
NOT KNOWING THINGS LIKE THIS DRIVES ME CRAZY!
THE CUS-TOMERS DON'T CARE EITHER WAY.
WELL, WRITERS DO.
MUST BE A TOUGH GIG.
WHY DOES THE MASTER CARPENTER BLOW HIS TOP RIGHT THEN?
THE CLASSICS REALLY ARE WELL POLISHED...
WHY DOES HE BLOW HIS TOP?
I NEVER REALLY GAVE IT ANY THOUGHT.
BUT THAT REMINDS ME.
THERE'S ONE THING SHISHO COMPLIMENTED ME ON.

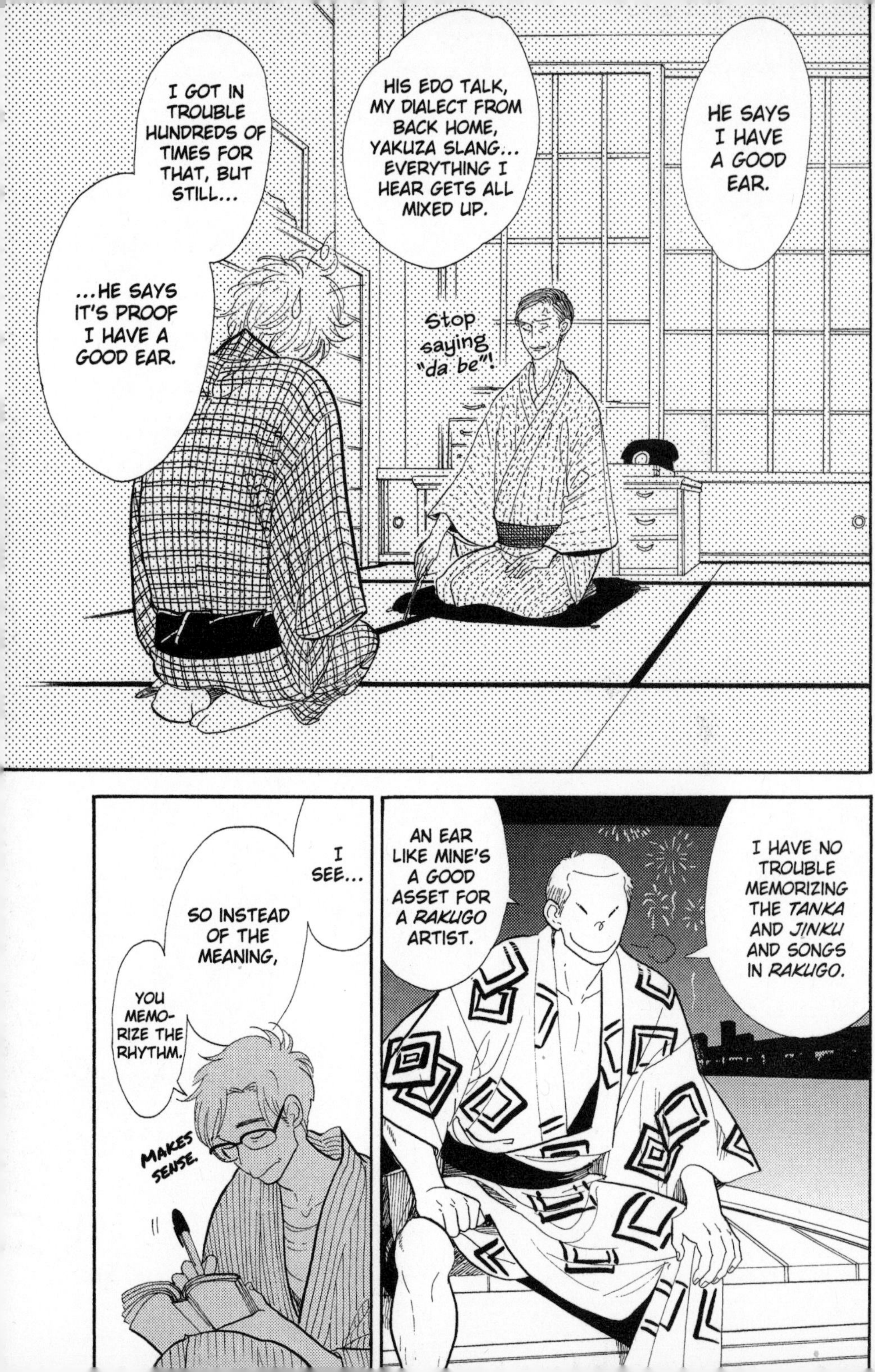
HE SAYS I HAVE A GOOD EAR.
HIS EDO TALK, MY DIALECT FROM BACK HOME, YAKUZA SLANG... EVERYTHING I HEAR GETS ALL MIXED UP.
I GOT IN TROUBLE HUNDREDS OF TIMES FOR THAT, BUT STILL...
...HE SAYS IT'S PROOF I HAVE A GOOD EAR.
Stop saying "da be"!
I HAVE NO TROUBLE MEMORIZING THE *TANKA* AND *JINKU* AND SONGS IN *RAKUGO*.
AN EAR LIKE MINE'S A GOOD ASSET FOR A *RAKUGO* ARTIST.
I SEE...
SO INSTEAD OF THE MEANING,
YOU MEMORIZE THE RHYTHM.
MAKES SENSE.

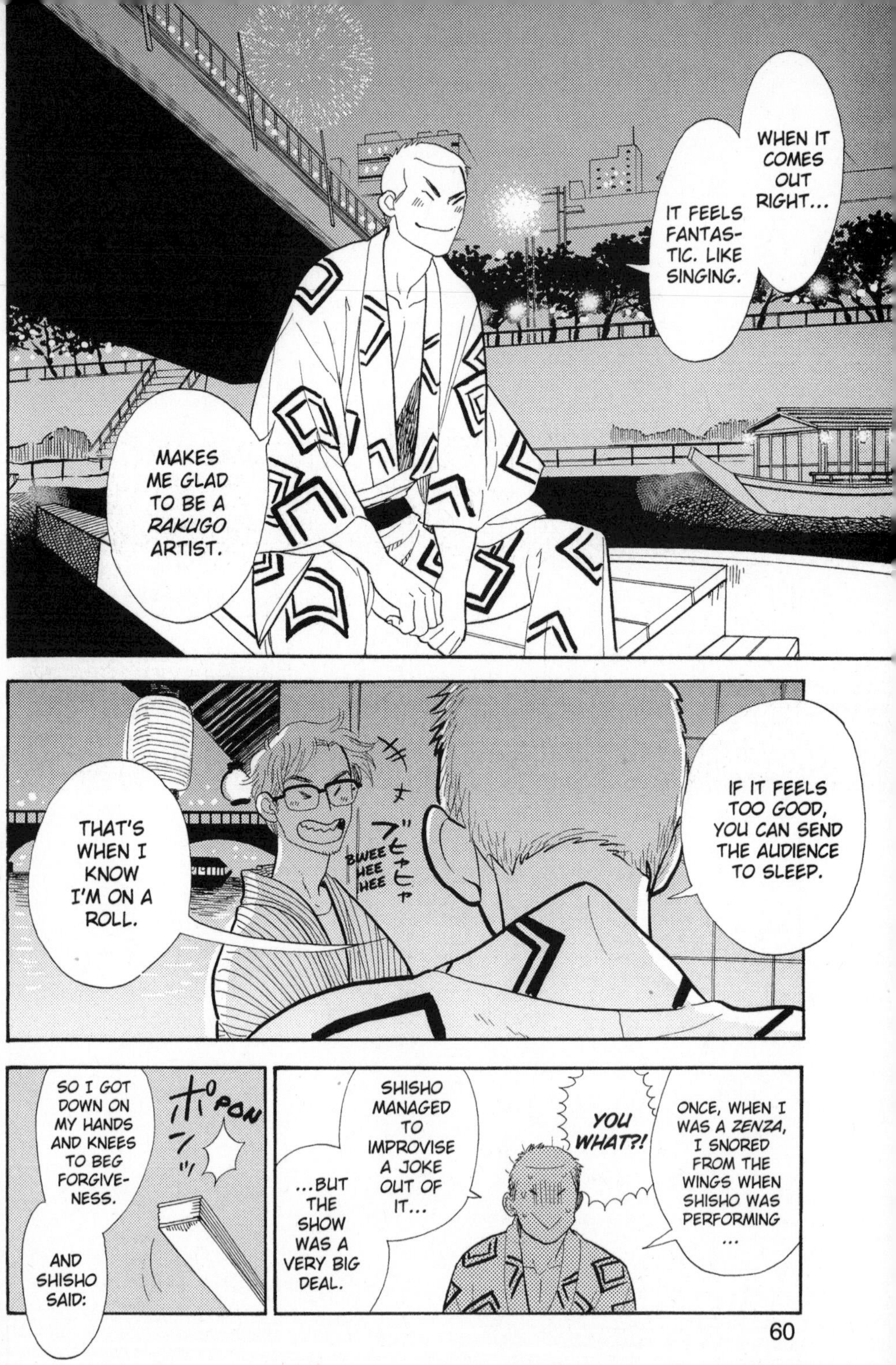
WHEN IT COMES OUT RIGHT...
IT FEELS FANTASTIC. LIKE SINGING.
MAKES ME GLAD TO BE A *RAKUGO* ARTIST.
IF IT FEELS TOO GOOD, YOU CAN SEND THE AUDIENCE TO SLEEP.
BWEE HEE HEE
THAT'S WHEN I KNOW I'M ON A ROLL.
ONCE, WHEN I WAS A *ZENZA*, I SNORED FROM THE WINGS WHEN SHISHO WAS PERFORMING ...
YOU WHAT?!
SHISHO MANAGED TO IMPROVISE A JOKE OUT OF IT...
...BUT THE SHOW WAS A VERY BIG DEAL.
PON
SO I GOT DOWN ON MY HANDS AND KNEES TO BEG FORGIVE-NESS.
AND SHISHO SAID:

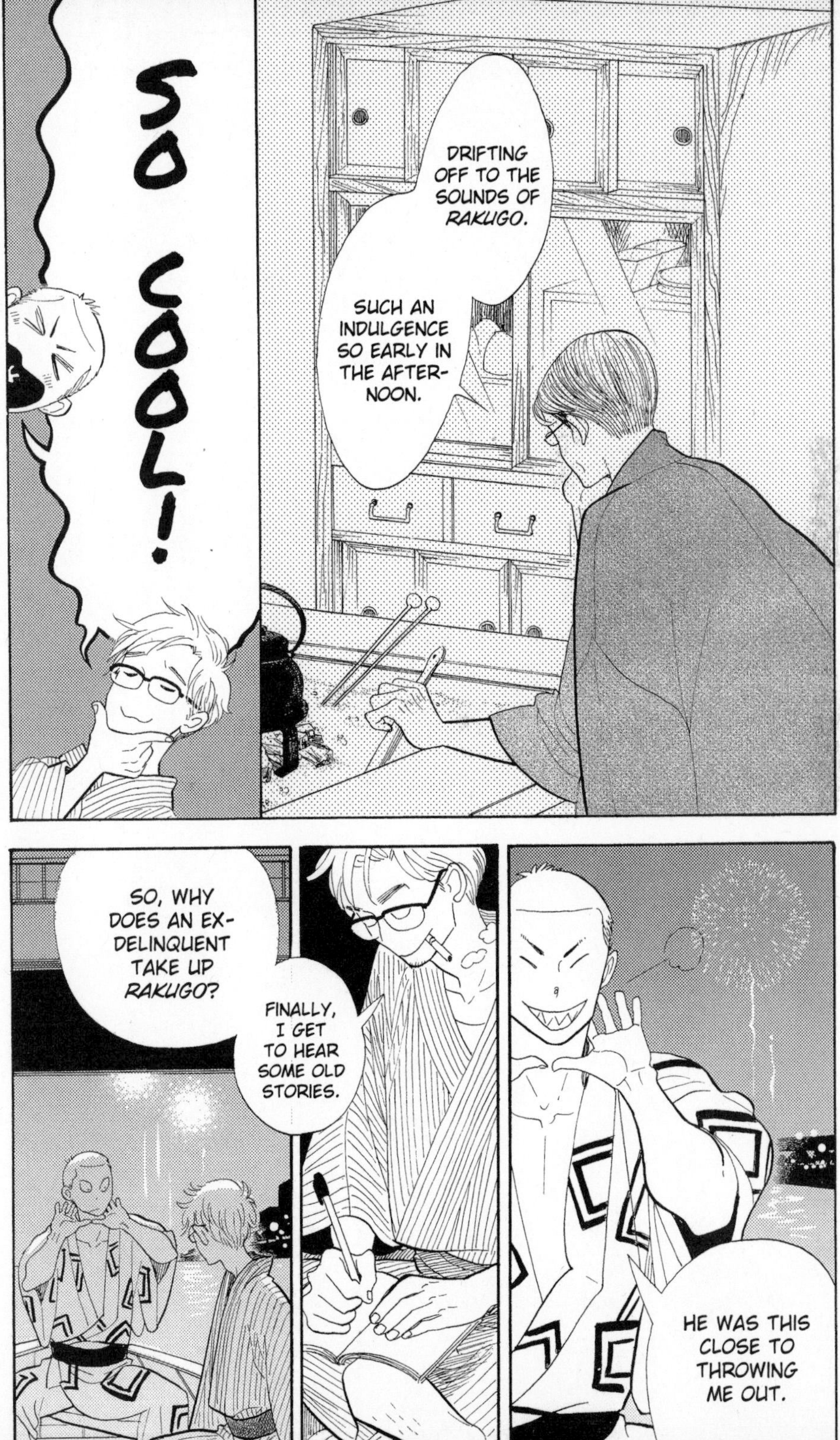
DRIFTING OFF TO THE SOUNDS OF *RAKUGO*.
SUCH AN INDULGENCE SO EARLY IN THE AFTER-NOON.
SO COOL!
HE WAS THIS CLOSE TO THROWING ME OUT.
FINALLY, I GET TO HEAR SOME OLD STORIES.
SO, WHY DOES AN EX-DELINQUENT TAKE UP *RAKUGO*?

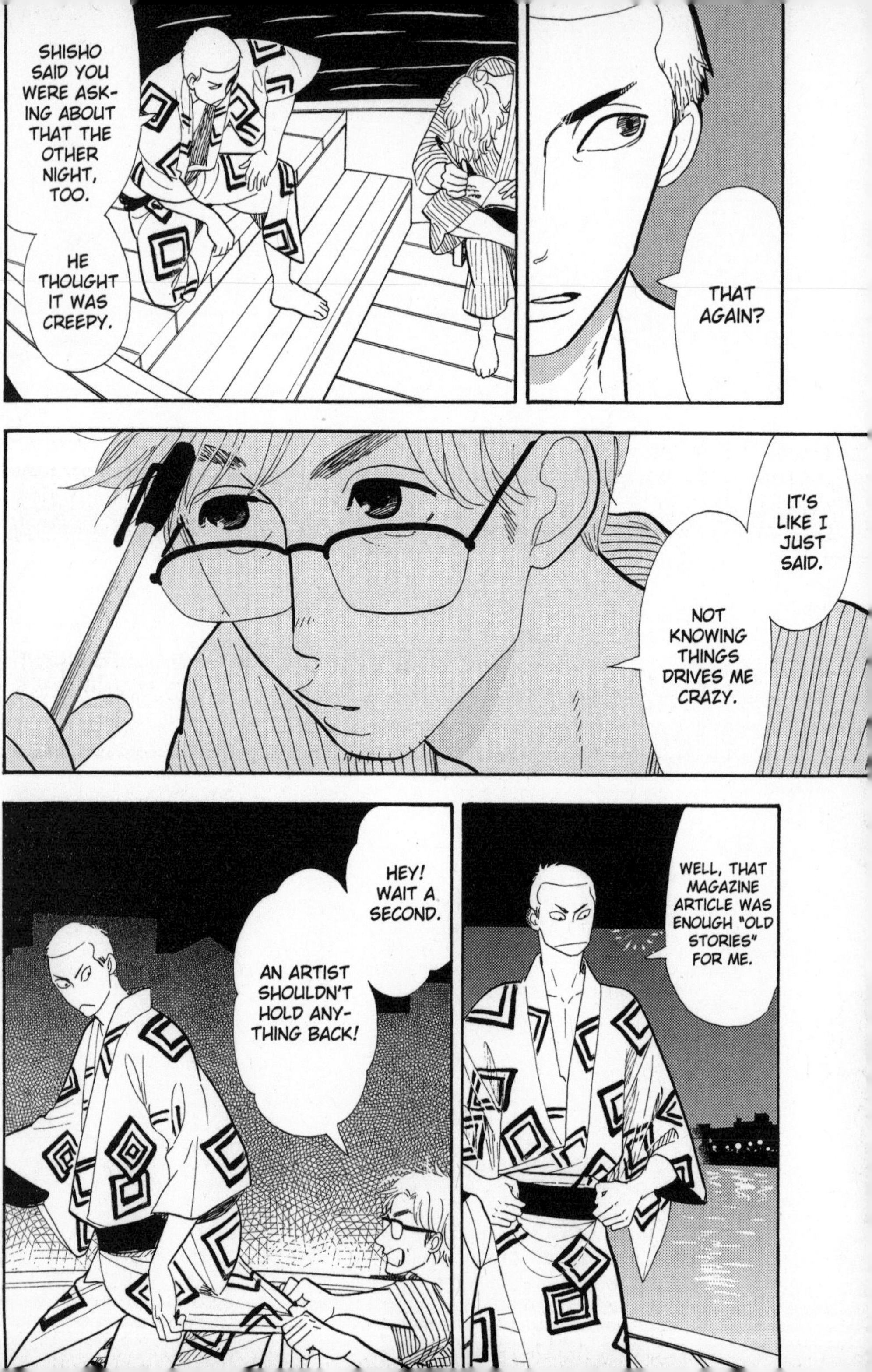
THAT AGAIN?
SHISHO SAID YOU WERE ASK-ING ABOUT THAT THE OTHER NIGHT, TOO.
HE THOUGHT IT WAS CREEPY.
IT'S LIKE I JUST SAID.
NOT KNOWING THINGS DRIVES ME CRAZY.
WELL, THAT MAGAZINE ARTICLE WAS ENOUGH "OLD STORIES" FOR ME.
HEY! WAIT A SECOND.
AN ARTIST SHOULDN'T HOLD ANY-THING BACK!

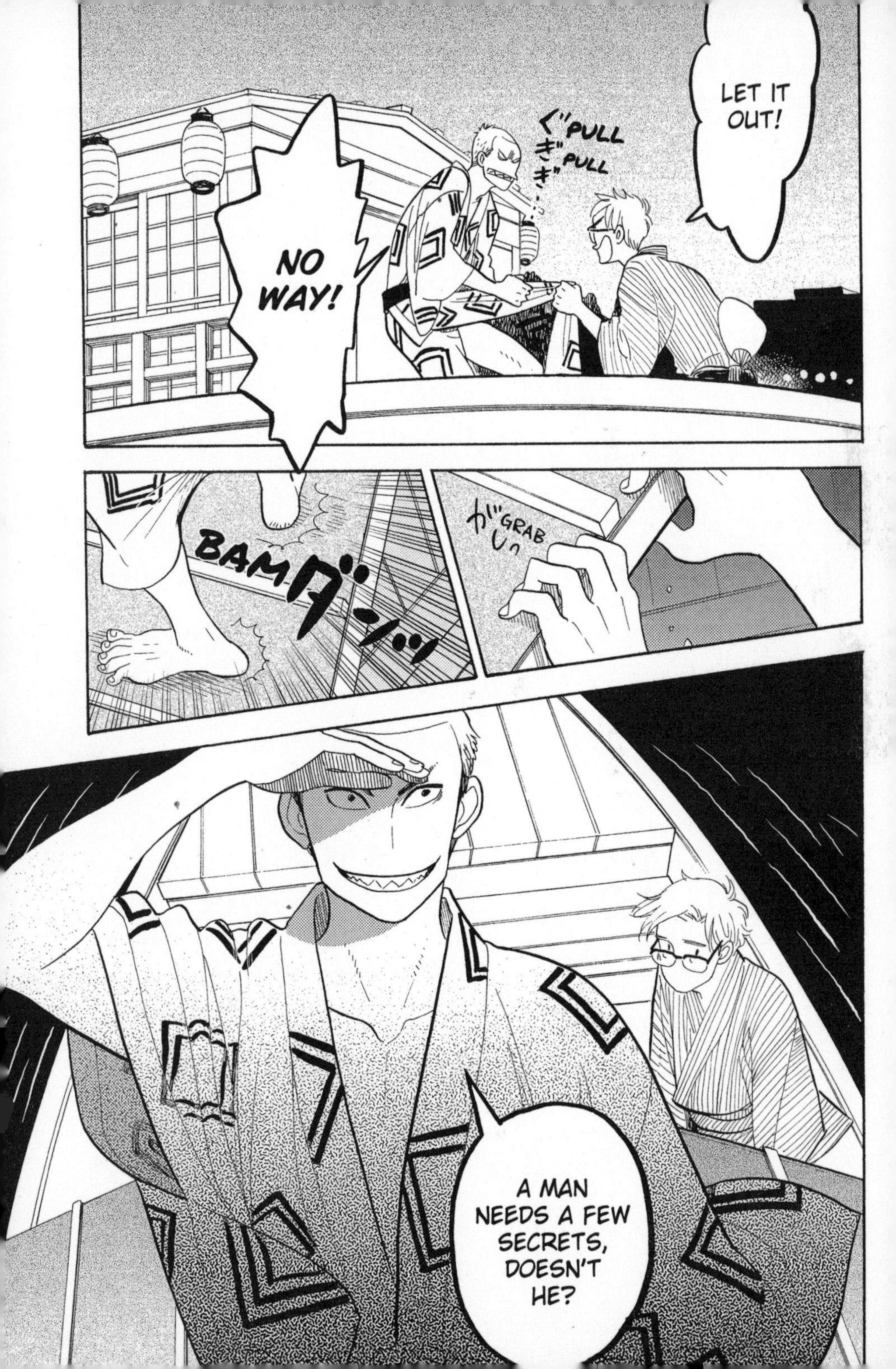
LET IT OUT!
ぐ" PULL
ぎ" PULL
NO WAY!
が" GRAB
しっ
BAM ダンッ
A MAN NEEDS A FEW SECRETS, DOESN'T HE?

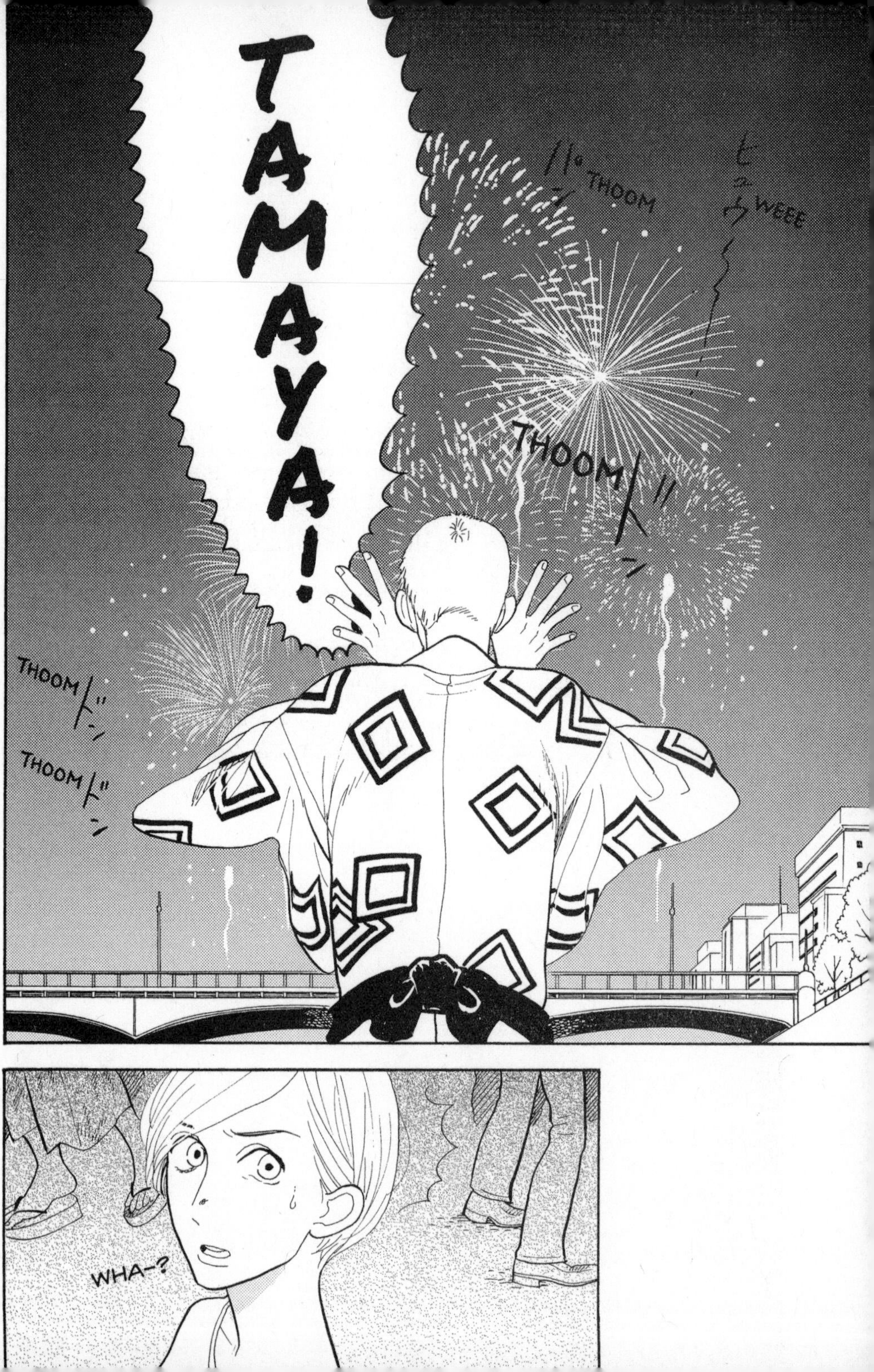
WEEE
THOOM
TAMAYA!
THOOM
THOOM
THOOM
WHA-?

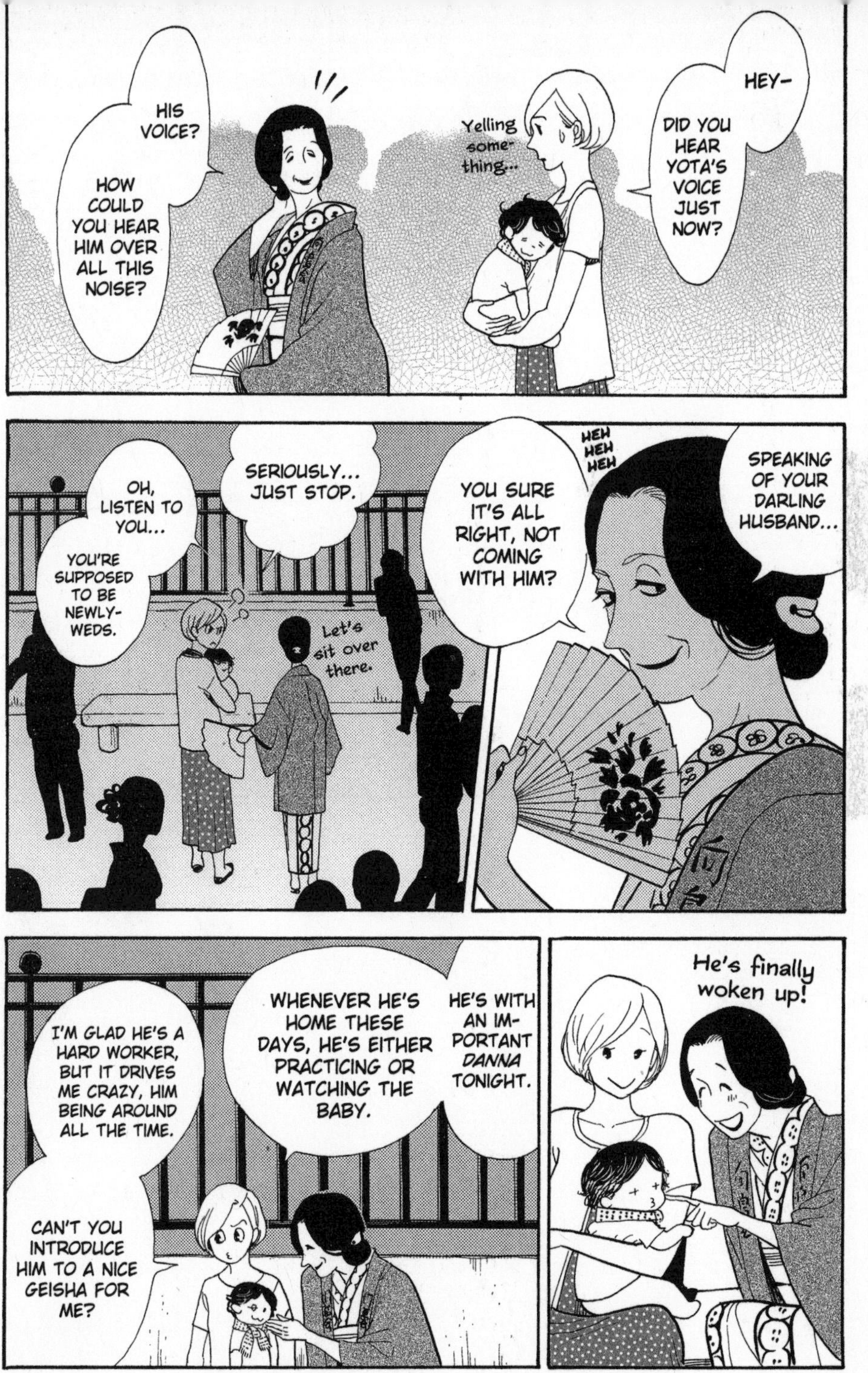
HEY—
DID YOU HEAR YOTA'S VOICE JUST NOW?
Yelling something...
HIS VOICE?
HOW COULD YOU HEAR HIM OVER ALL THIS NOISE?
SPEAKING OF YOUR DARLING HUSBAND...
HEH HEH HEH
YOU SURE IT'S ALL RIGHT, NOT COMING WITH HIM?
SERIOUSLY... JUST STOP.
OH, LISTEN TO YOU...
YOU'RE SUPPOSED TO BE NEWLYWEDS.
Let's sit over there.
He's finally woken up!
HE'S WITH AN IMPORTANT *DANNA* TONIGHT.
WHENEVER HE'S HOME THESE DAYS, HE'S EITHER PRACTICING OR WATCHING THE BABY.
I'M GLAD HE'S A HARD WORKER, BUT IT DRIVES ME CRAZY, HIM BEING AROUND ALL THE TIME.
CAN'T YOU INTRODUCE HIM TO A NICE GEISHA FOR ME?

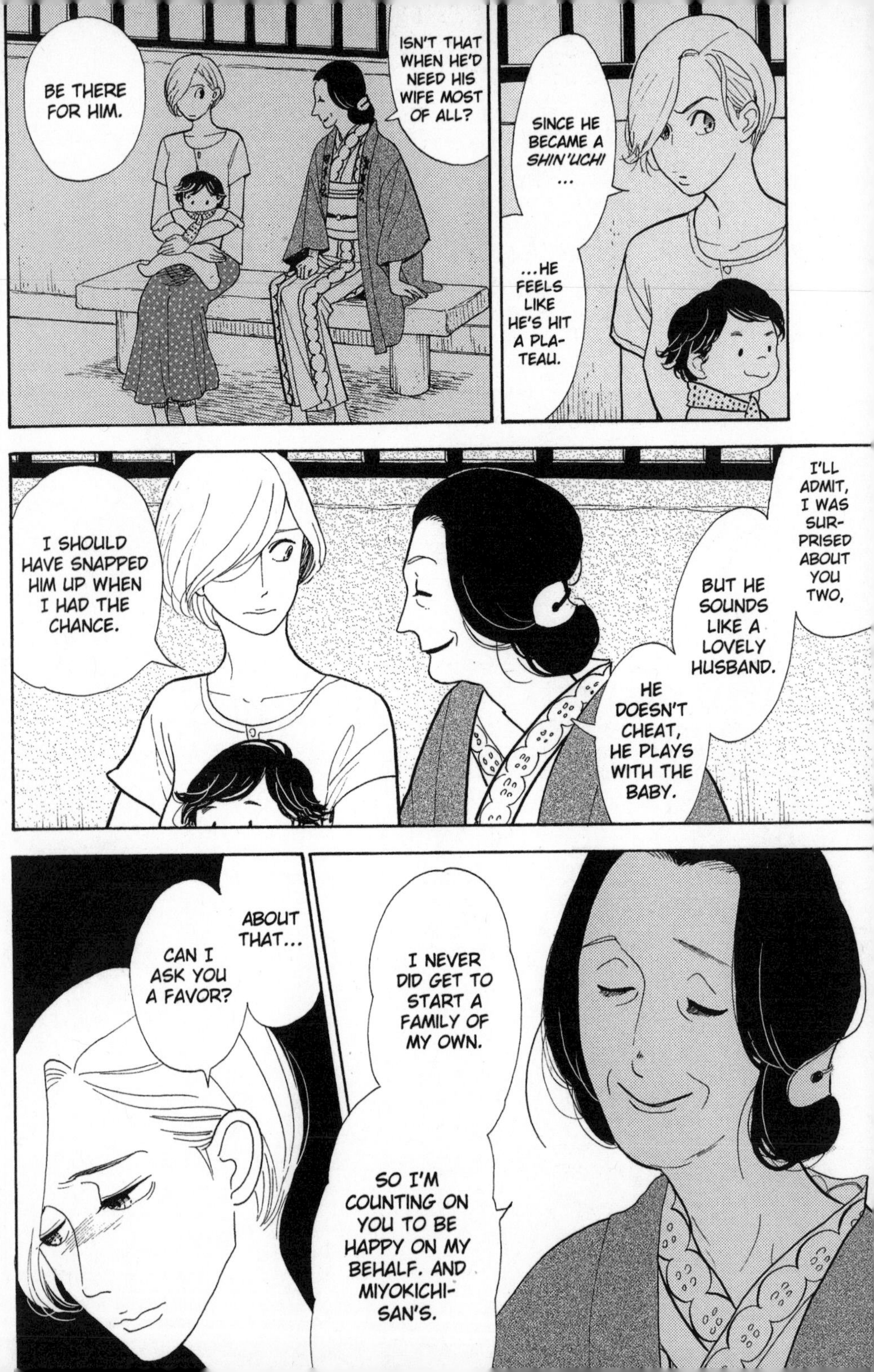
SINCE HE BECAME A *SHIN'UCHI* ...
...HE FEELS LIKE HE'S HIT A PLA-TEAU.
ISN'T THAT WHEN HE'D NEED HIS WIFE MOST OF ALL?
BE THERE FOR HIM.
I'LL ADMIT, I WAS SUR-PRISED ABOUT YOU TWO,
BUT HE SOUNDS LIKE A LOVELY HUSBAND.
HE DOESN'T CHEAT, HE PLAYS WITH THE BABY.
I SHOULD HAVE SNAPPED HIM UP WHEN I HAD THE CHANCE.
I NEVER DID GET TO START A FAMILY OF MY OWN.
SO I'M COUNTING ON YOU TO BE HAPPY ON MY BEHALF. AND MIYOKICHI-SAN'S.
ABOUT THAT...
CAN I ASK YOU A FAVOR?

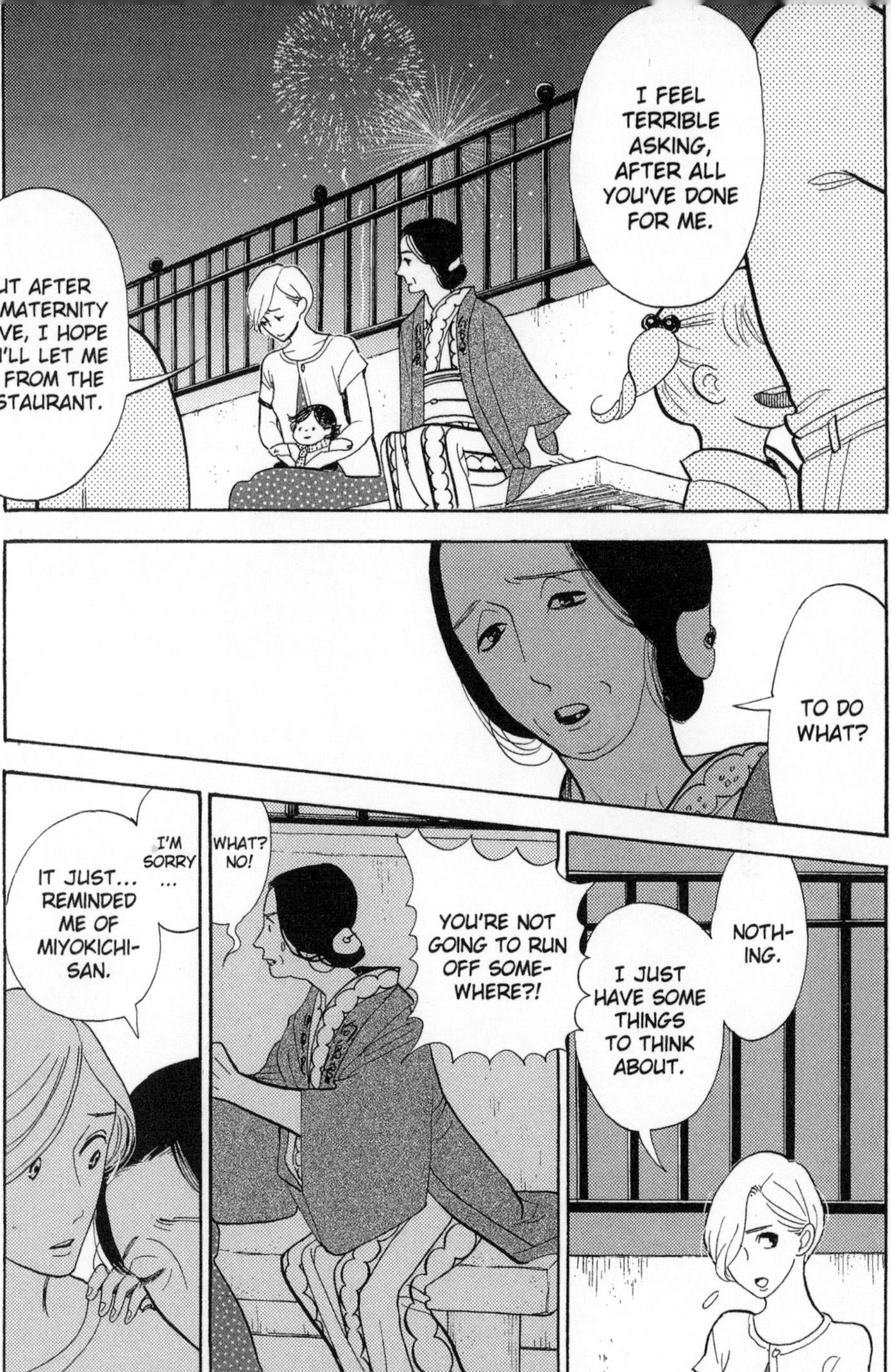
I FEEL TERRIBLE ASKING, AFTER ALL YOU'VE DONE FOR ME.
BUT AFTER MY MATERNITY LEAVE, I HOPE YOU'LL LET ME GO FROM THE RESTAURANT.
TO DO WHAT?
NOTH-ING.
I JUST HAVE SOME THINGS TO THINK ABOUT.
YOU'RE NOT GOING TO RUN OFF SOME-WHERE?!
WHAT? NO!
I'M SORRY...
IT JUST... REMINDED ME OF MIYOKICHI-SAN.

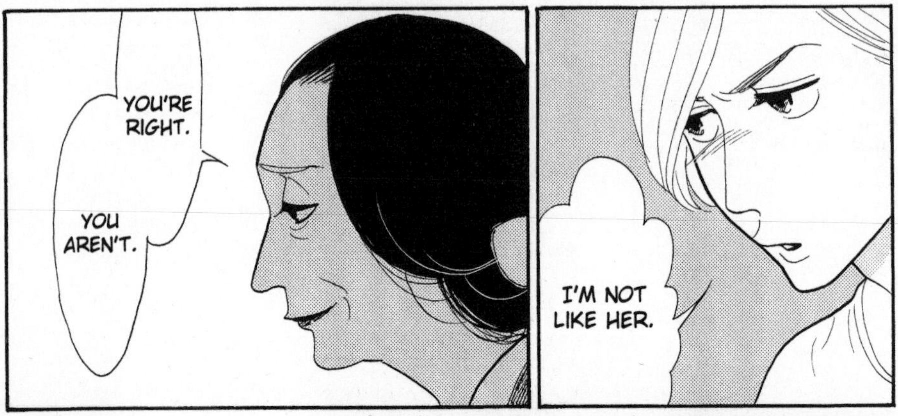
I'M NOT LIKE HER.
YOU'RE RIGHT.
YOU AREN'T.

Jacket lapels: Mukojima Association

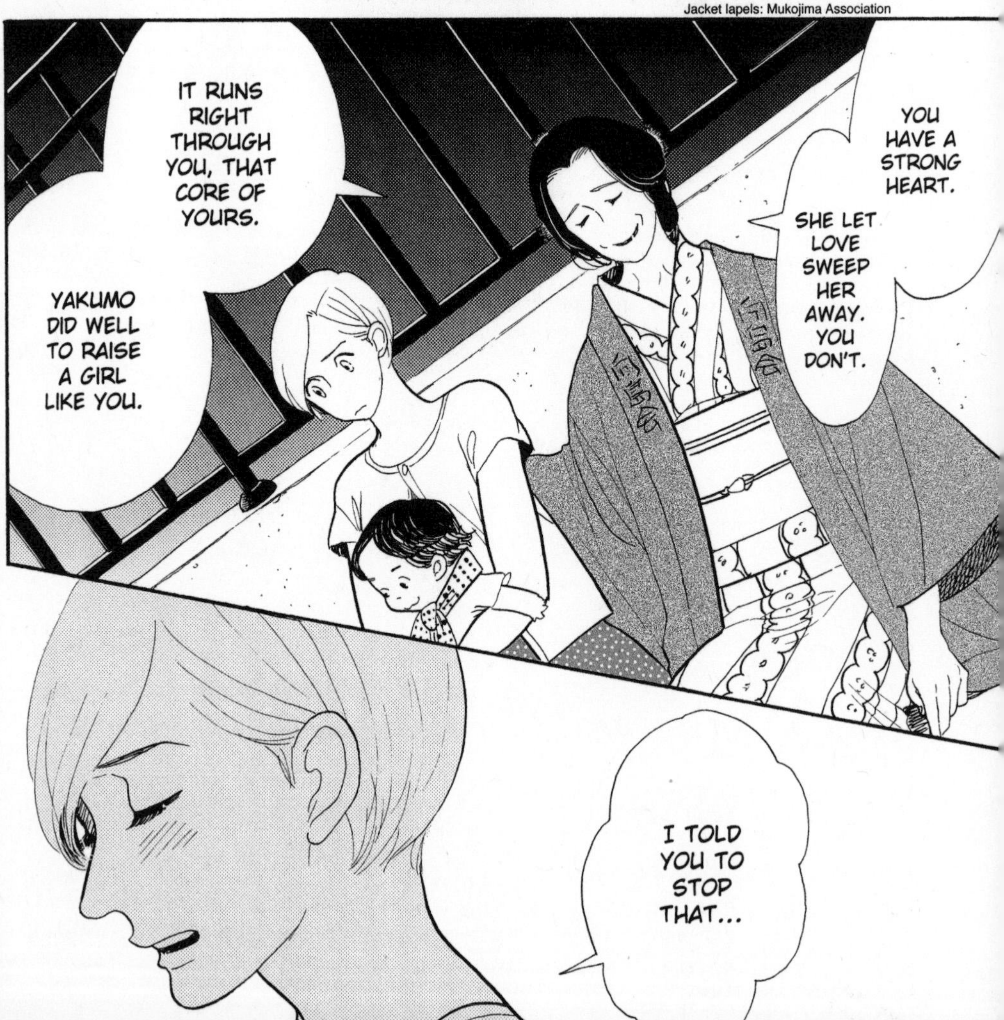
YOU HAVE A STRONG HEART.
SHE LET LOVE SWEEP HER AWAY. YOU DON'T.
IT RUNS RIGHT THROUGH YOU, THAT CORE OF YOURS.
YAKUMO DID WELL TO RAISE A GIRL LIKE YOU.
I TOLD YOU TO STOP THAT...

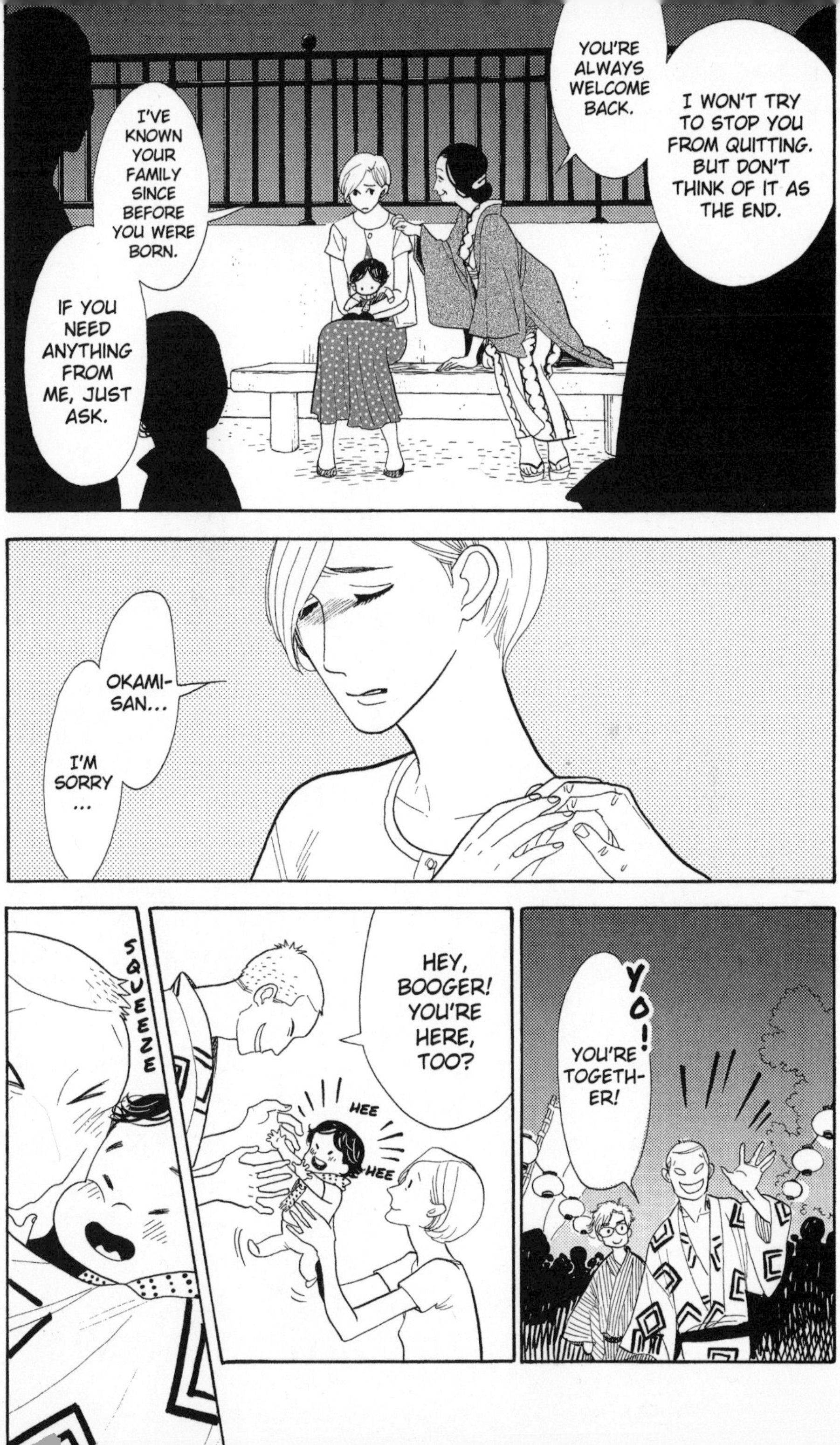
I WON'T TRY TO STOP YOU FROM QUITTING. BUT DON'T THINK OF IT AS THE END.
YOU'RE ALWAYS WELCOME BACK.
I'VE KNOWN YOUR FAMILY SINCE BEFORE YOU WERE BORN.
IF YOU NEED ANYTHING FROM ME, JUST ASK.
OKAMI-SAN...
I'M SORRY ...
YO!
YOU'RE TOGETHER!
HEY, BOOGER! YOU'RE HERE, TOO?
HEE HEE
SQUEEZE

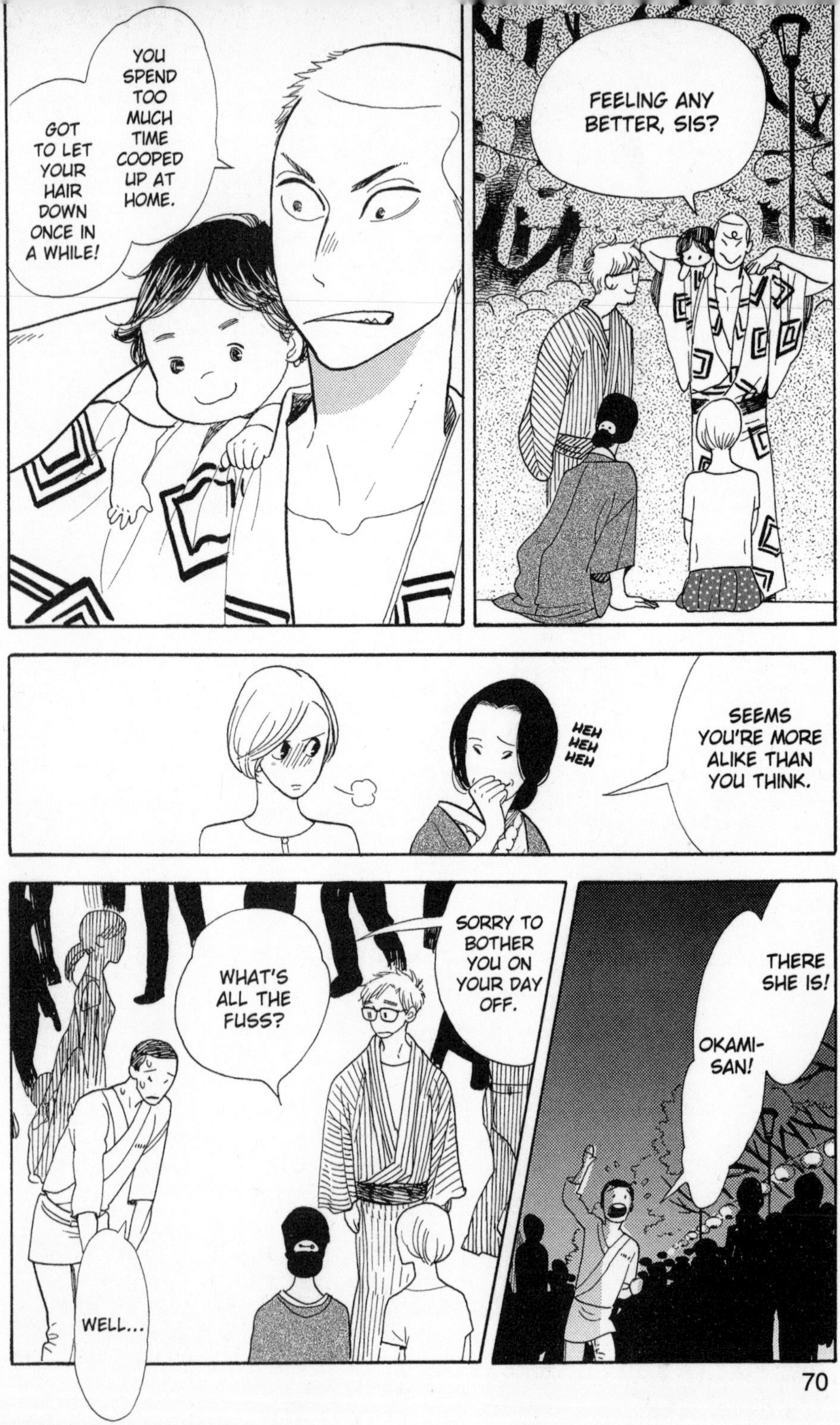
FEELING ANY BETTER, SIS?
YOU SPEND TOO MUCH TIME COOPED UP AT HOME.
GOT TO LET YOUR HAIR DOWN ONCE IN A WHILE!
SEEMS YOU'RE MORE ALIKE THAN YOU THINK.
HEH HEH HEH
THERE SHE IS!
OKAMI-SAN!
SORRY TO BOTHER YOU ON YOUR DAY OFF.
WHAT'S ALL THE FUSS?
WELL...

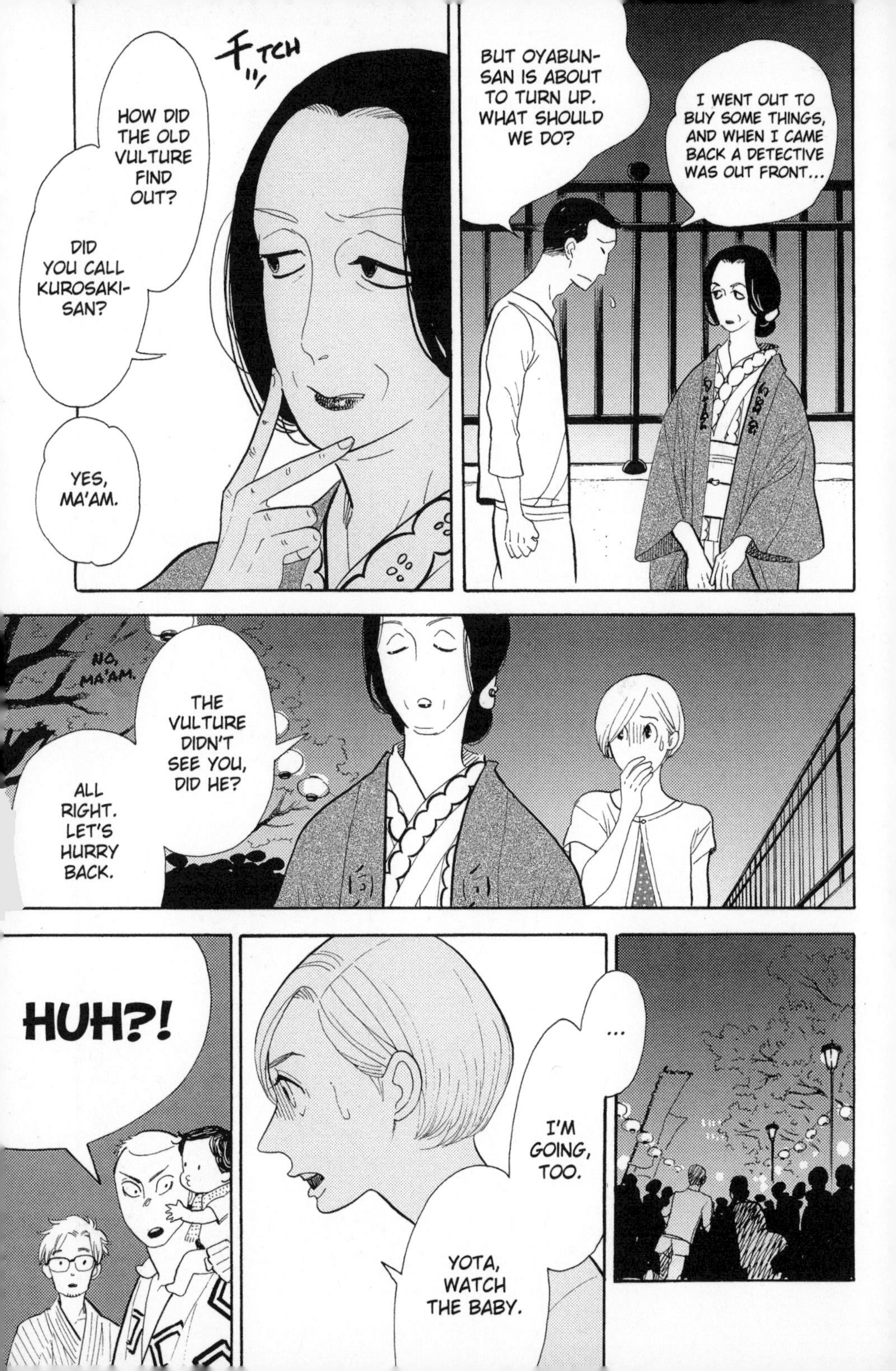

I WENT OUT TO BUY SOME THINGS, AND WHEN I CAME BACK A DETECTIVE WAS OUT FRONT...
BUT OYABUN-SAN IS ABOUT TO TURN UP. WHAT SHOULD WE DO?
チTCH
HOW DID THE OLD VULTURE FIND OUT?
DID YOU CALL KUROSAKI-SAN?
YES, MA'AM.
THE VULTURE DIDN'T SEE YOU, DID HE?
NO, MA'AM.
ALL RIGHT. LET'S HURRY BACK.
...
I'M GOING, TOO.
YOTA, WATCH THE BABY.
HUH?!

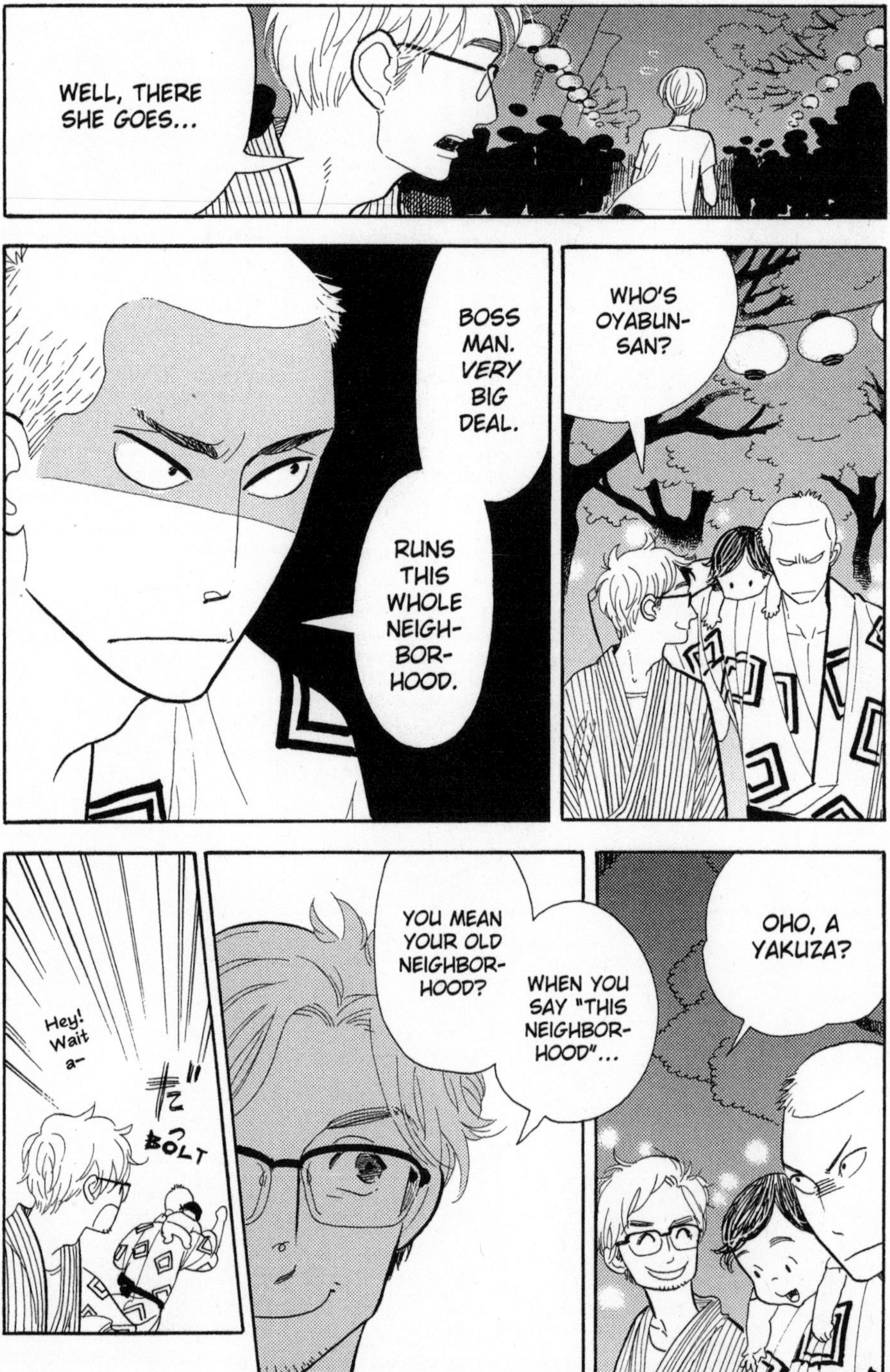
WELL, THERE SHE GOES...
WHO'S OYABUN-SAN?
BOSS MAN. VERY BIG DEAL.
RUNS THIS WHOLE NEIGHBOR-HOOD.
OHO, A YAKUZA?
WHEN YOU SAY "THIS NEIGHBOR-HOOD"...
YOU MEAN YOUR OLD NEIGHBOR-HOOD?
Hey! Wait a-
BOLT

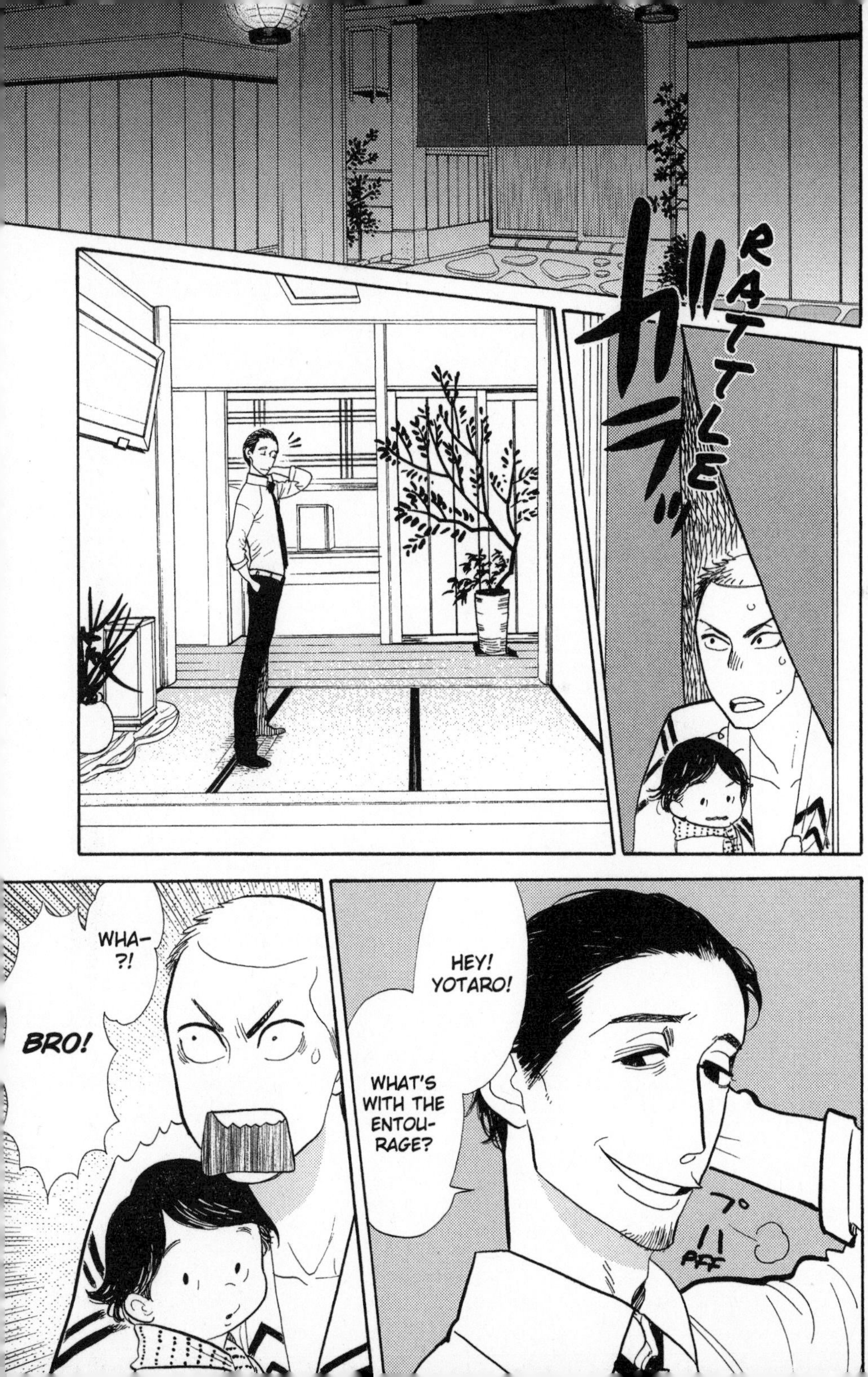
ガラッ
RATTLE
HEY! YOTARO!
WHAT'S WITH THE ENTOU-RAGE?
PFF
WHA- ?!
BRO!

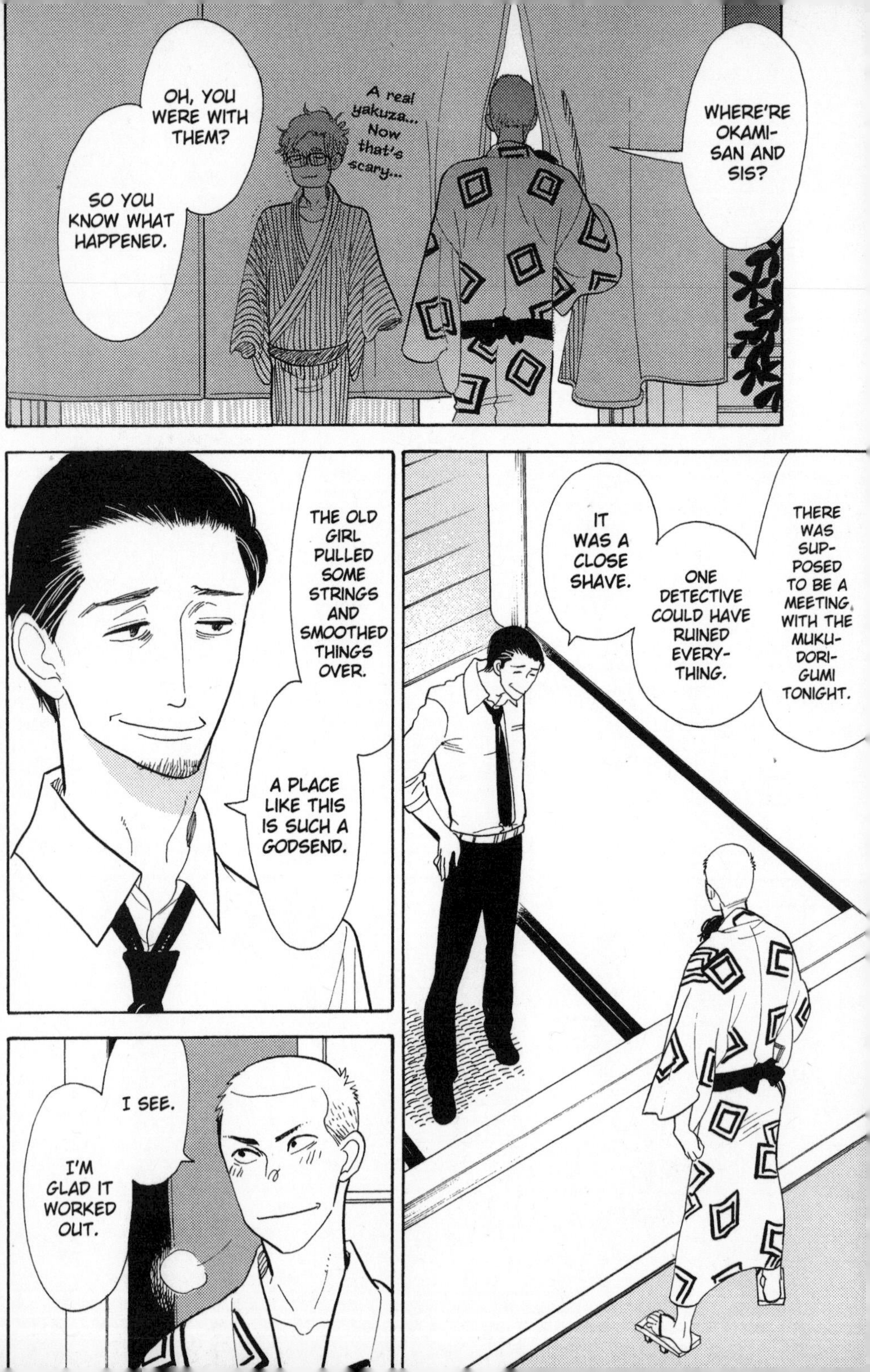

WHERE'RE OKAMI-SAN AND SIS?
A real yakuza... Now that's scary...
OH, YOU WERE WITH THEM?
SO YOU KNOW WHAT HAPPENED.
THERE WAS SUPPOSED TO BE A MEETING WITH THE MUKUDORI-GUMI TONIGHT.
IT WAS A CLOSE SHAVE.
ONE DETECTIVE COULD HAVE RUINED EVERYTHING.
THE OLD GIRL PULLED SOME STRINGS AND SMOOTHED THINGS OVER.
A PLACE LIKE THIS IS SUCH A GODSEND.
I SEE.
I'M GLAD IT WORKED OUT.

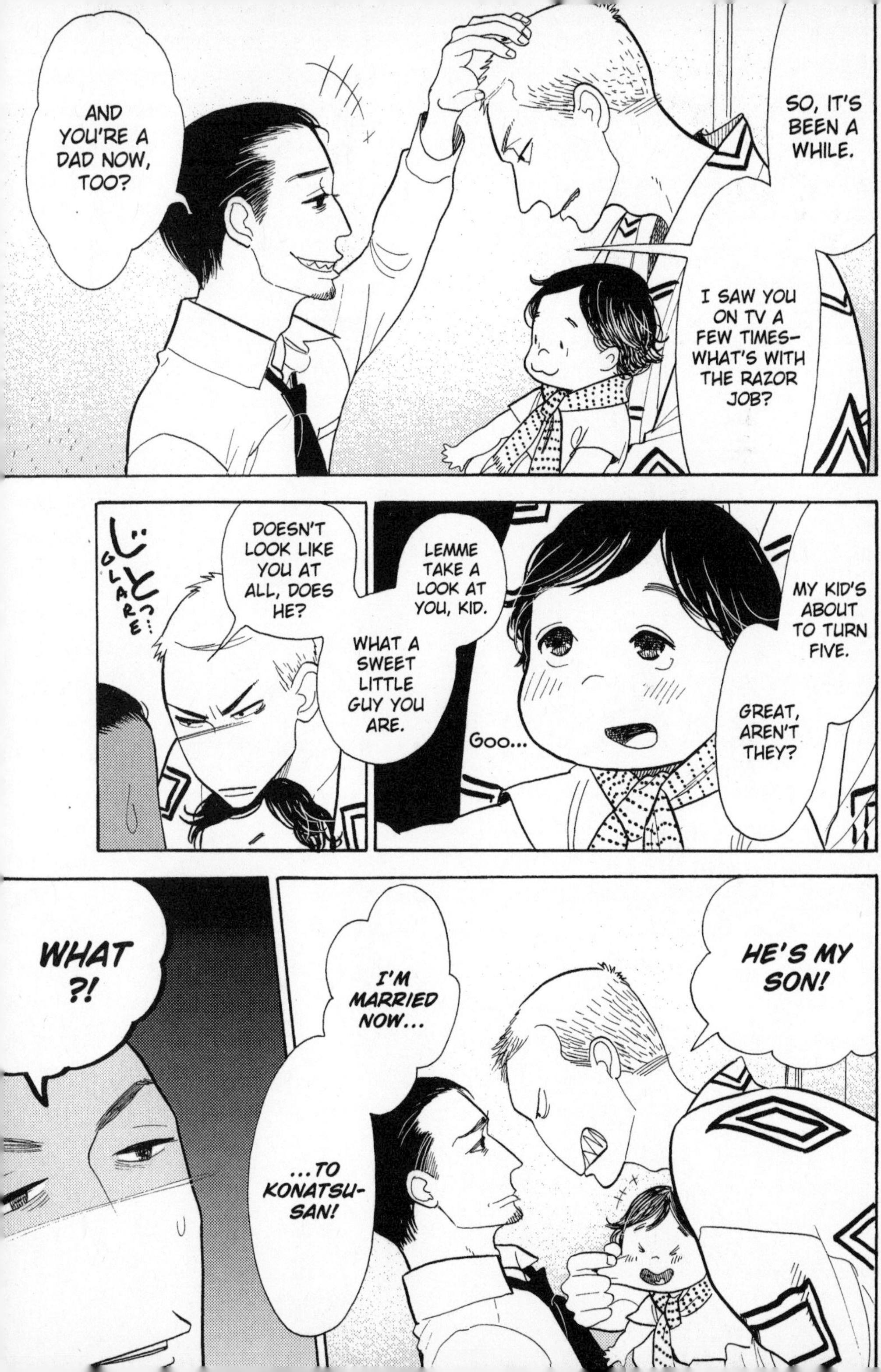
SO, IT'S BEEN A WHILE.
I SAW YOU ON TV A FEW TIMES—WHAT'S WITH THE RAZOR JOB?
AND YOU'RE A DAD NOW, TOO?
MY KID'S ABOUT TO TURN FIVE.
GREAT, AREN'T THEY?
LEMME TAKE A LOOK AT YOU, KID.
WHAT A SWEET LITTLE GUY YOU ARE.
Goo...
DOESN'T LOOK LIKE YOU AT ALL, DOES HE?
GLARE
HE'S MY SON!
I'M MARRIED NOW...
...TO KONATSU-SAN!
WHAT?!

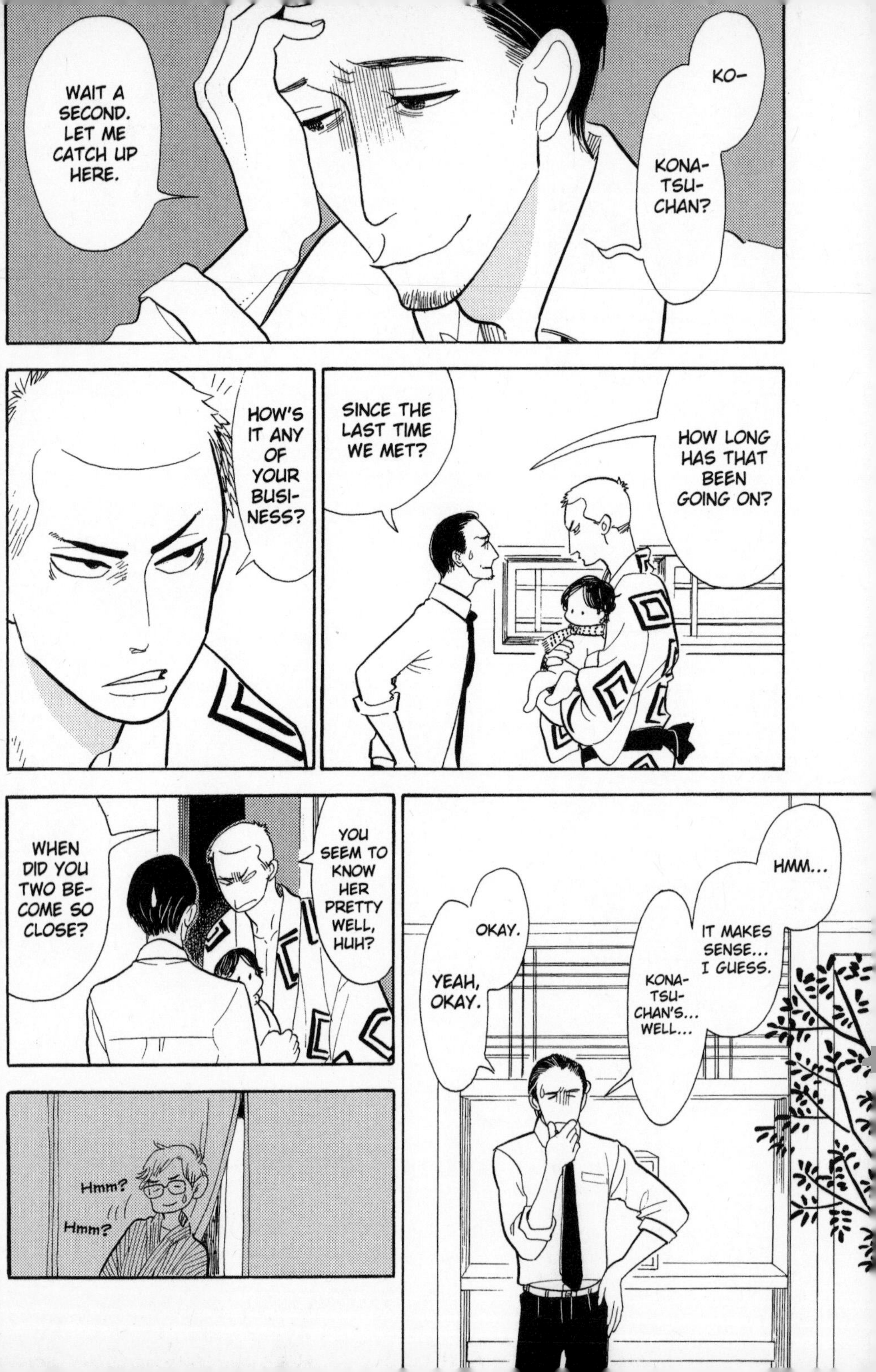
KO-
KONA-TSU-CHAN?
WAIT A SECOND. LET ME CATCH UP HERE.
HOW LONG HAS THAT BEEN GOING ON?
SINCE THE LAST TIME WE MET?
HOW'S IT ANY OF YOUR BUSI-NESS?
HMM...
IT MAKES SENSE... I GUESS.
KONA-TSU-CHAN'S... WELL...
OKAY.
YEAH, OKAY.
YOU SEEM TO KNOW HER PRETTY WELL, HUH?
WHEN DID YOU TWO BE-COME SO CLOSE?
Hmm?
Hmm?

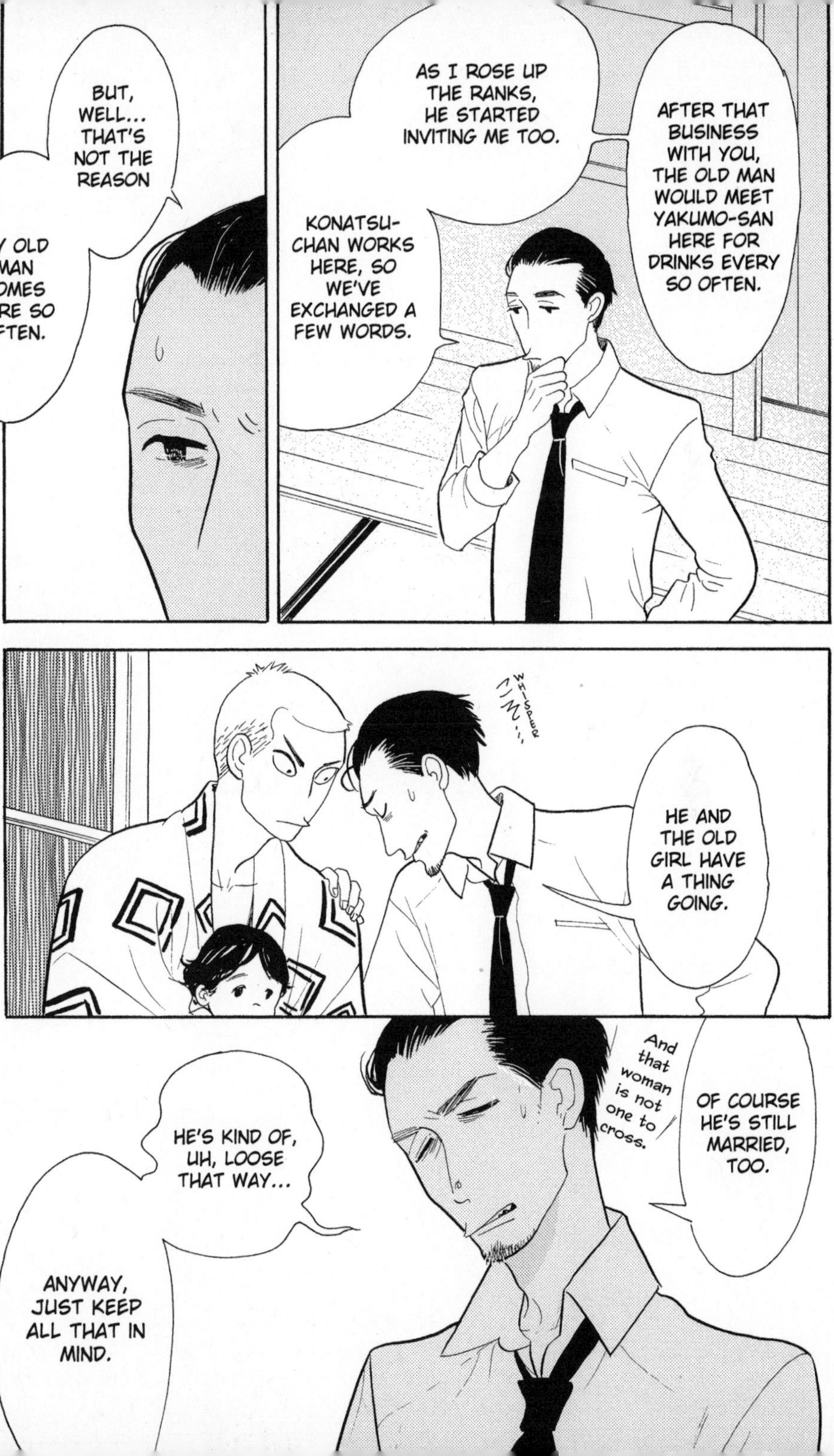
AFTER THAT BUSINESS WITH YOU, THE OLD MAN WOULD MEET YAKUMO-SAN HERE FOR DRINKS EVERY SO OFTEN.
AS I ROSE UP THE RANKS, HE STARTED INVITING ME TOO.
KONATSU-CHAN WORKS HERE, SO WE'VE EXCHANGED A FEW WORDS.
BUT, WELL... THAT'S NOT THE REASON
MY OLD MAN COMES HERE SO OFTEN.
WHISPER
HE AND THE OLD GIRL HAVE A THING GOING.
OF COURSE HE'S STILL MARRIED, TOO.
And that woman is not one to cross.
HE'S KIND OF, UH, LOOSE THAT WAY...
ANYWAY, JUST KEEP ALL THAT IN MIND.

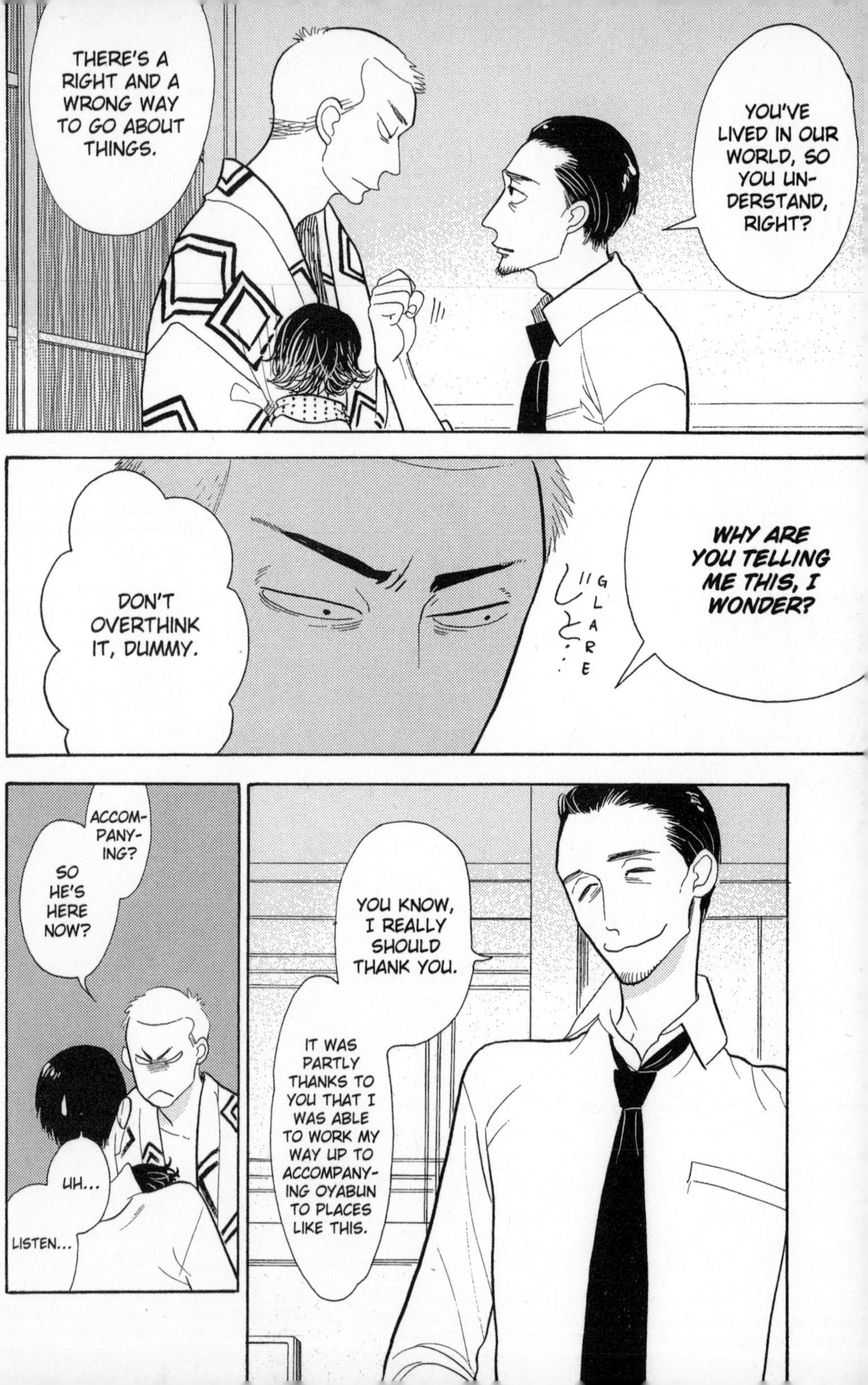
YOU'VE LIVED IN OUR WORLD, SO YOU UNDERSTAND, RIGHT?
THERE'S A RIGHT AND A WRONG WAY TO GO ABOUT THINGS.
WHY ARE YOU TELLING ME THIS, I WONDER?
GLARE
DON'T OVERTHINK IT, DUMMY.
YOU KNOW, I REALLY SHOULD THANK YOU.
IT WAS PARTLY THANKS TO YOU THAT I WAS ABLE TO WORK MY WAY UP TO ACCOMPANYING OYABUN TO PLACES LIKE THIS.
ACCOMPANYING?
SO HE'S HERE NOW?
UH...
LISTEN...

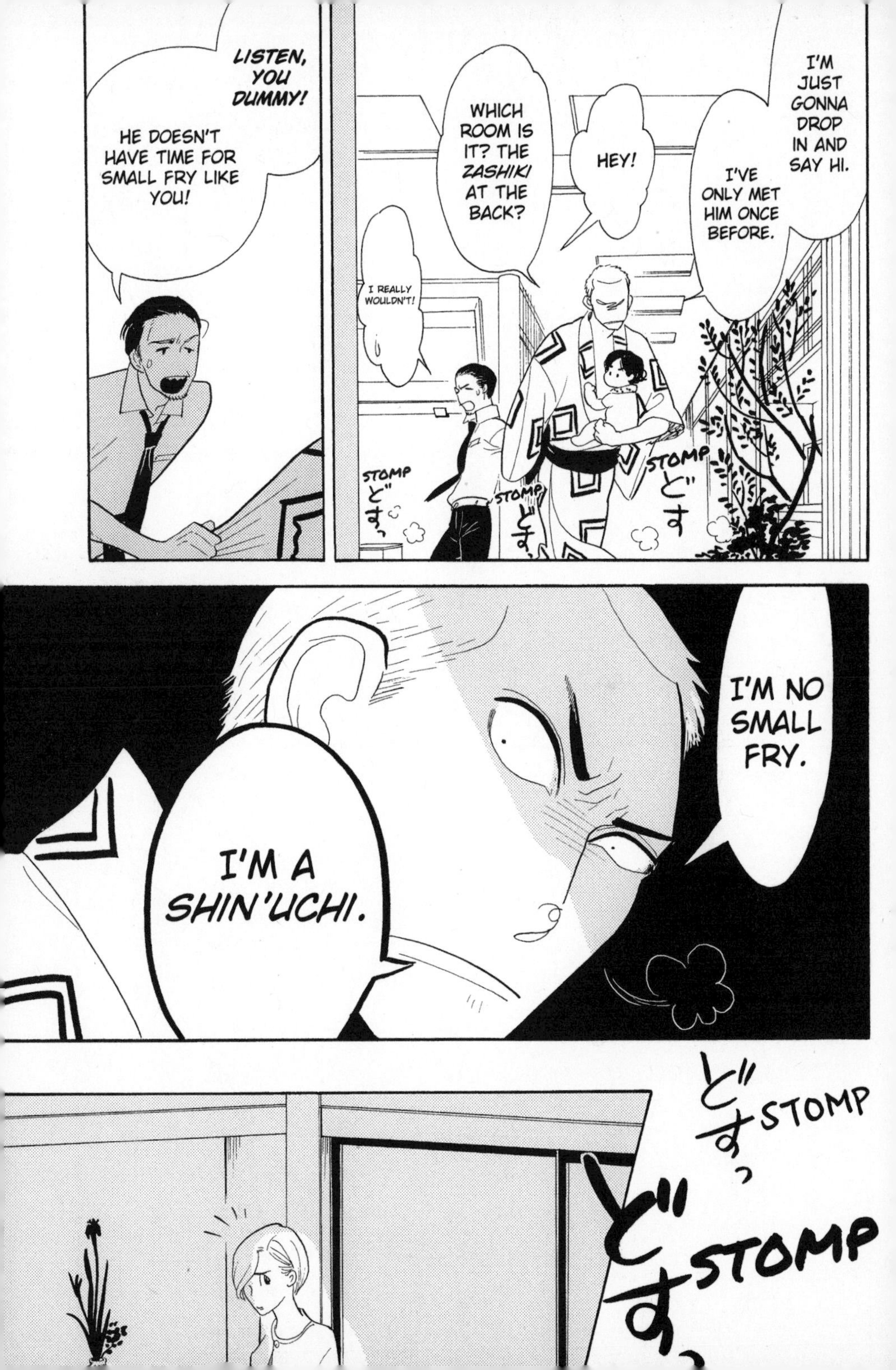
I'M JUST GONNA DROP IN AND SAY HI.
I'VE ONLY MET HIM ONCE BEFORE.
HEY!
WHICH ROOM IS IT? THE *ZASHIKI* AT THE BACK?
I REALLY WOULDN'T!
STOMP どす
STOMP どすっ
STOMP どすっ
LISTEN, YOU DUMMY!
HE DOESN'T HAVE TIME FOR SMALL FRY LIKE YOU!
I'M NO SMALL FRY.
I'M A *SHIN'UCHI*.
どすっ STOMP
どすっ STOMP

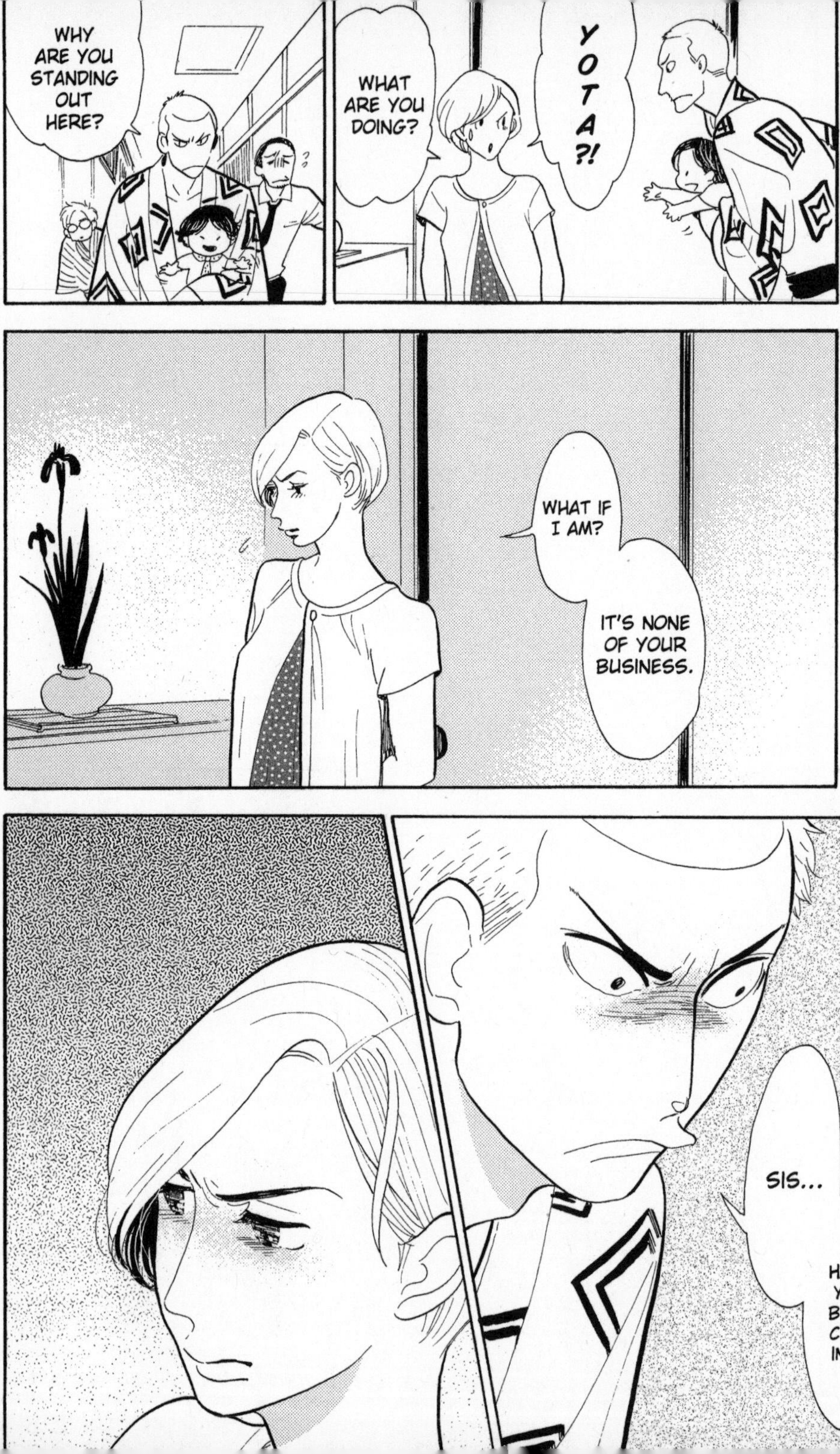
YOTA?!
WHAT ARE YOU DOING?
WHY ARE YOU STANDING OUT HERE?
WHAT IF I AM?
IT'S NONE OF YOUR BUSINESS.
SIS...
HAVE YOU BEEN CRY-ING?

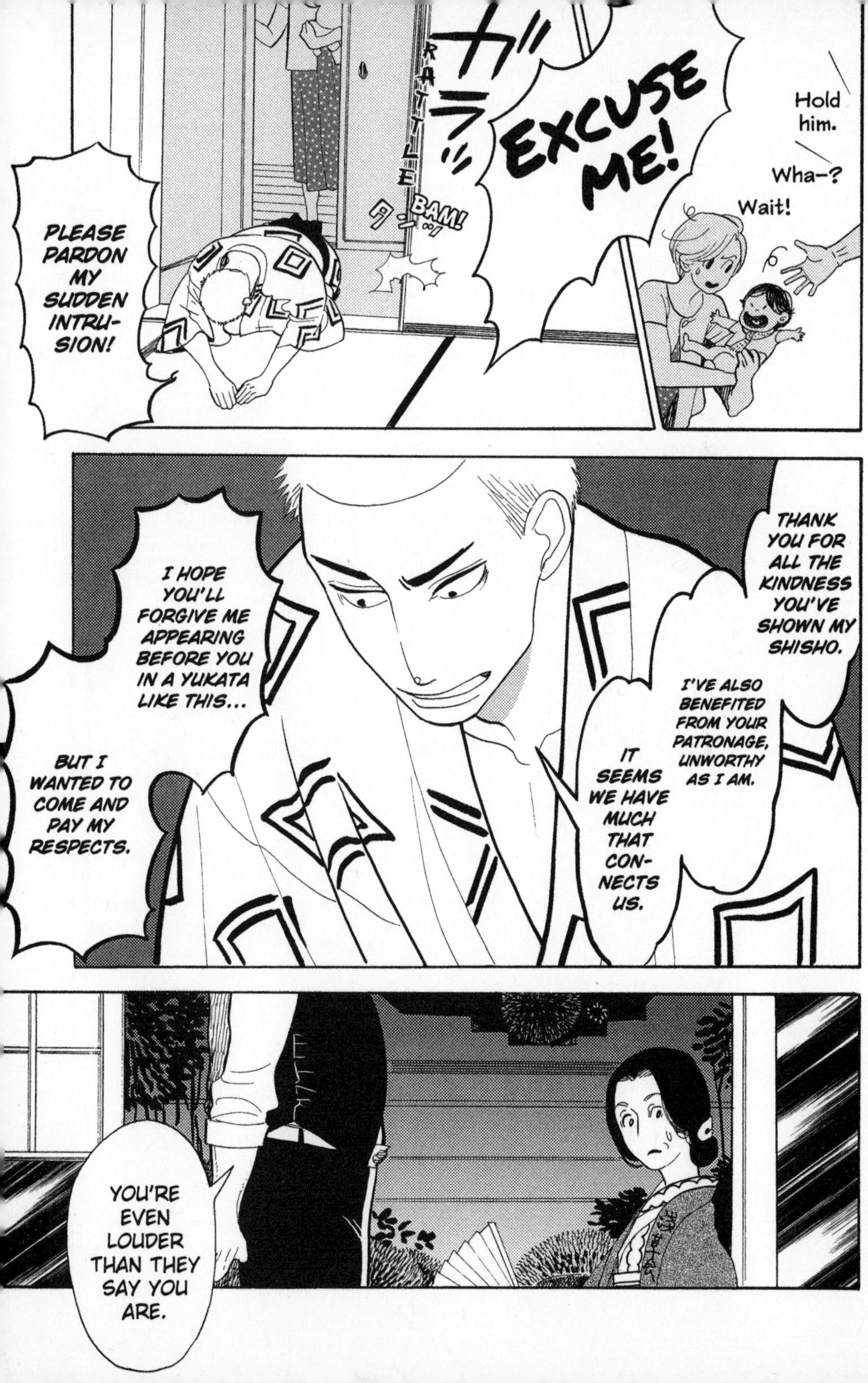
Hold him.
Wha–?
Wait!
EXCUSE ME!
RATTLE
BAM!
PLEASE PARDON MY SUDDEN INTRUSION!
THANK YOU FOR ALL THE KINDNESS YOU'VE SHOWN MY SHISHO.
I'VE ALSO BENEFITED FROM YOUR PATRONAGE, UNWORTHY AS I AM.
IT SEEMS WE HAVE MUCH THAT CONNECTS US.
I HOPE YOU'LL FORGIVE ME APPEARING BEFORE YOU IN A YUKATA LIKE THIS...
BUT I WANTED TO COME AND PAY MY RESPECTS.
YOU'RE EVEN LOUDER THAN THEY SAY YOU ARE.

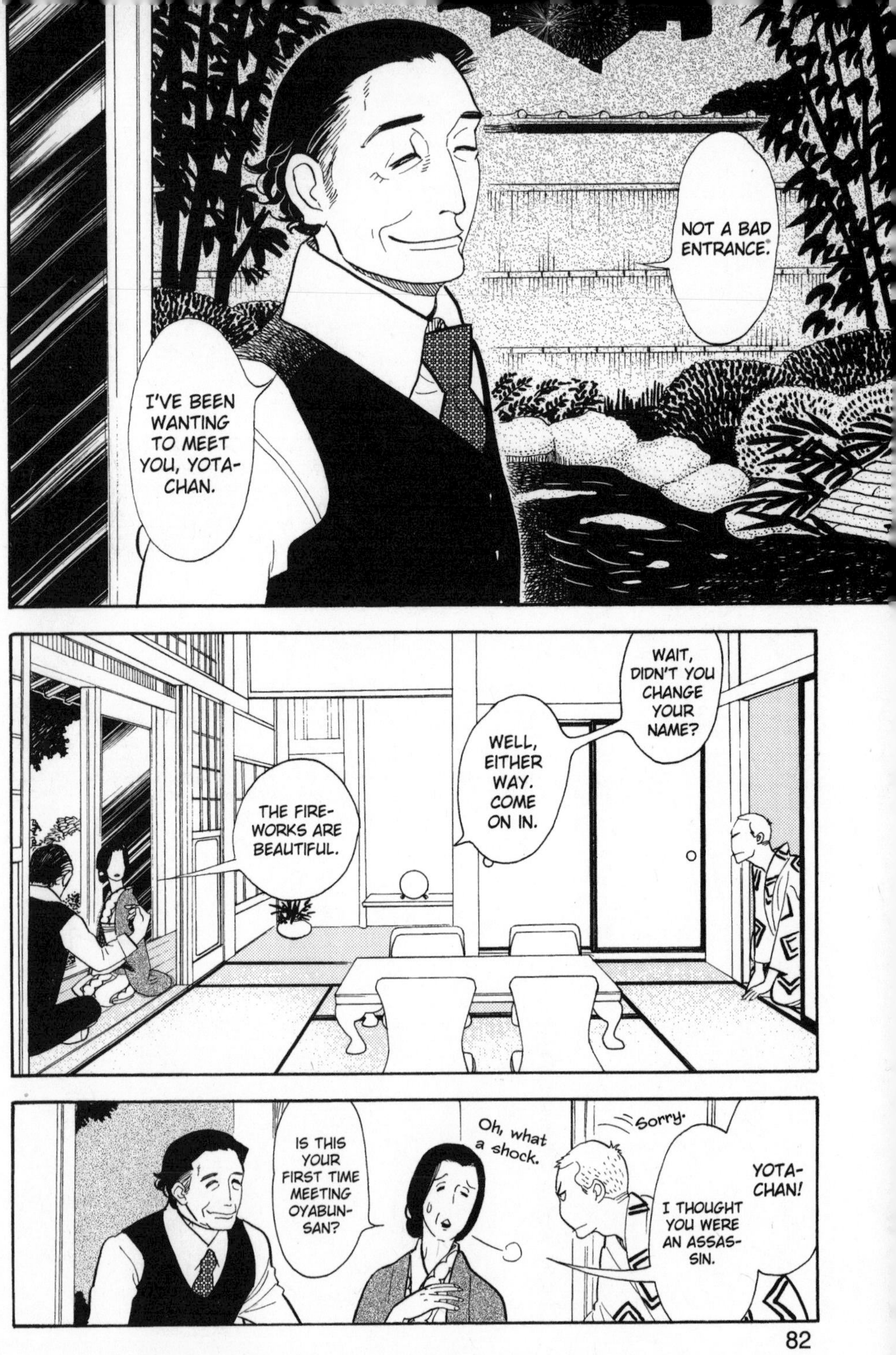
NOT A BAD ENTRANCE.
I'VE BEEN WANTING TO MEET YOU, YOTA-CHAN.
WAIT, DIDN'T YOU CHANGE YOUR NAME?
WELL, EITHER WAY. COME ON IN.
THE FIRE-WORKS ARE BEAUTIFUL.
YOTA-CHAN!
I THOUGHT YOU WERE AN ASSAS-SIN.
Sorry.
Oh, what a shock.
IS THIS YOUR FIRST TIME MEETING OYABUN-SAN?

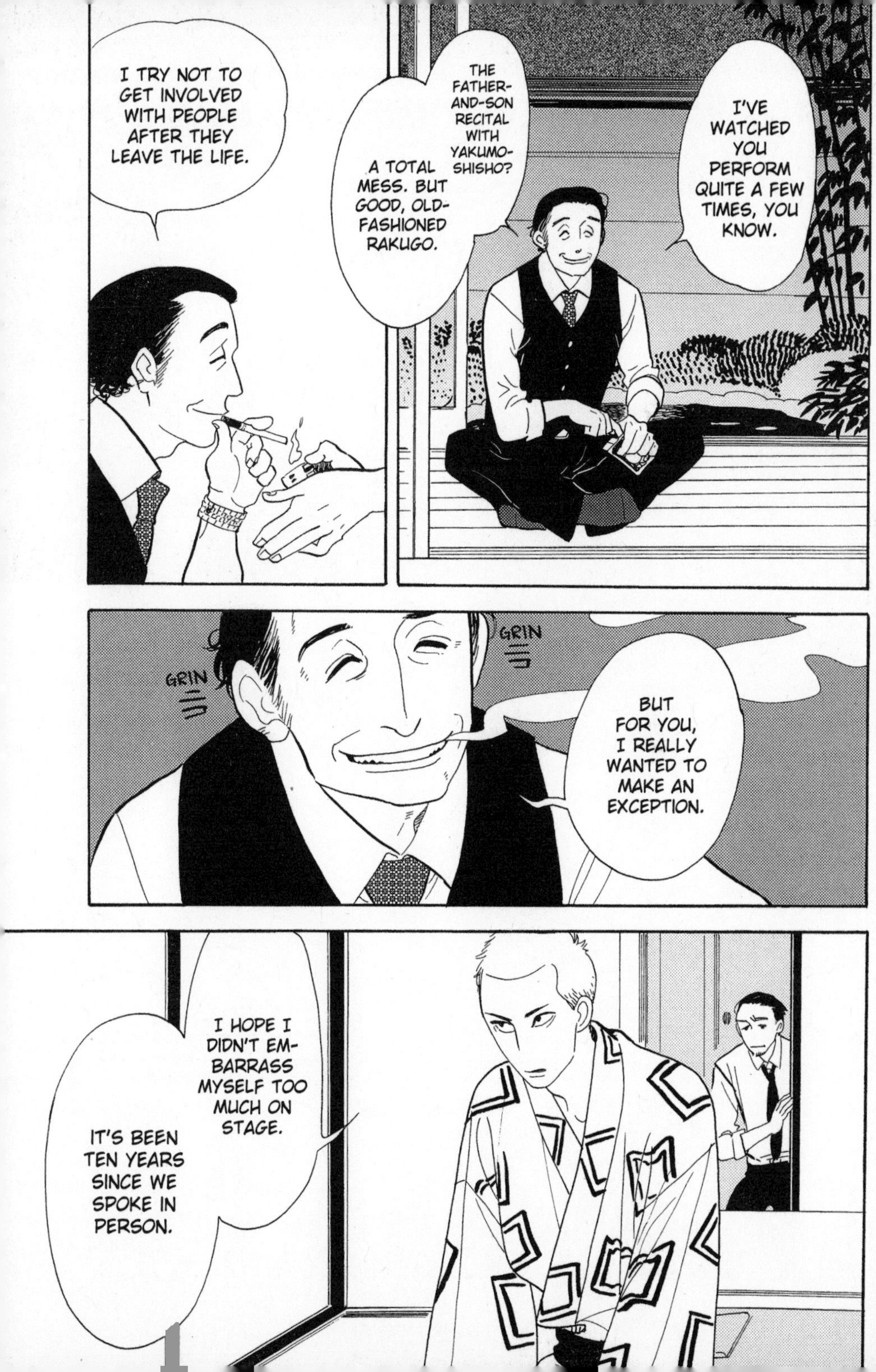
I'VE WATCHED YOU PERFORM QUITE A FEW TIMES, YOU KNOW.
THE FATHER-AND-SON RECITAL WITH YAKUMO-SHISHO?
A TOTAL MESS. BUT GOOD, OLD-FASHIONED RAKUGO.
I TRY NOT TO GET INVOLVED WITH PEOPLE AFTER THEY LEAVE THE LIFE.
GRIN
BUT FOR YOU, I REALLY WANTED TO MAKE AN EXCEPTION.
GRIN
I HOPE I DIDN'T EM-BARRASS MYSELF TOO MUCH ON STAGE.
IT'S BEEN TEN YEARS SINCE WE SPOKE IN PERSON.

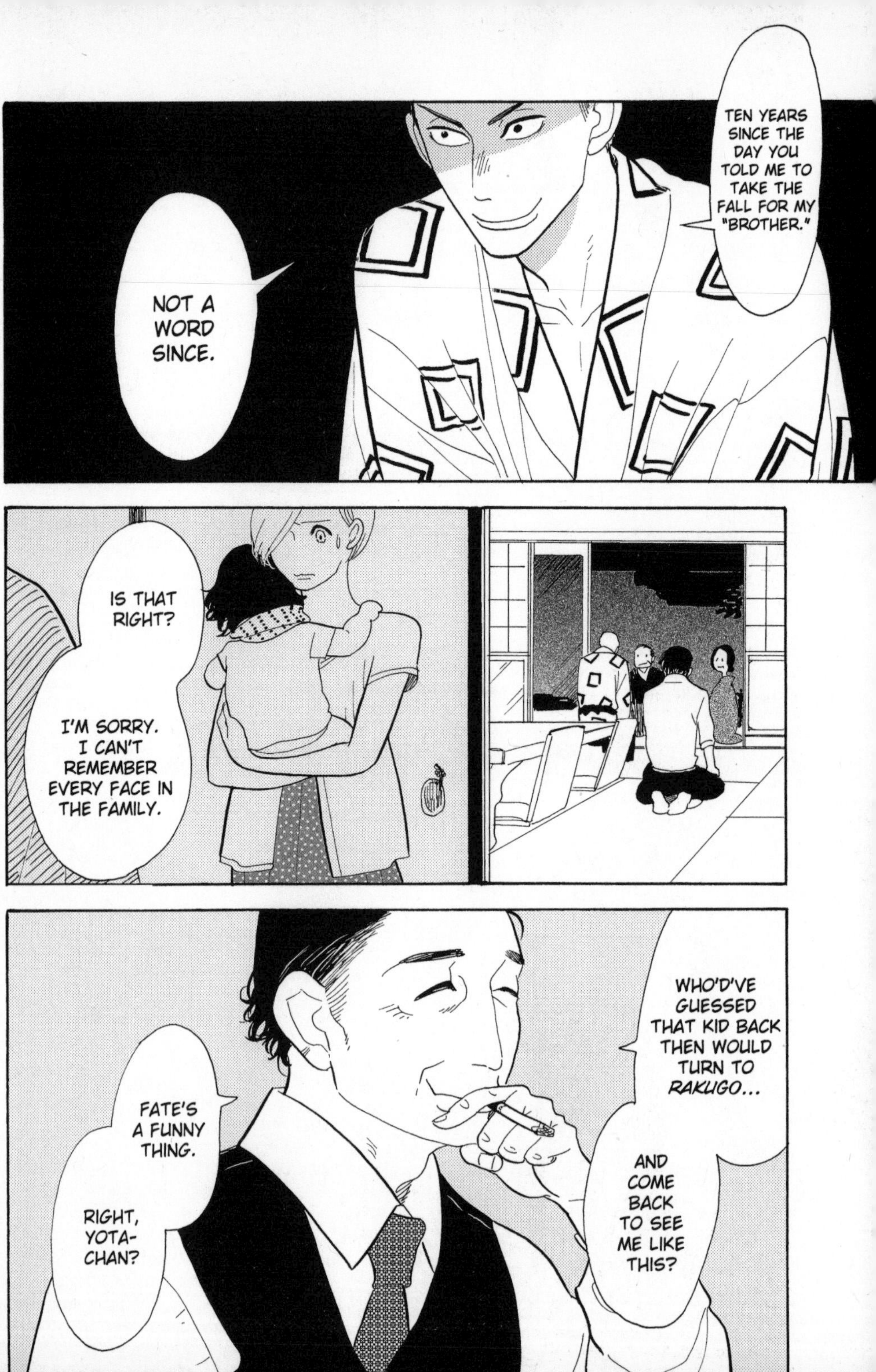
TEN YEARS SINCE THE DAY YOU TOLD ME TO TAKE THE FALL FOR MY "BROTHER."
NOT A WORD SINCE.
IS THAT RIGHT?
I'M SORRY. I CAN'T REMEMBER EVERY FACE IN THE FAMILY.
WHO'D'VE GUESSED THAT KID BACK THEN WOULD TURN TO *RAKUGO*...
AND COME BACK TO SEE ME LIKE THIS?
FATE'S A FUNNY THING.
RIGHT, YOTA-CHAN?

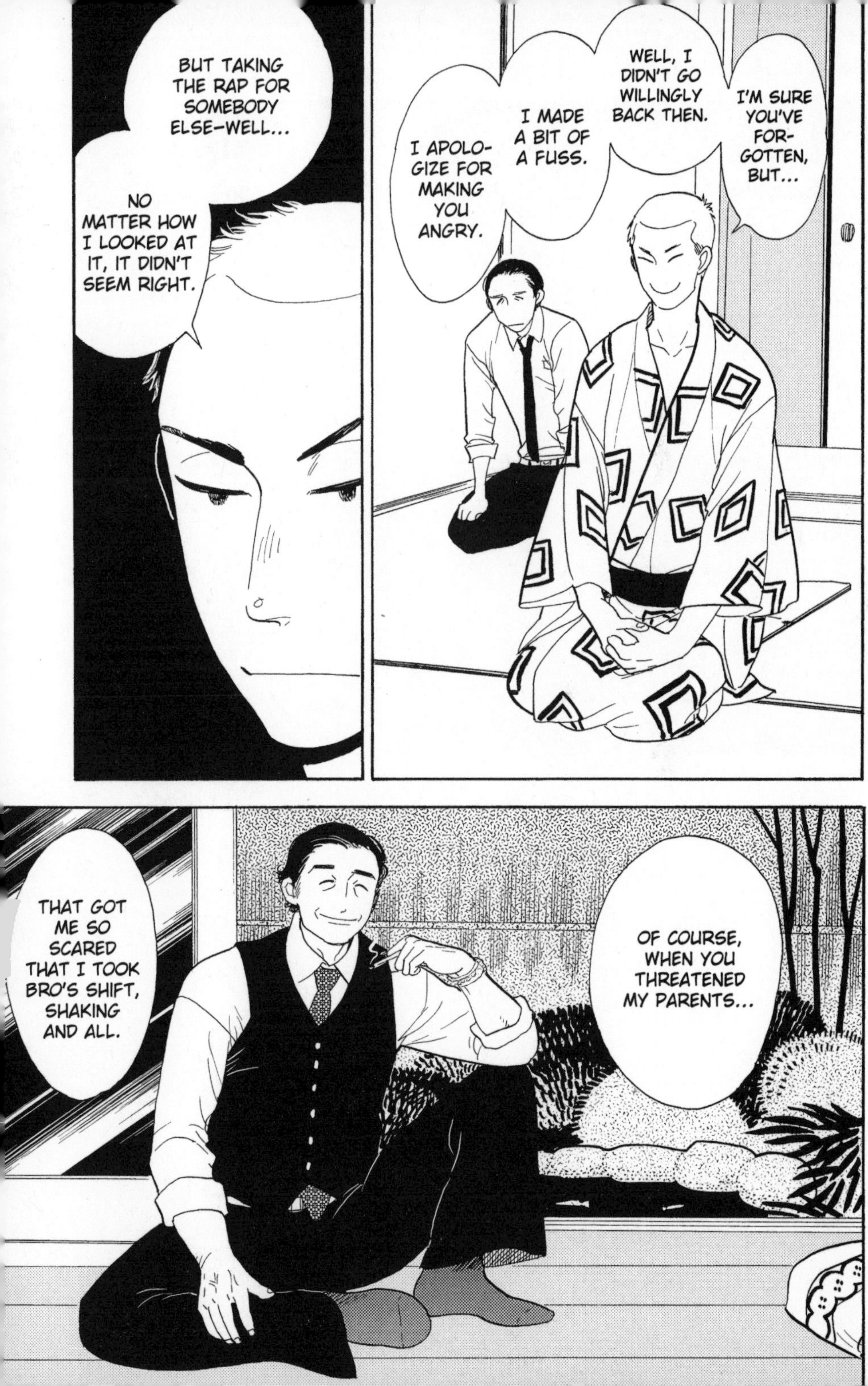
I'M SURE YOU'VE FOR-GOTTEN, BUT...
WELL, I DIDN'T GO WILLINGLY BACK THEN.
I MADE A BIT OF A FUSS.
I APOLOGIZE FOR MAKING YOU ANGRY.
BUT TAKING THE RAP FOR SOMEBODY ELSE—WELL...
NO MATTER HOW I LOOKED AT IT, IT DIDN'T SEEM RIGHT.
OF COURSE, WHEN YOU THREATENED MY PARENTS...
THAT GOT ME SO SCARED THAT I TOOK BRO'S SHIFT, SHAKING AND ALL.

I WAS EVEN MORE OF A YOTARO—MORE OF A FOOL—BACK THEN THAN I AM NOW.

AND THEN, WHILE I WAS IN PRISON,

MY OLD MAN GOT SICK AND DIED.

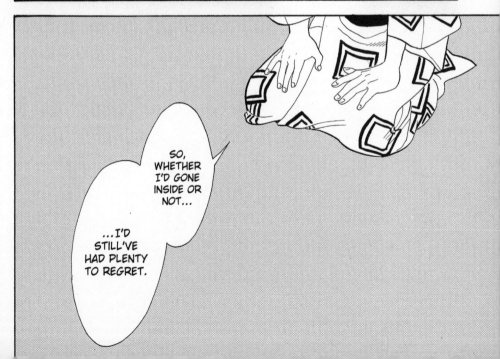

SO, WHETHER I'D GONE INSIDE OR NOT...

...I'D STILL'VE HAD PLENTY TO REGRET.

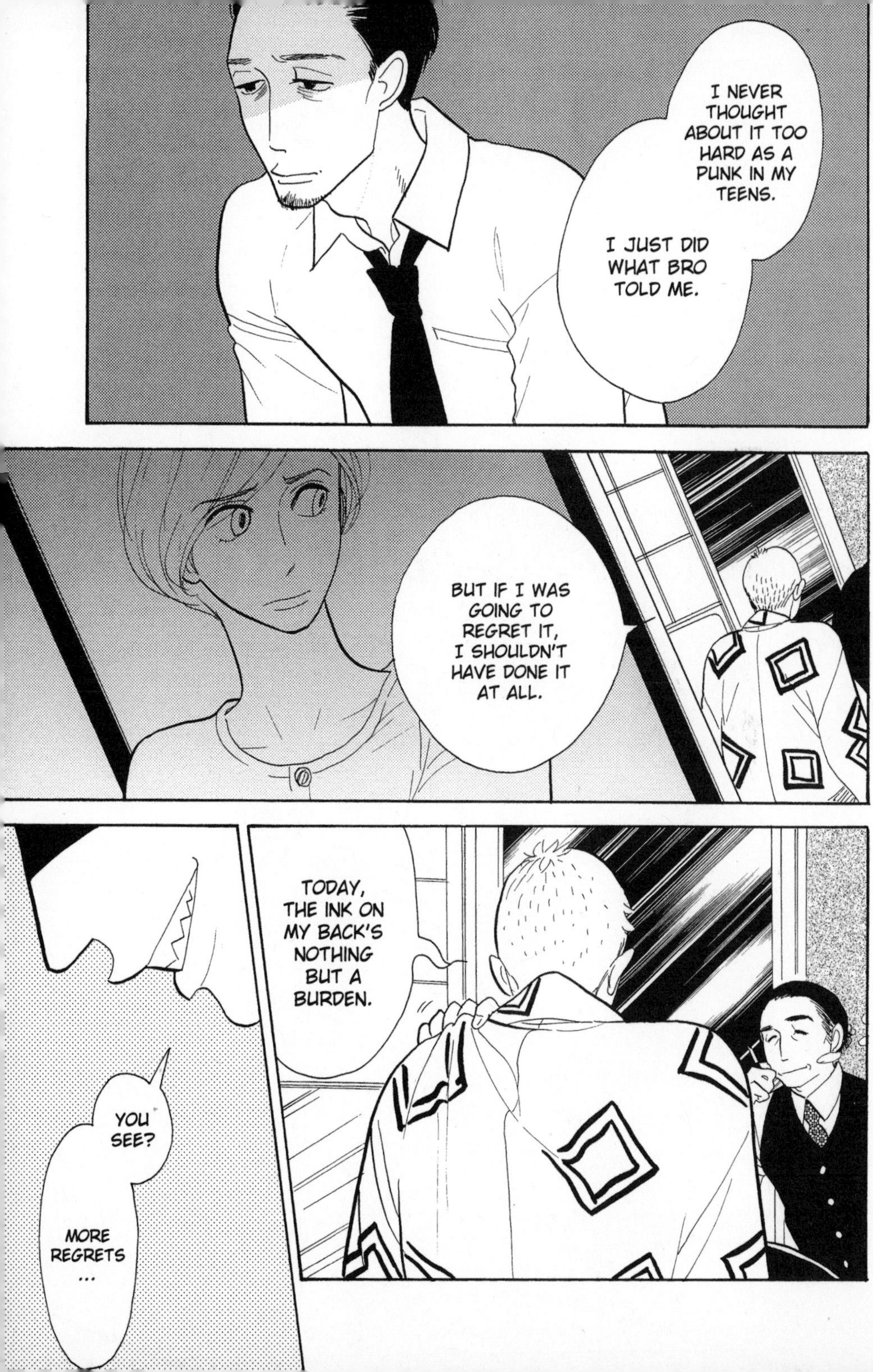
I NEVER THOUGHT ABOUT IT TOO HARD AS A PUNK IN MY TEENS.
I JUST DID WHAT BRO TOLD ME.
BUT IF I WAS GOING TO REGRET IT, I SHOULDN'T HAVE DONE IT AT ALL.
TODAY, THE INK ON MY BACK'S NOTHING BUT A BURDEN.
YOU SEE?
MORE REGRETS ...

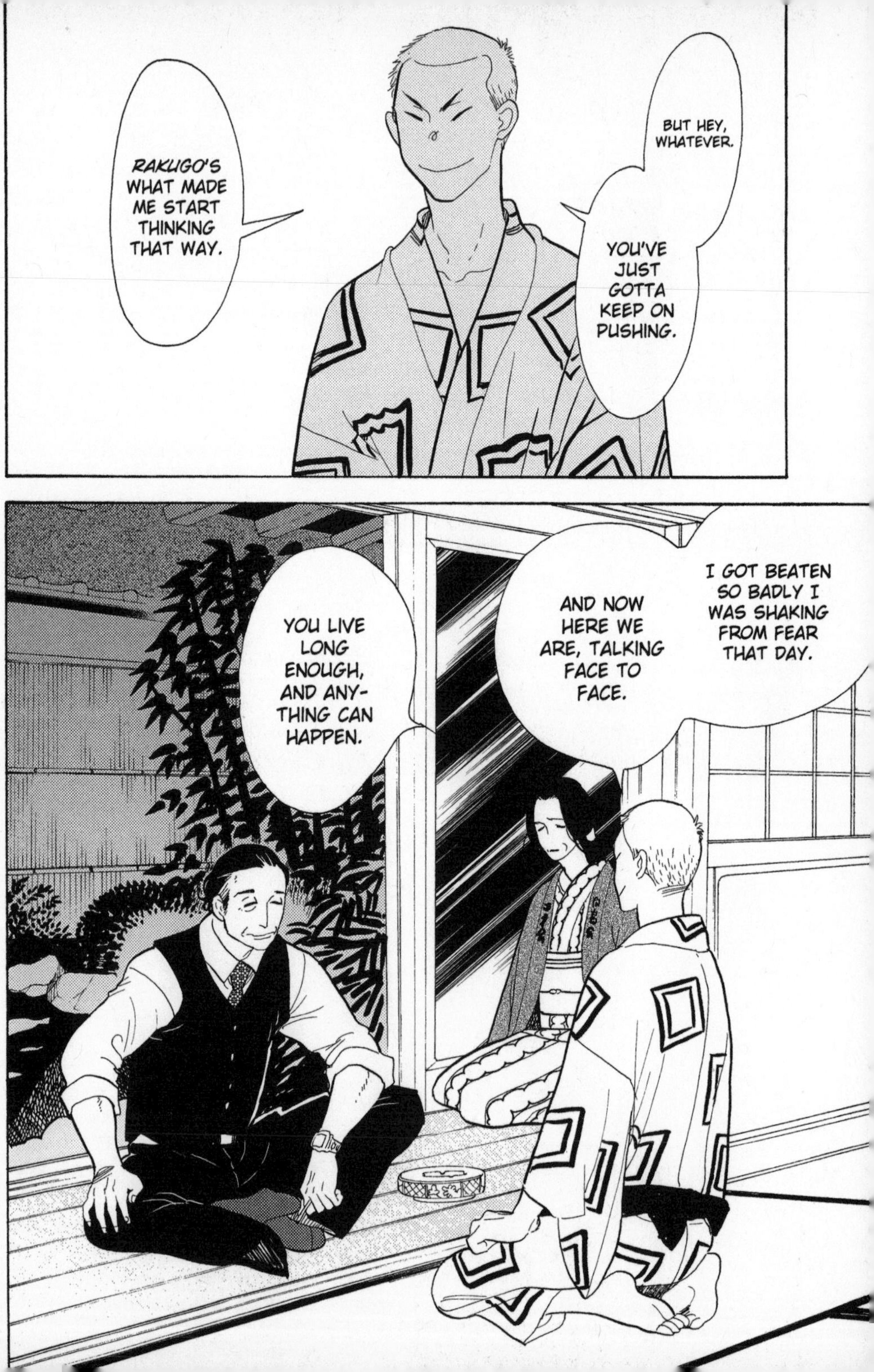
BUT HEY, WHATEVER.
YOU'VE JUST GOTTA KEEP ON PUSHING.
RAKUGO'S WHAT MADE ME START THINKING THAT WAY.
I GOT BEATEN SO BADLY I WAS SHAKING FROM FEAR THAT DAY.
AND NOW HERE WE ARE, TALKING FACE TO FACE.
YOU LIVE LONG ENOUGH, AND ANYTHING CAN HAPPEN.

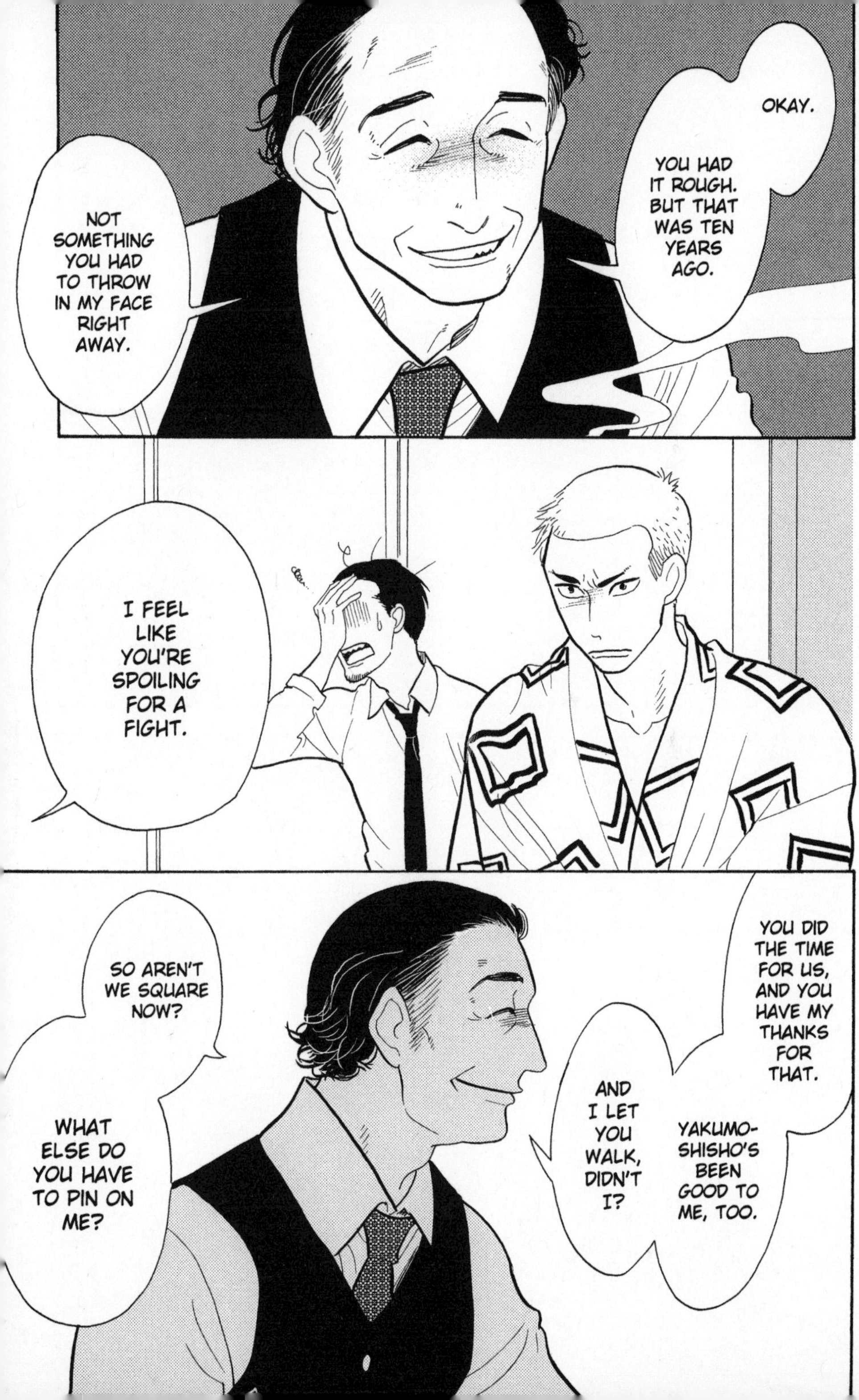
OKAY.
YOU HAD IT ROUGH. BUT THAT WAS TEN YEARS AGO.
NOT SOMETHING YOU HAD TO THROW IN MY FACE RIGHT AWAY.
I FEEL LIKE YOU'RE SPOILING FOR A FIGHT.
YOU DID THE TIME FOR US, AND YOU HAVE MY THANKS FOR THAT.
YAKUMO-SHISHO'S BEEN GOOD TO ME, TOO.
AND I LET YOU WALK, DIDN'T I?
SO AREN'T WE SQUARE NOW?
WHAT ELSE DO YOU HAVE TO PIN ON ME?

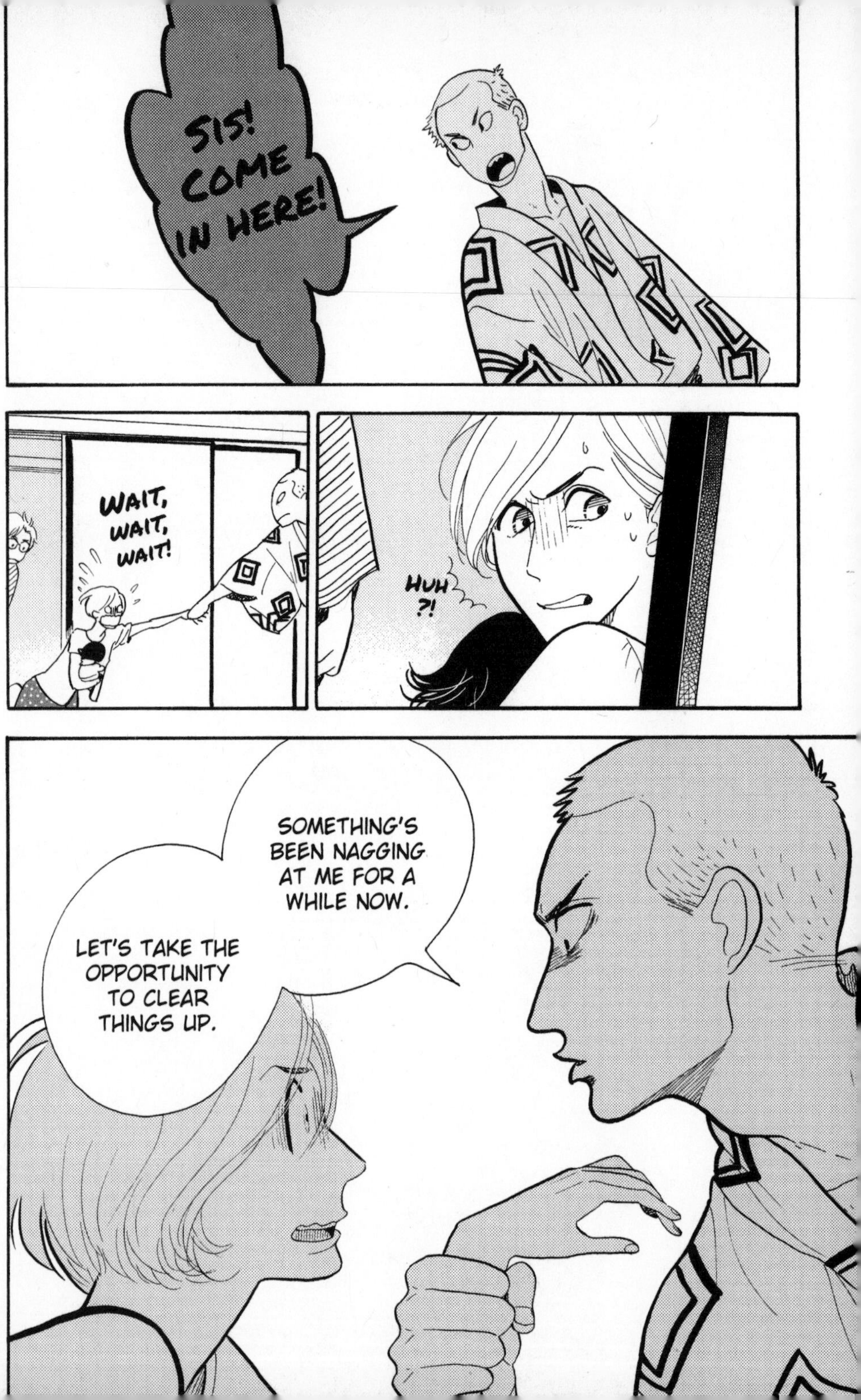
SIS! COME IN HERE!
HUH?!
WAIT, WAIT, WAIT!
SOMETHING'S BEEN NAGGING AT ME FOR A WHILE NOW.
LET'S TAKE THE OPPORTUNITY TO CLEAR THINGS UP.

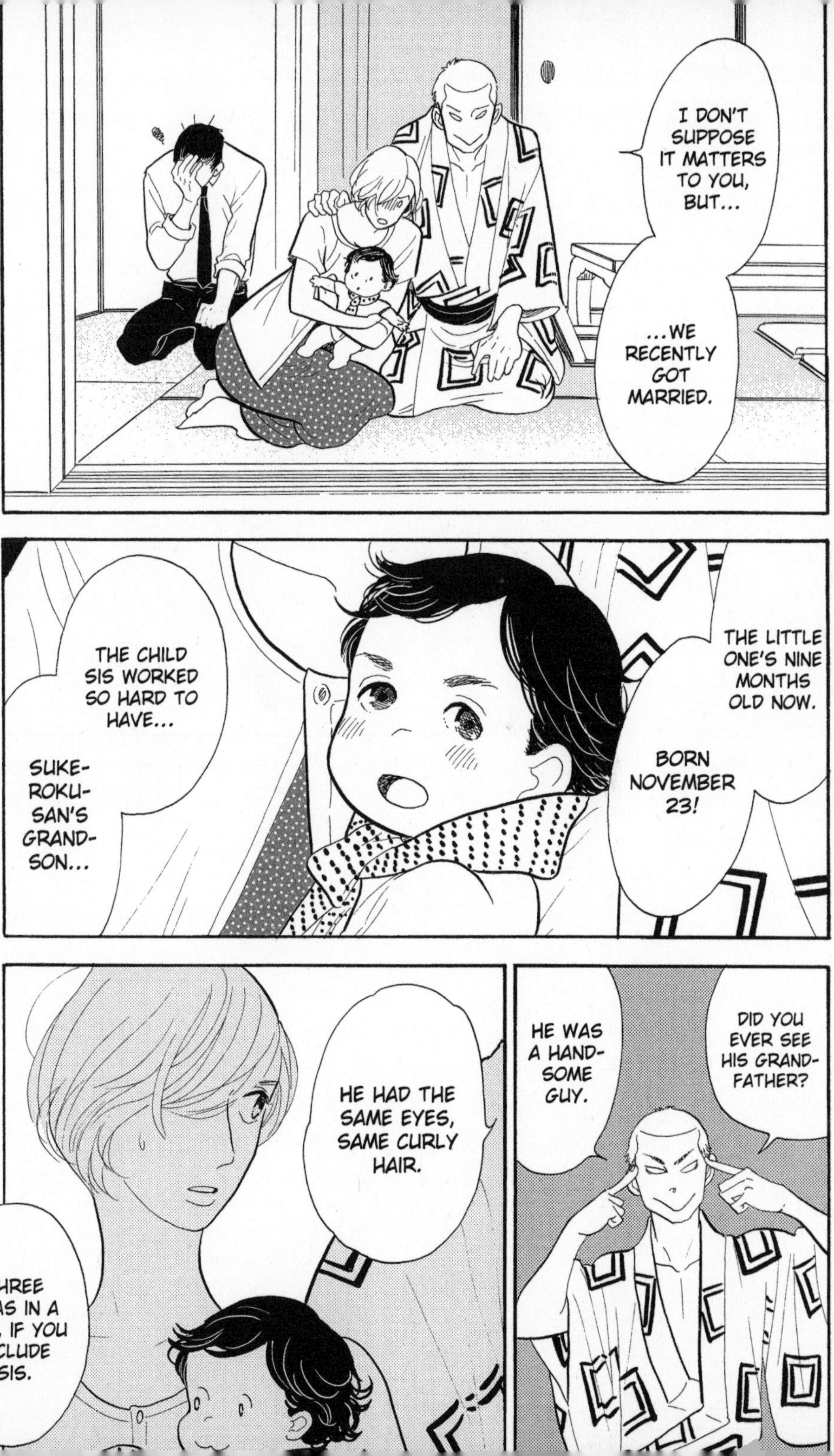
I DON'T SUPPOSE IT MATTERS TO YOU, BUT...
...WE RECENTLY GOT MARRIED.
THE LITTLE ONE'S NINE MONTHS OLD NOW.
BORN NOVEMBER 23!
THE CHILD SIS WORKED SO HARD TO HAVE...
SUKE-ROKU-SAN'S GRAND-SON...
DID YOU EVER SEE HIS GRAND-FATHER?
HE WAS A HAND-SOME GUY.
HE HAD THE SAME EYES, SAME CURLY HAIR.
THREE PEAS IN A POD, IF YOU INCLUDE SIS.

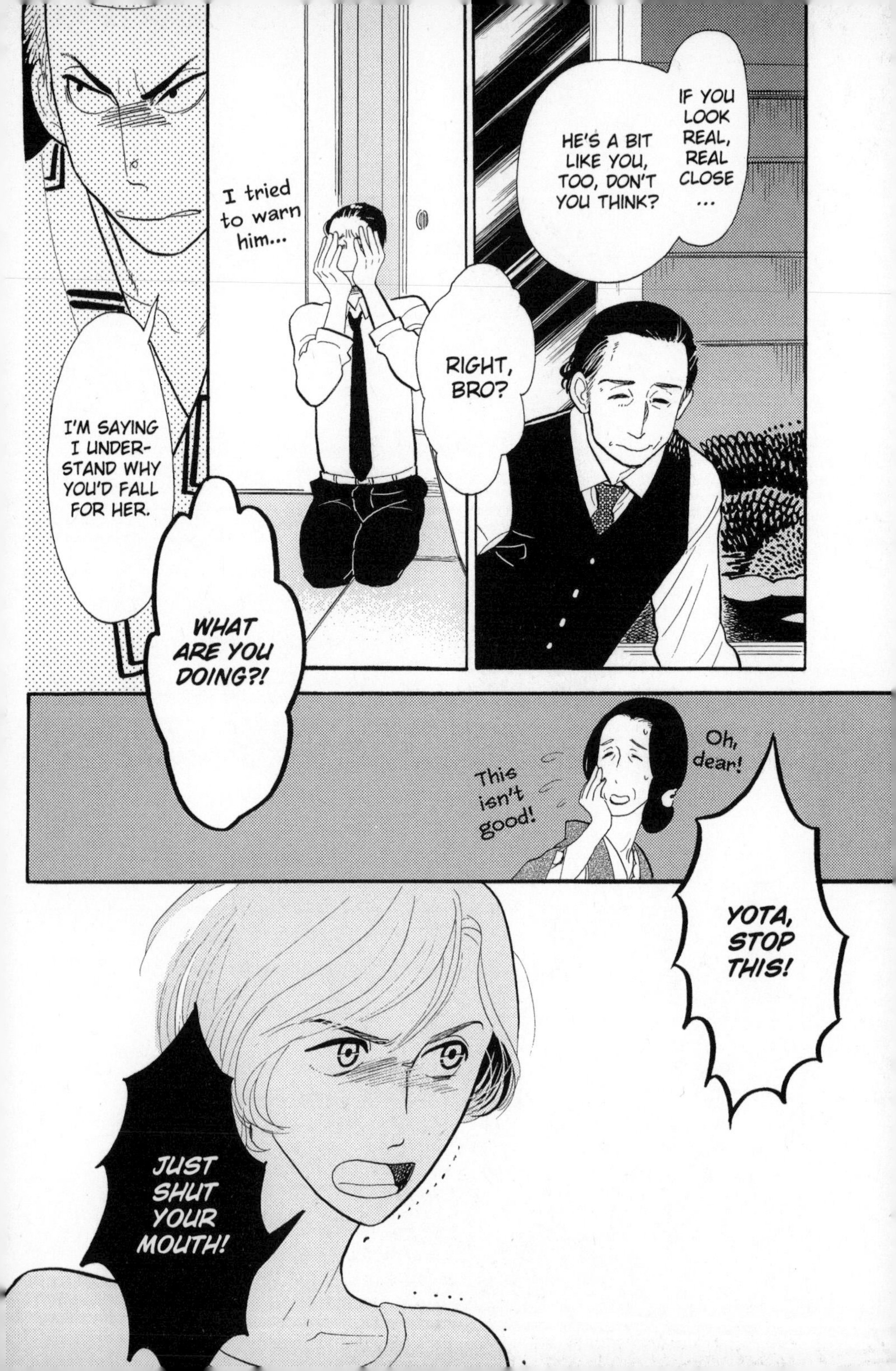
IF YOU LOOK REAL, REAL CLOSE...
HE'S A BIT LIKE YOU, TOO, DON'T YOU THINK?
RIGHT, BRO?
I tried to warn him...
I'M SAYING I UNDERSTAND WHY YOU'D FALL FOR HER.
WHAT ARE YOU DOING?!
Oh, dear!
This isn't good!
YOTA, STOP THIS!
JUST SHUT YOUR MOUTH!

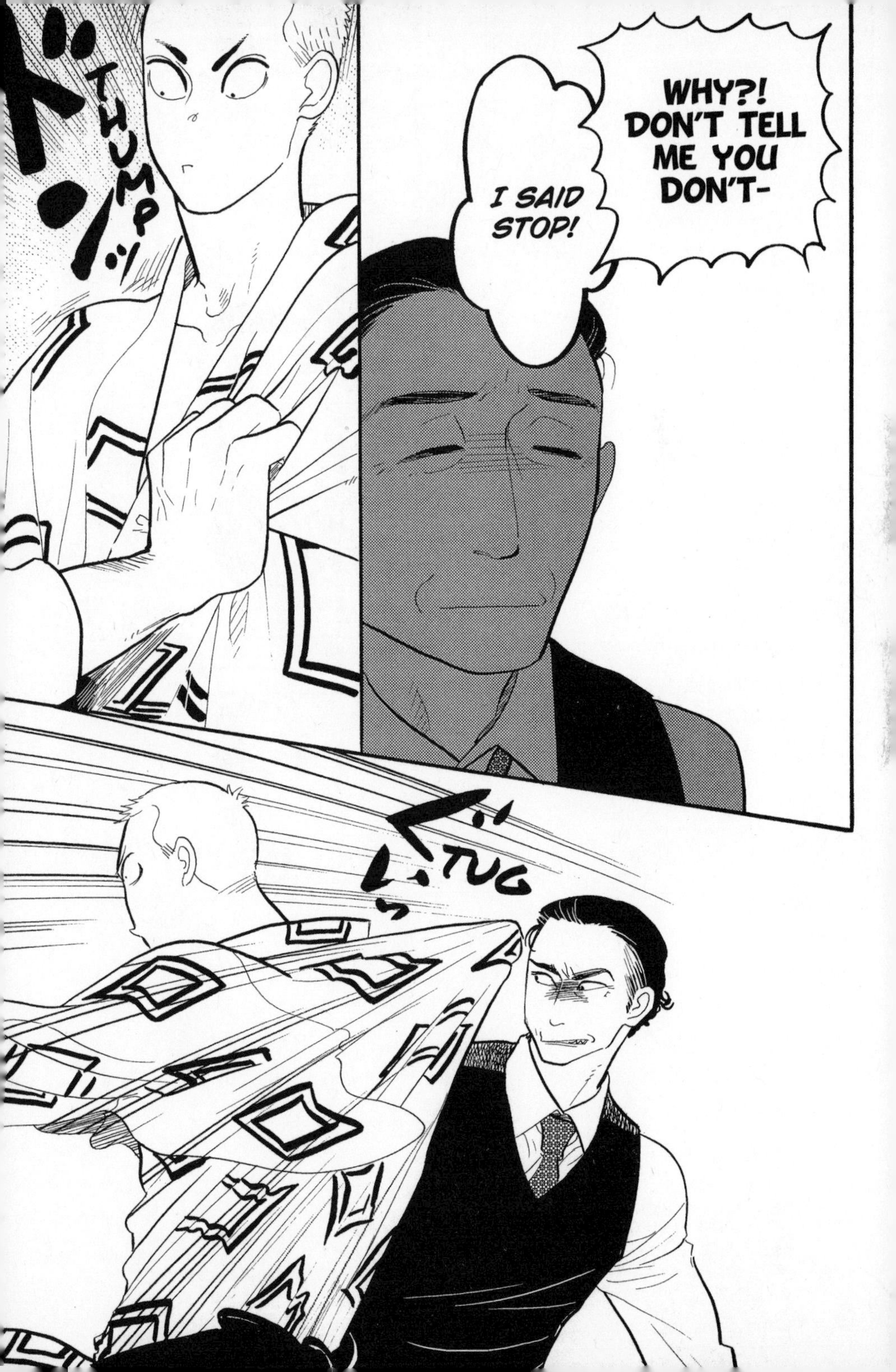
WHY?! DON'T TELL ME YOU DON'T-
I SAID STOP!
THUMP
TUG

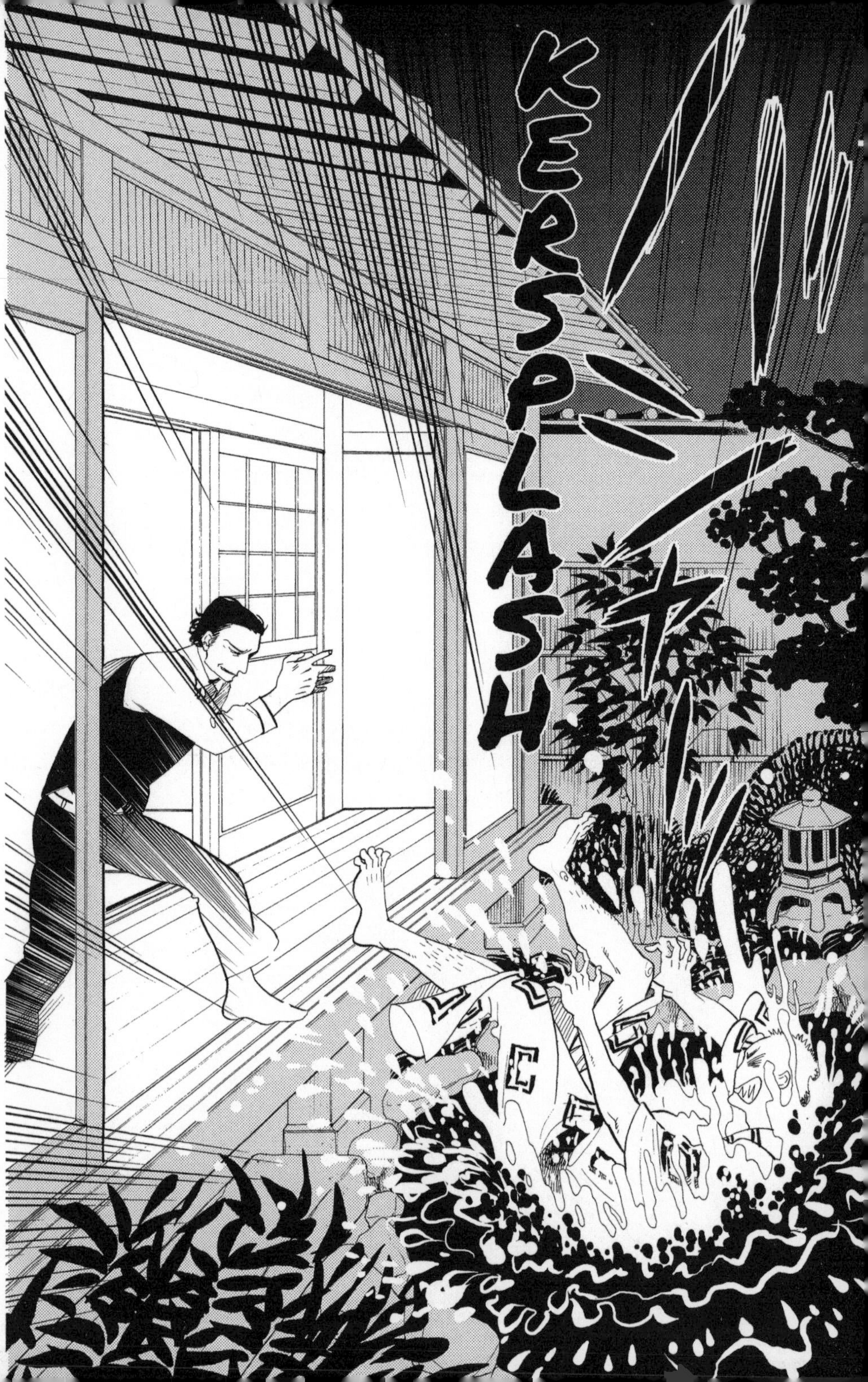
KERSPLASH

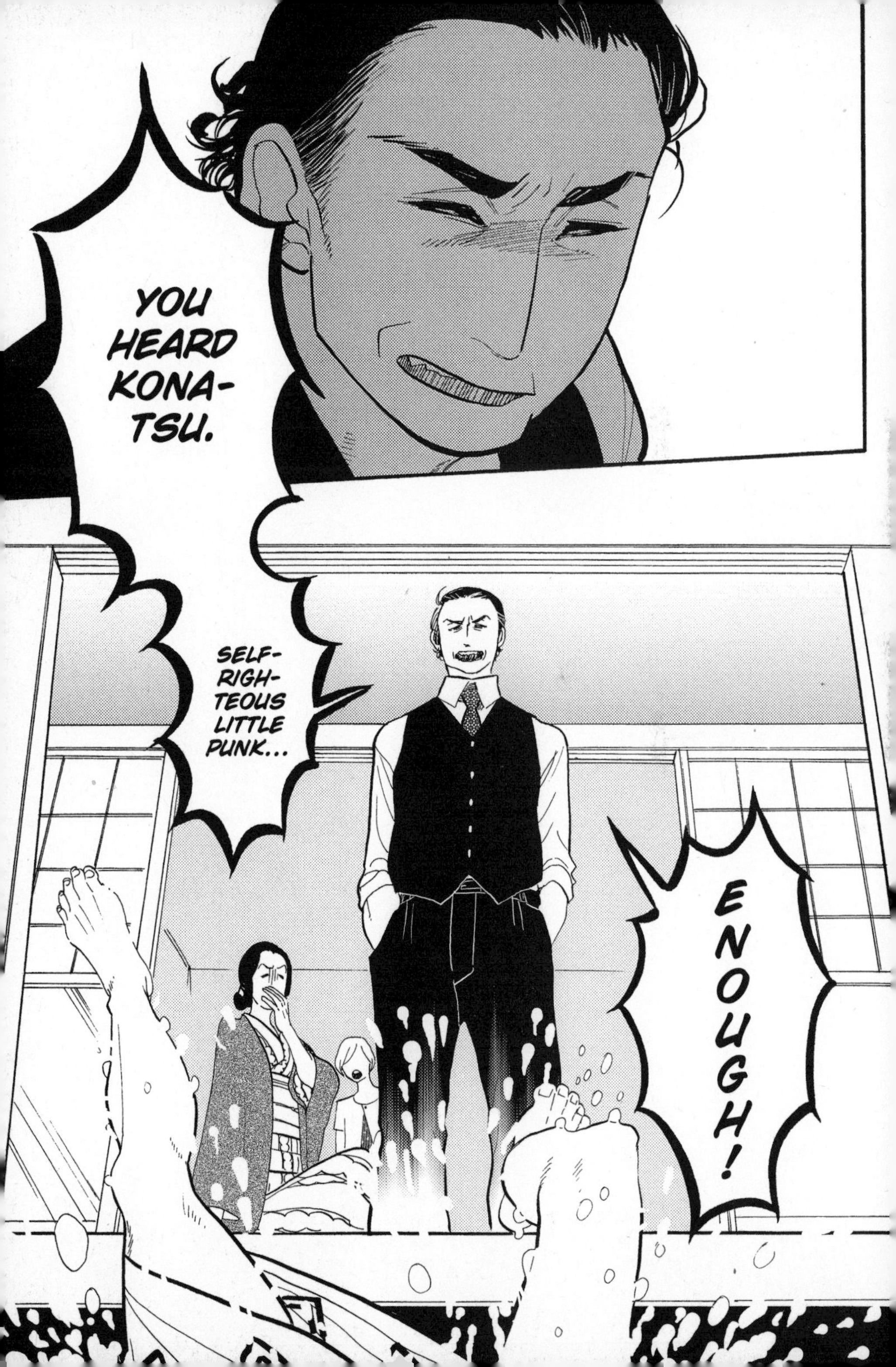
YOU HEARD KONATSU.
SELF-RIGHTEOUS LITTLE PUNK...
ENOUGH!

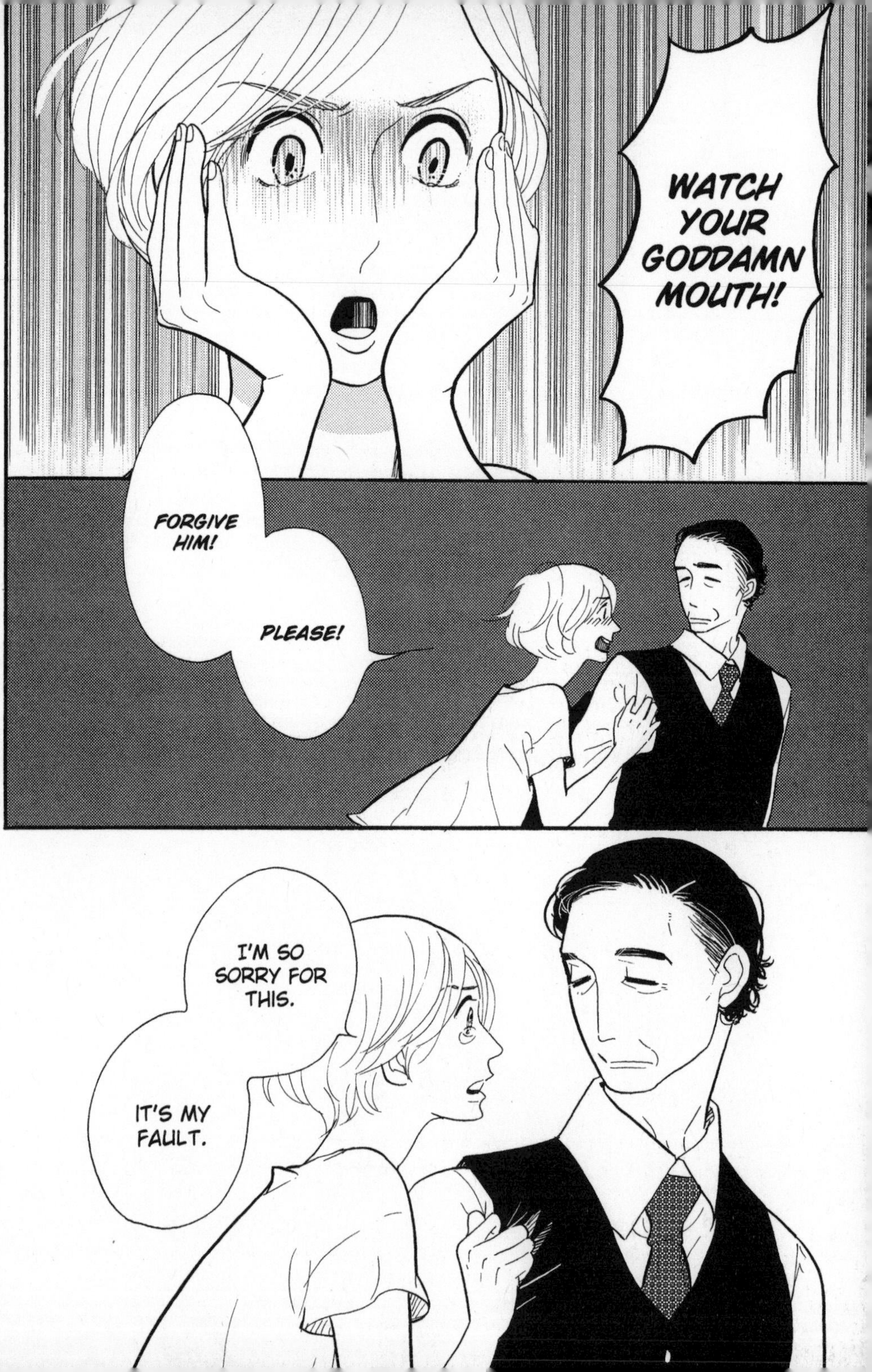
WATCH YOUR GODDAMN MOUTH!
FORGIVE HIM!
PLEASE!
I'M SO SORRY FOR THIS.
IT'S MY FAULT.

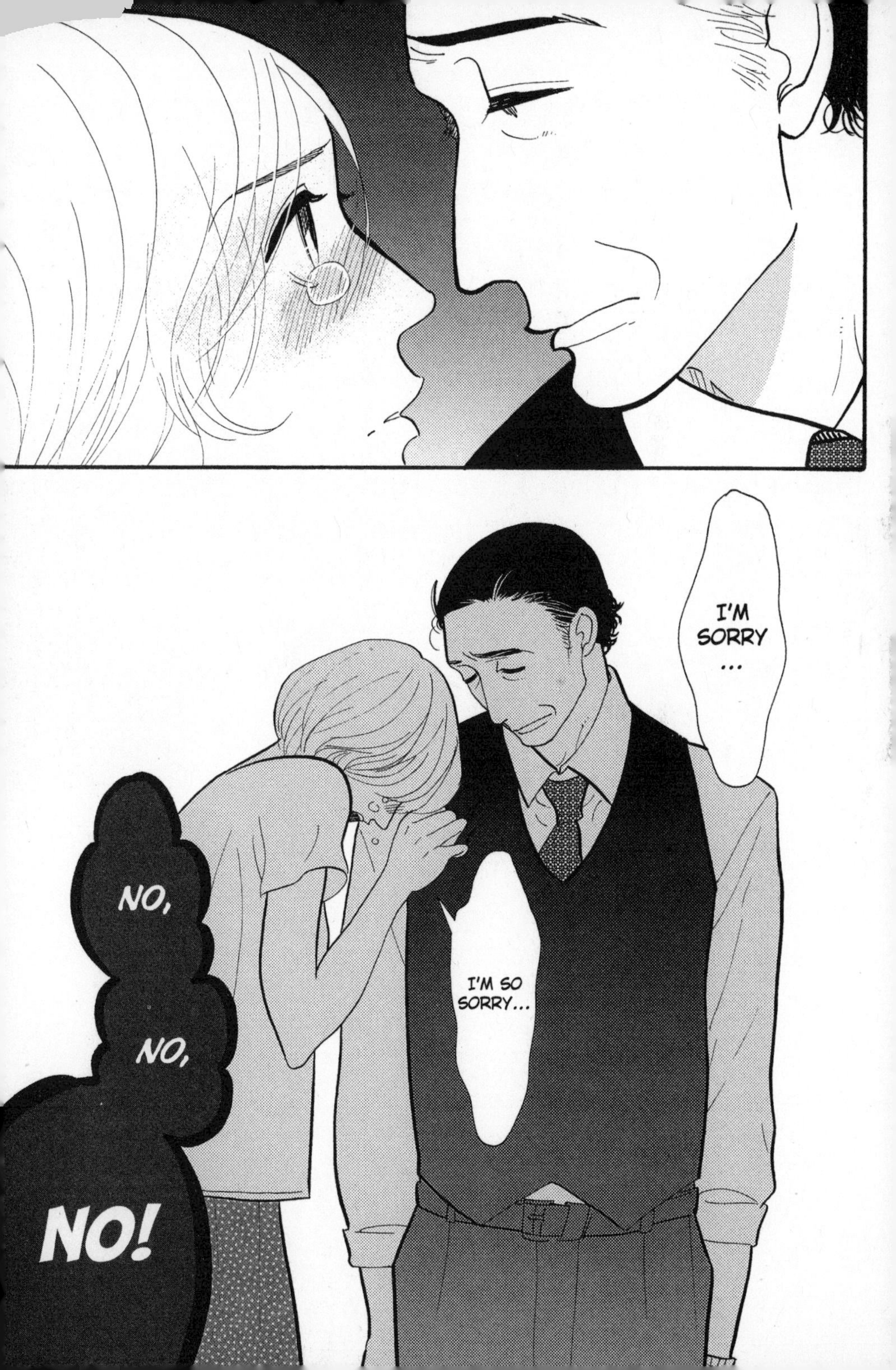
I'M SORRY ...
I'M SO SORRY...
NO,
NO,
NO!

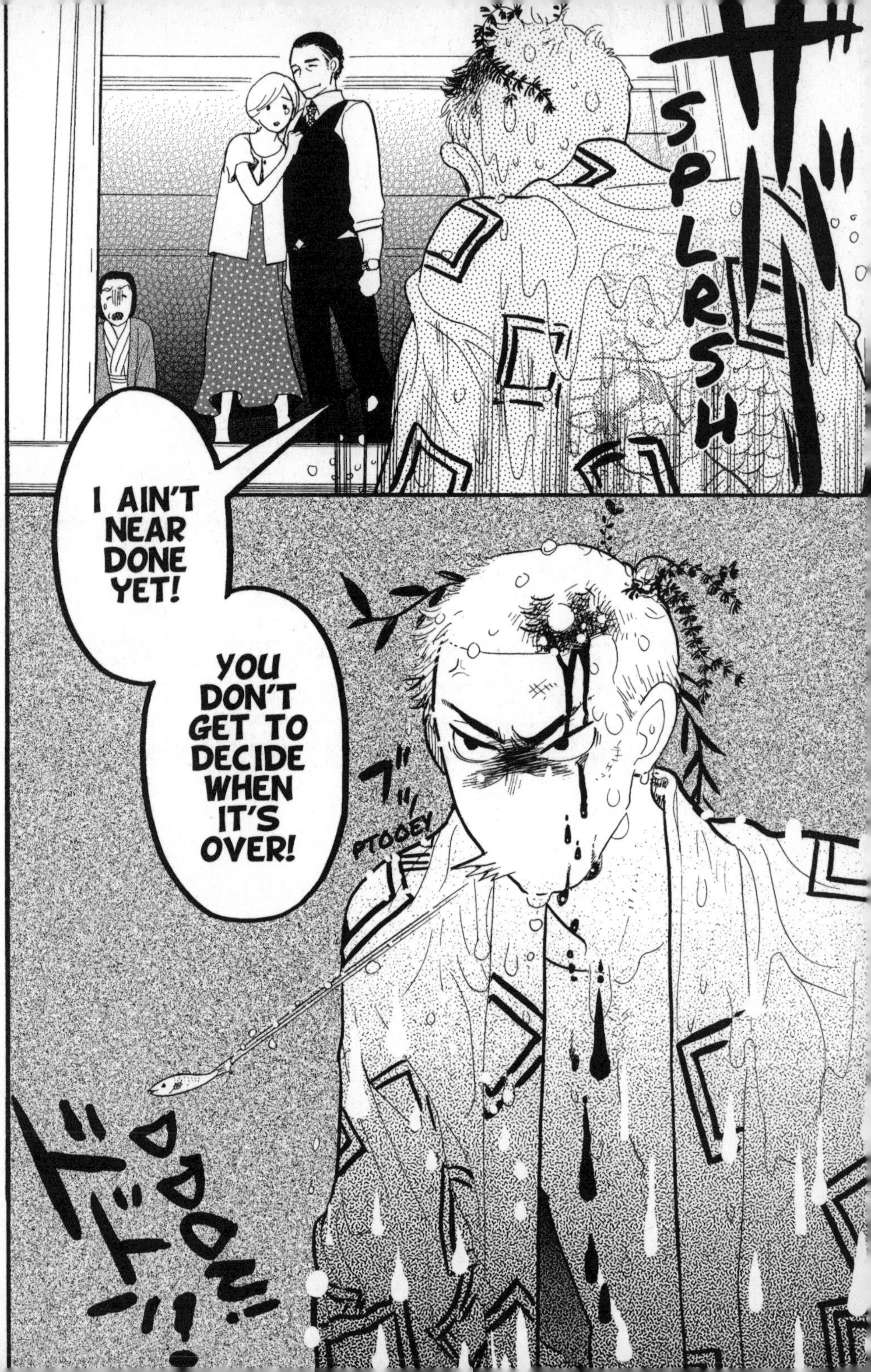
SPLRSH
I AIN'T NEAR DONE YET!
YOU DON'T GET TO DECIDE WHEN IT'S OVER!
PTOOEY
DON!!

DESCENDING
STORIES
SHOWA
GENROKU
RAKUGO
SHINJU

HARUKO KUMOTA

DESCENDING STORIES

SHOWA GENROKU RAKUGO SHINJU

SUKEROKU AGAIN: 5

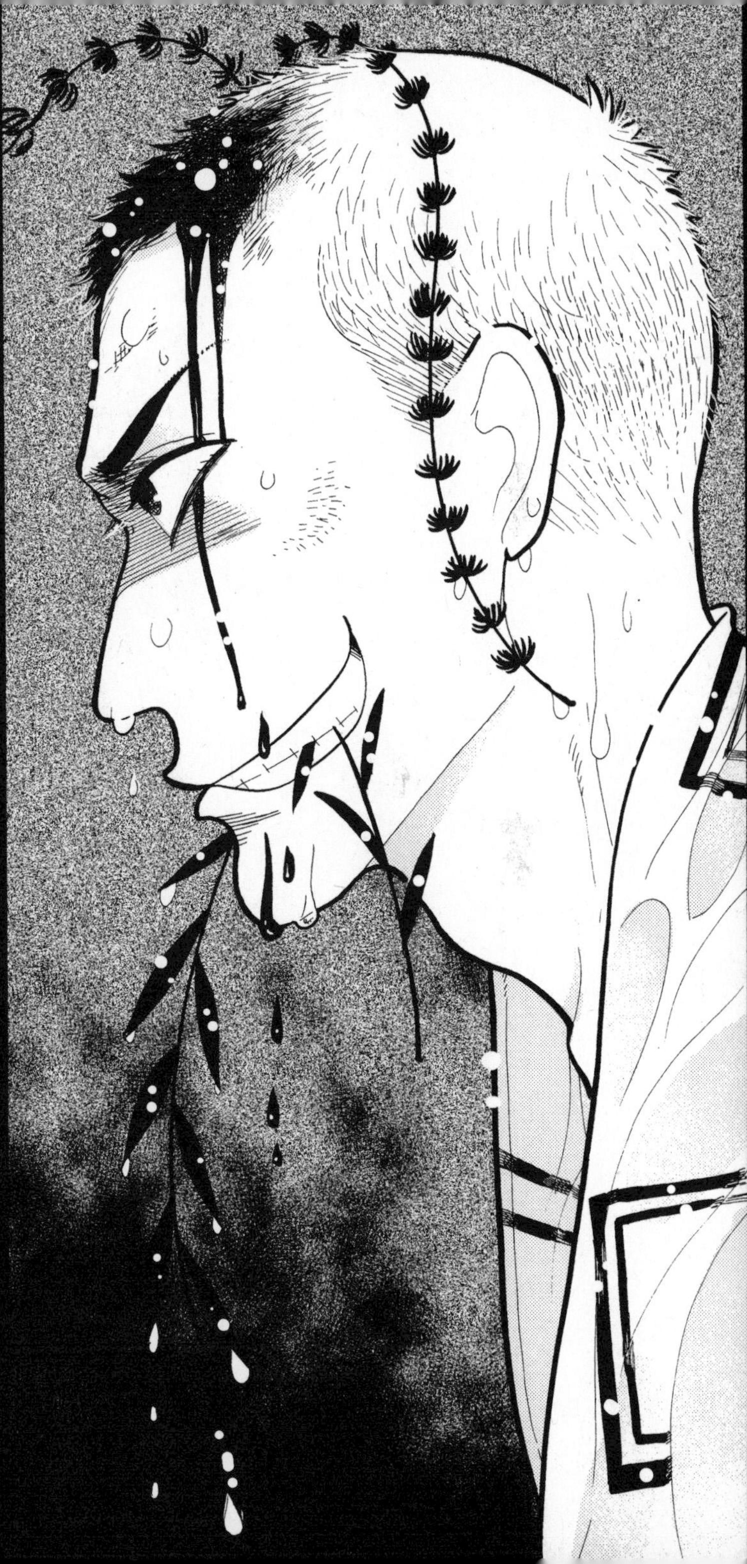

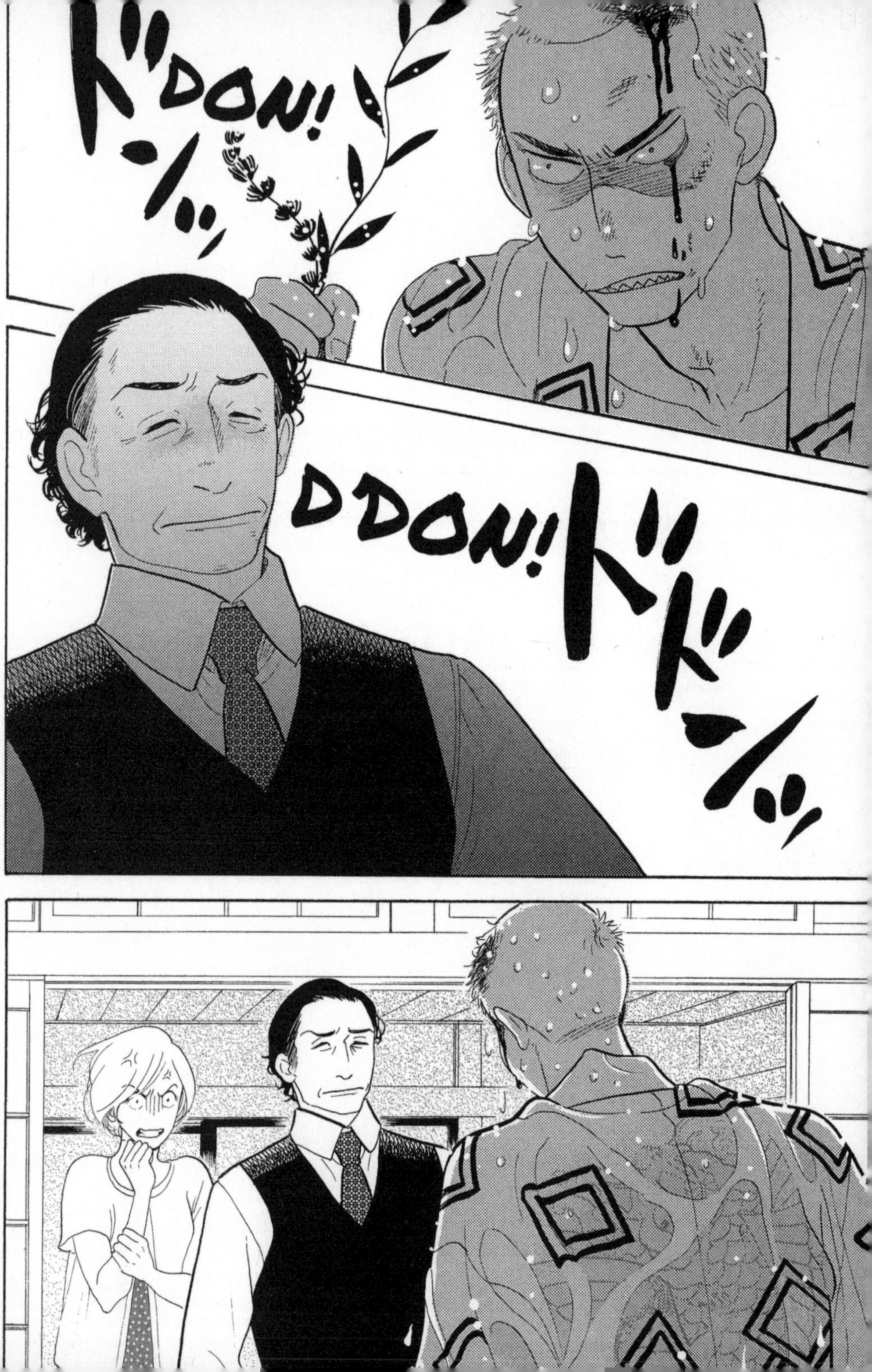
DON!
DDON!
ドドーンッ

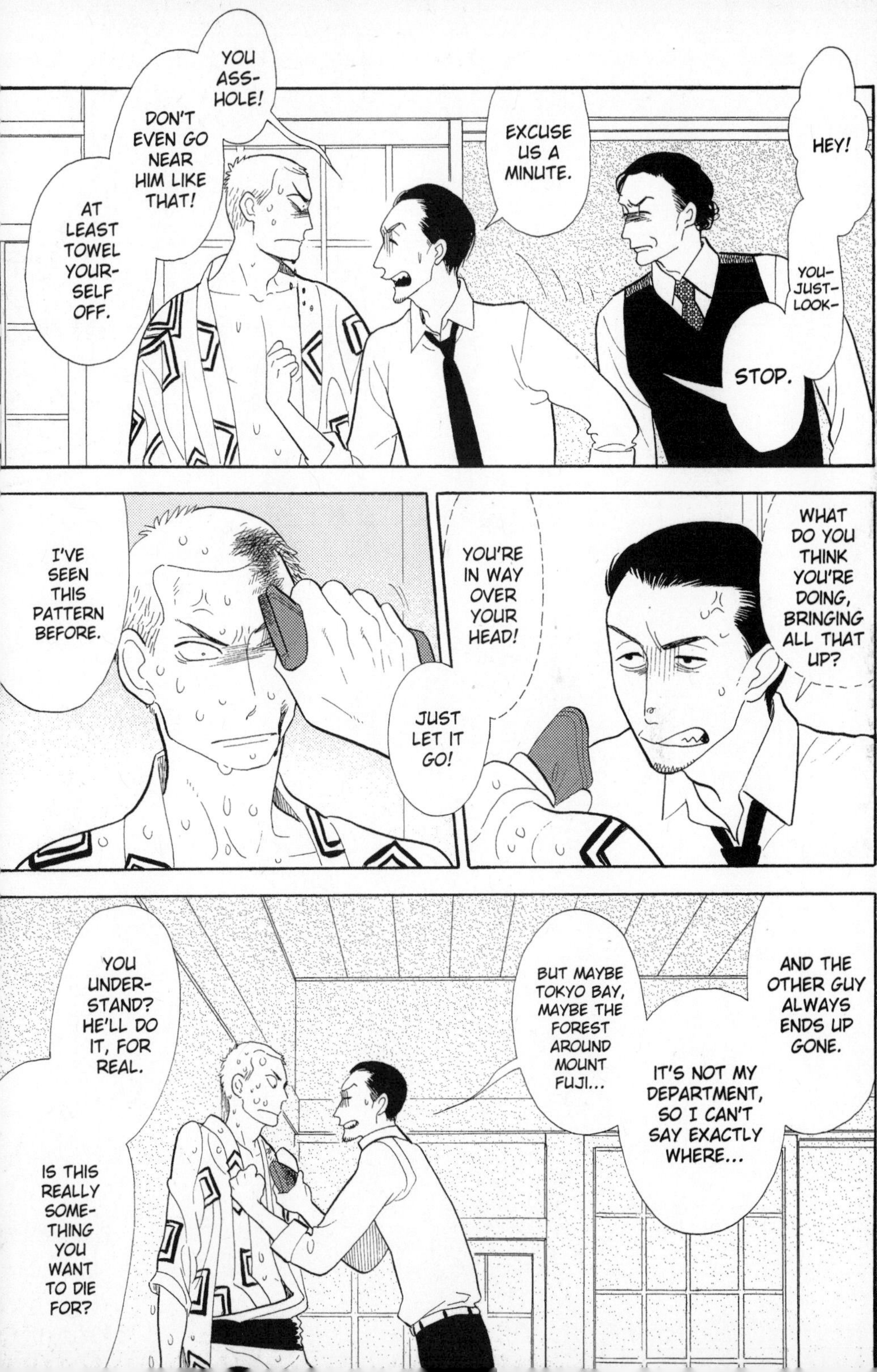
HEY!
YOU– JUST– LOOK–
STOP.
EXCUSE US A MINUTE.
YOU ASS-HOLE!
DON'T EVEN GO NEAR HIM LIKE THAT!
AT LEAST TOWEL YOUR-SELF OFF.
WHAT DO YOU THINK YOU'RE DOING, BRINGING ALL THAT UP?
YOU'RE IN WAY OVER YOUR HEAD!
JUST LET IT GO!
I'VE SEEN THIS PATTERN BEFORE.
AND THE OTHER GUY ALWAYS ENDS UP GONE.
IT'S NOT MY DEPARTMENT, SO I CAN'T SAY EXACTLY WHERE...
BUT MAYBE TOKYO BAY, MAYBE THE FOREST AROUND MOUNT FUJI...
YOU UNDER-STAND? HE'LL DO IT, FOR REAL.
IS THIS REALLY SOME-THING YOU WANT TO DIE FOR?

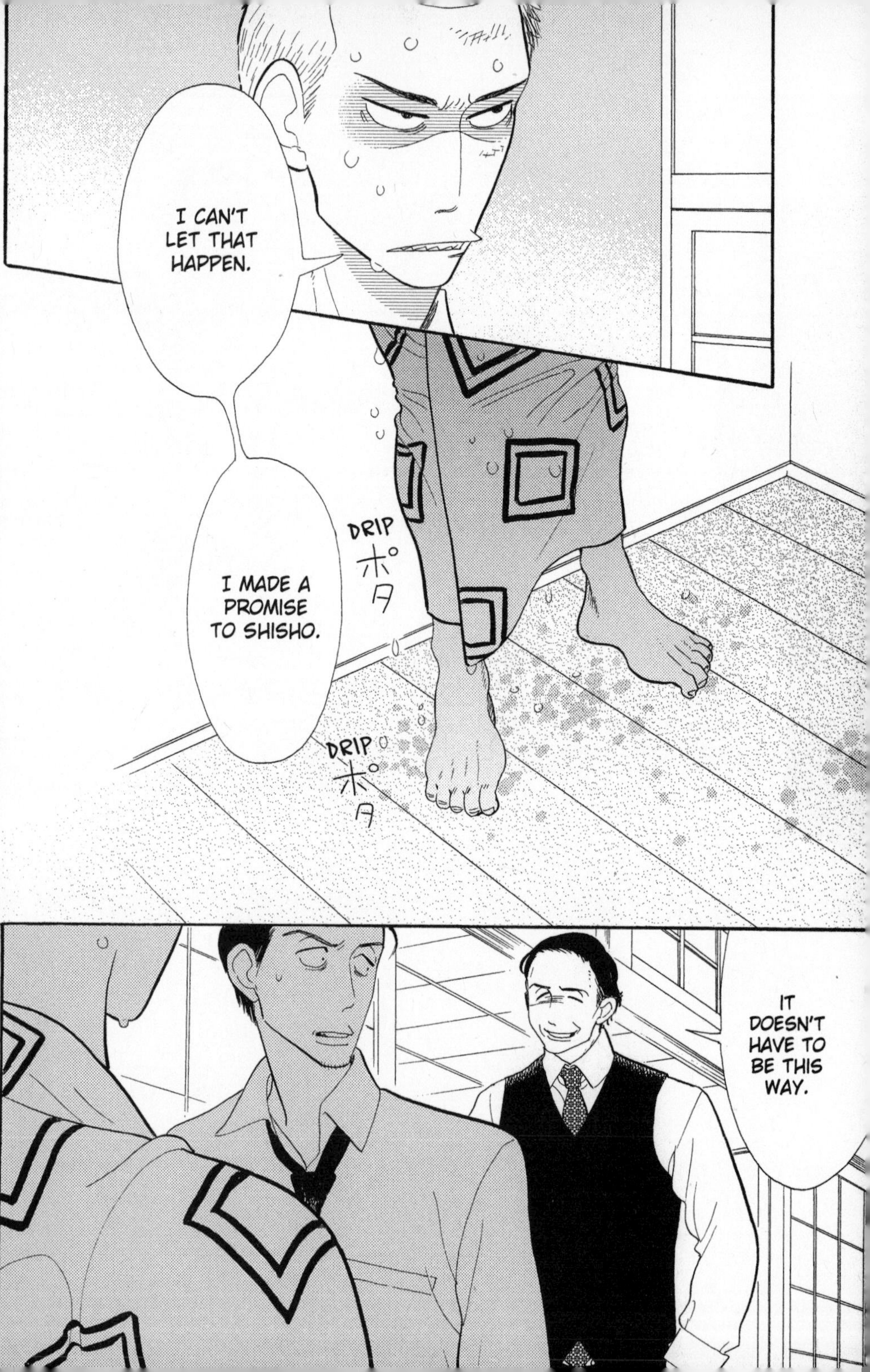
I CAN'T LET THAT HAPPEN.
I MADE A PROMISE TO SHISHO.
DRIP ポタ
DRIP ポタ
IT DOESN'T HAVE TO BE THIS WAY.

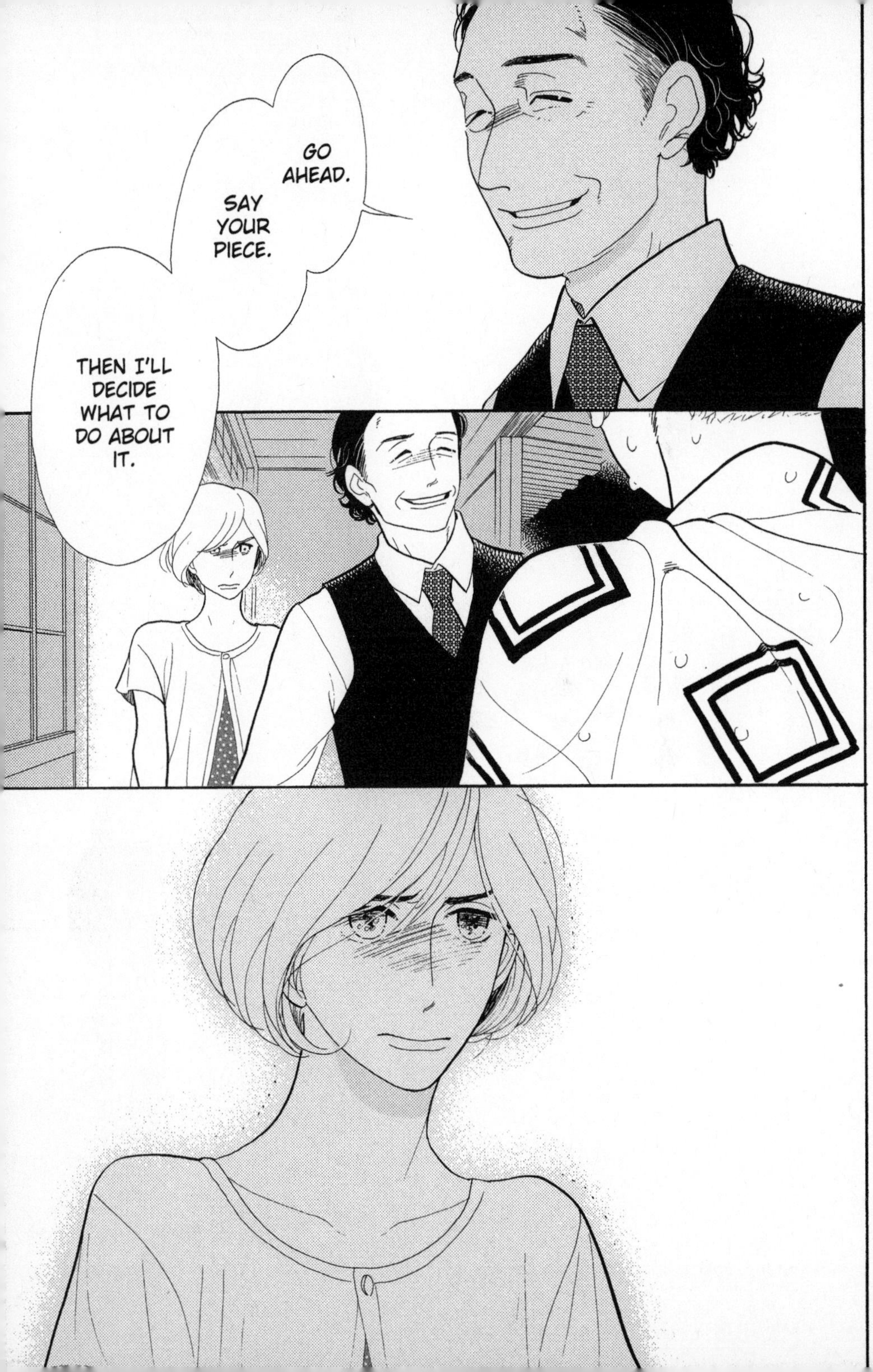
GO AHEAD.
SAY YOUR PIECE.
THEN I'LL DECIDE WHAT TO DO ABOUT IT.

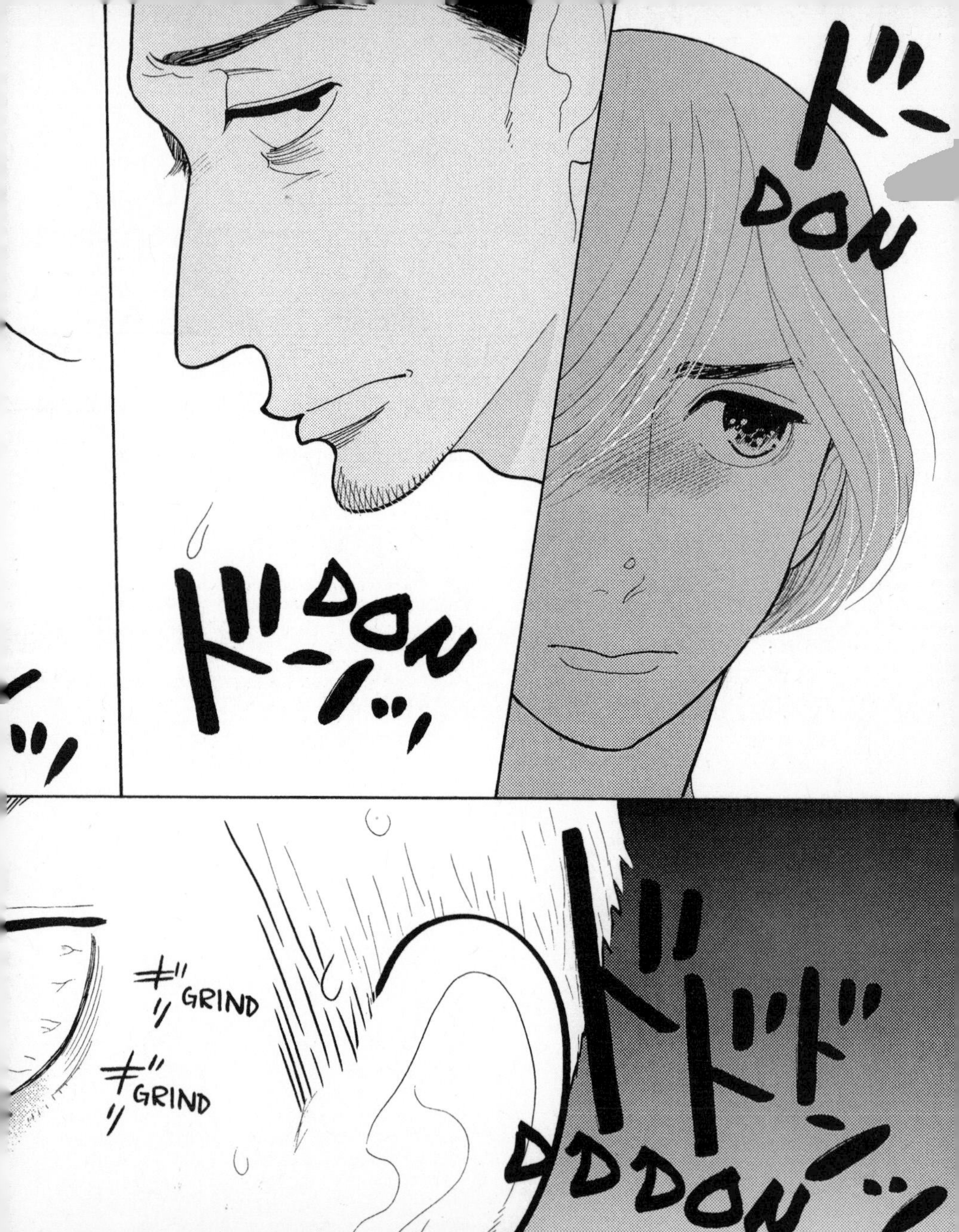
ドー DON
ドーンッ DON
ドドドーンッ DDDON
ギリ GRIND
ギリ GRIND

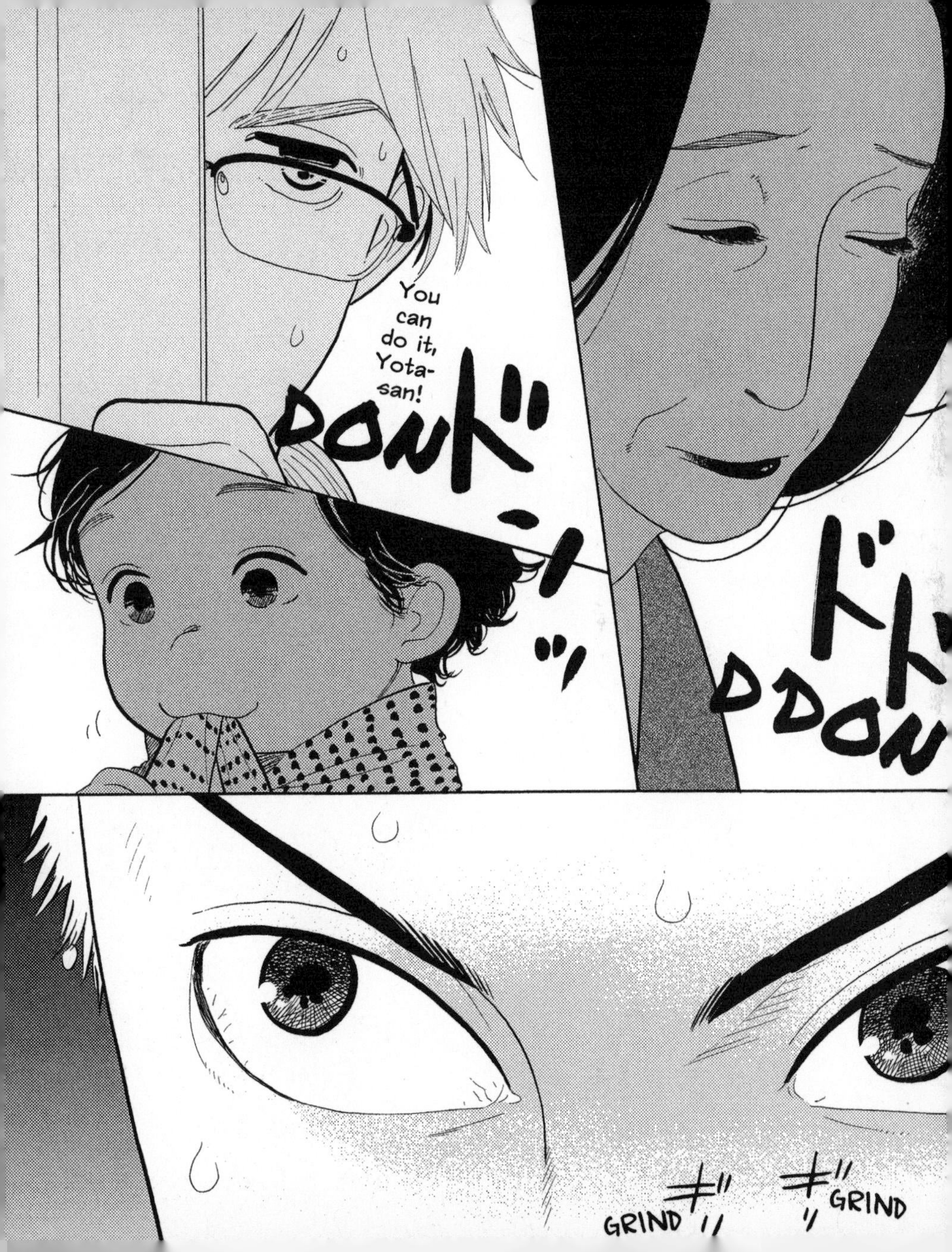
ドドDDON
You can do it, Yota-san!
DONドーンッ
ギッGRIND
ギッGRIND

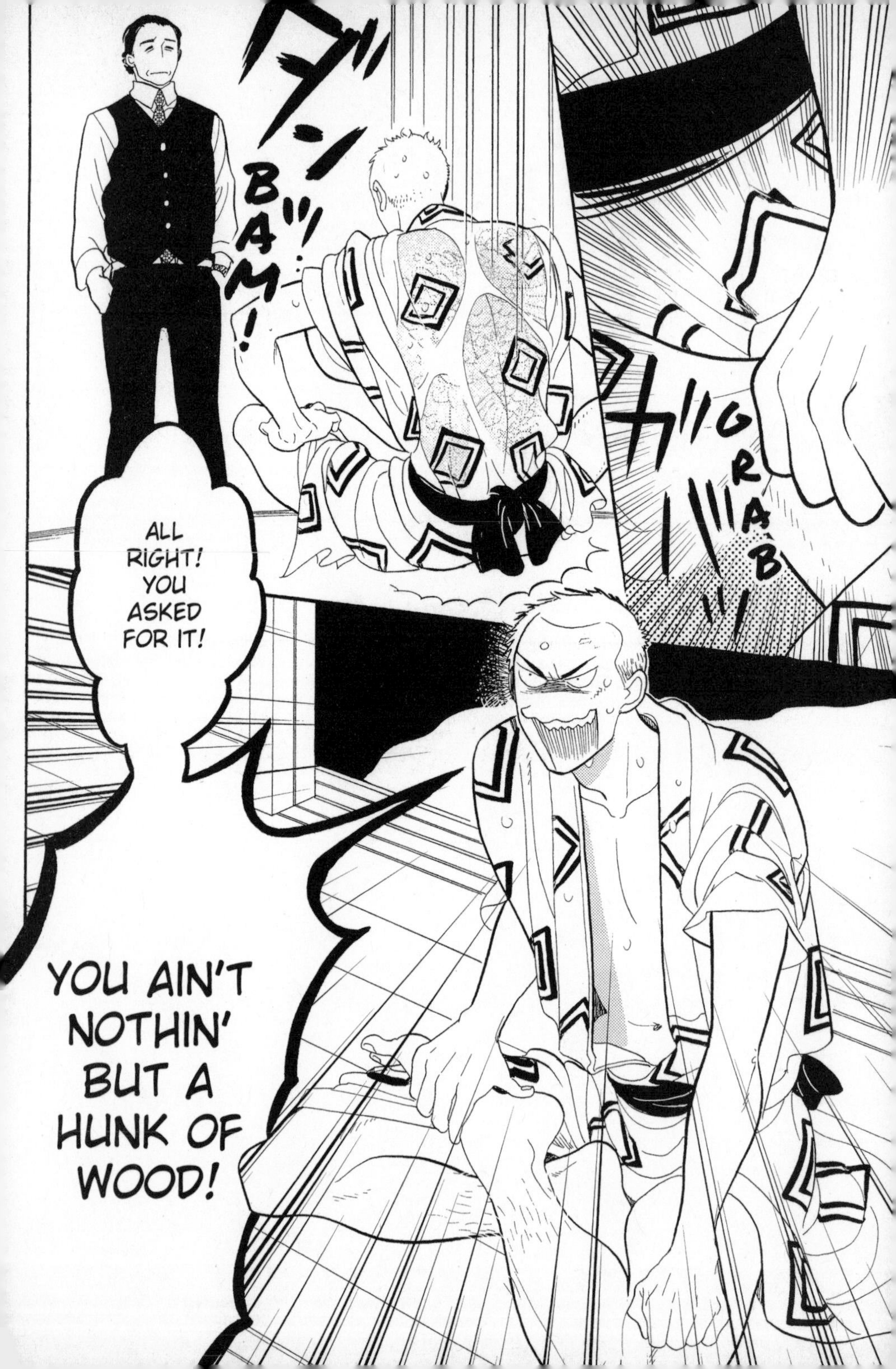
GRAB
BAM!
ALL RIGHT! YOU ASKED FOR IT!
YOU AIN'T NOTHIN' BUT A HUNK OF WOOD!

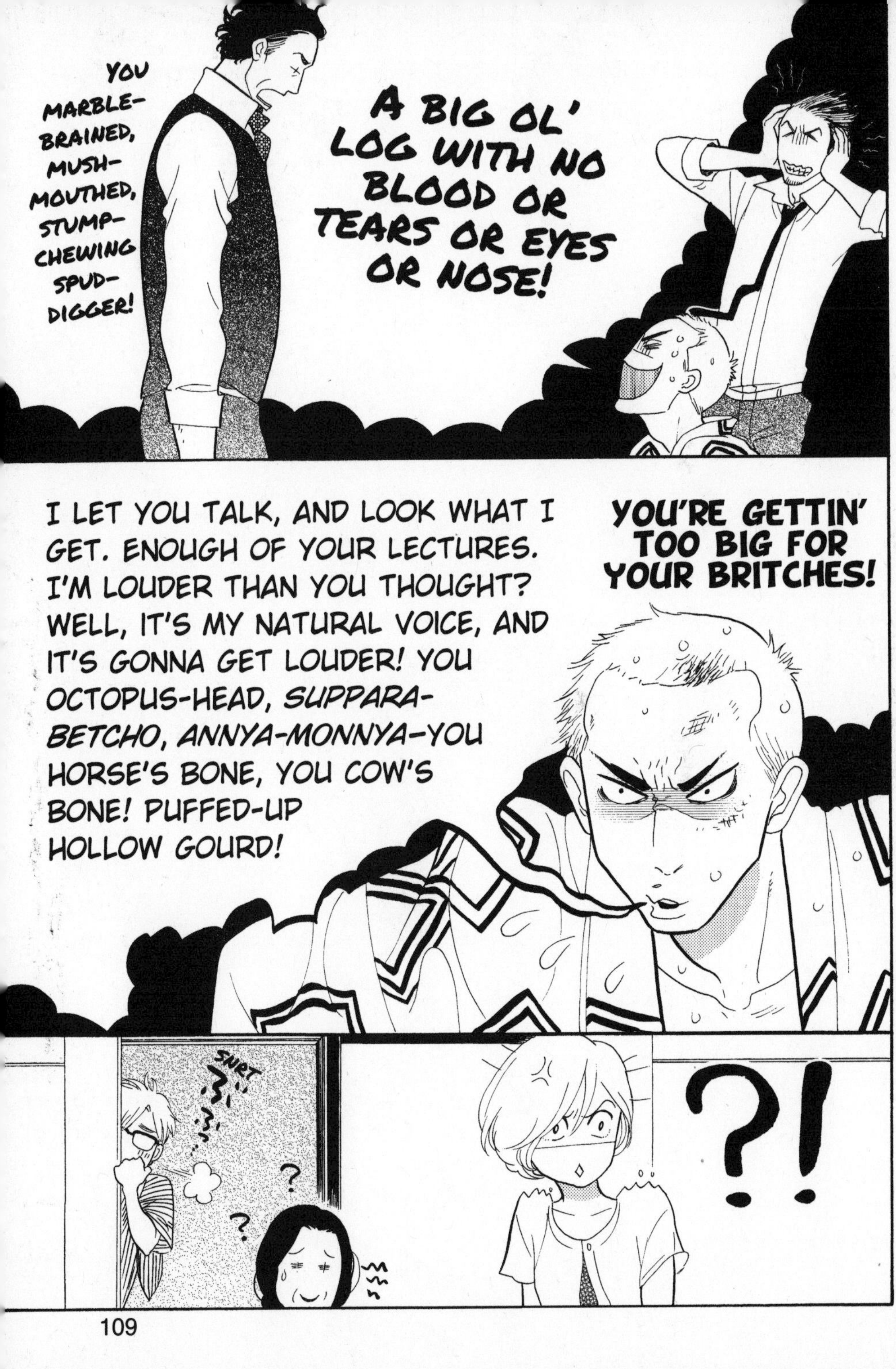

A BIG OL' LOG WITH NO BLOOD OR TEARS OR EYES OR NOSE!
YOU MARBLE-BRAINED, MUSH-MOUTHED, STUMP-CHEWING SPUD-DIGGER!
YOU'RE GETTIN' TOO BIG FOR YOUR BRITCHES!
I LET YOU TALK, AND LOOK WHAT I GET. ENOUGH OF YOUR LECTURES. I'M LOUDER THAN YOU THOUGHT? WELL, IT'S MY NATURAL VOICE, AND IT'S GONNA GET LOUDER! YOU OCTOPUS-HEAD, *SUPPARA-BETCHO*, *ANNYA-MONNYA*-YOU HORSE'S BONE, YOU COW'S BONE! PUFFED-UP HOLLOW GOURD!
?!
SWRT
?
?

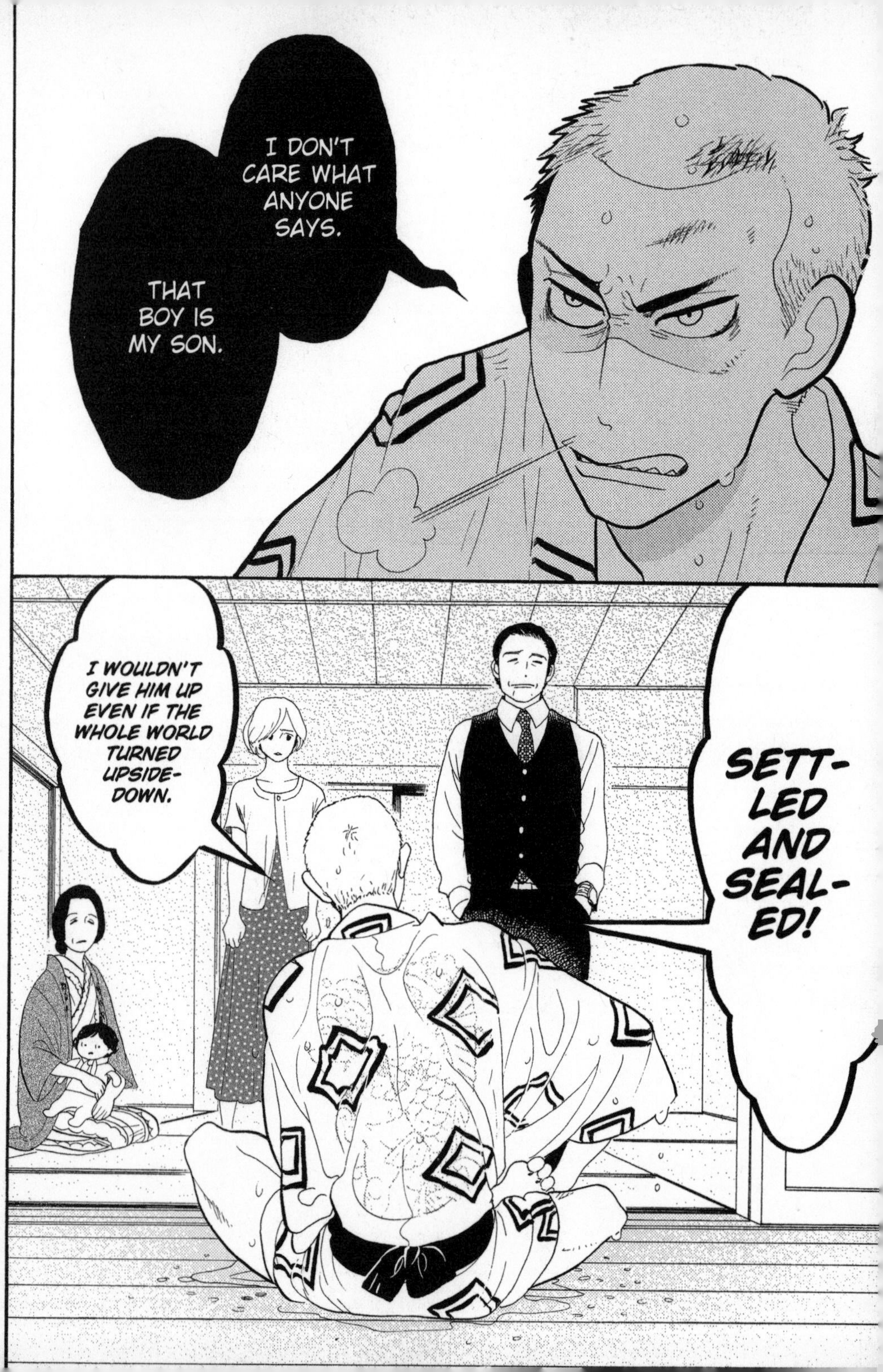
I DON'T CARE WHAT ANYONE SAYS.
THAT BOY IS MY SON.
SETT-LED AND SEAL-ED!
I WOULDN'T GIVE HIM UP EVEN IF THE WHOLE WORLD TURNED UPSIDE-DOWN.

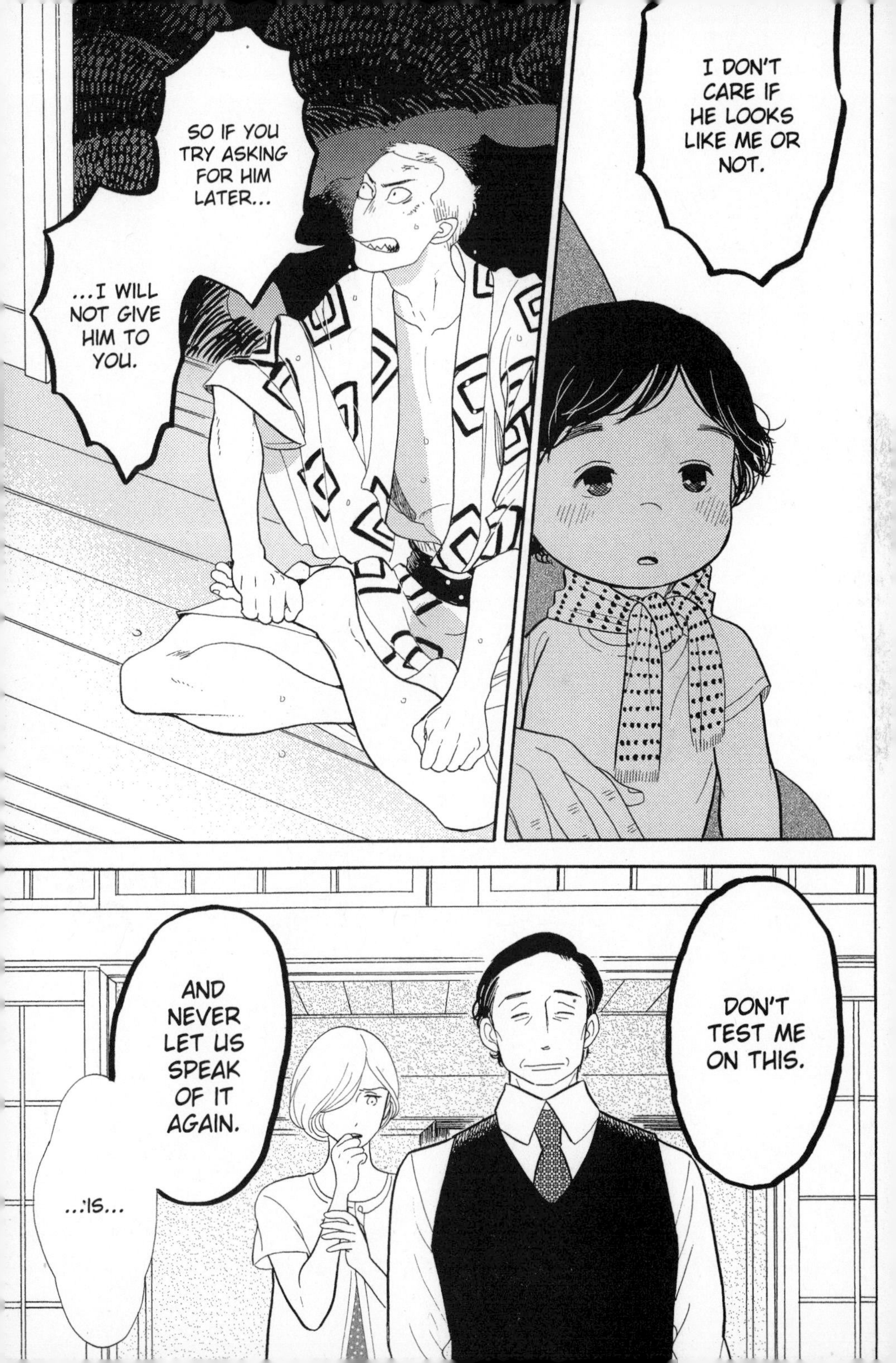
I DON'T CARE IF HE LOOKS LIKE ME OR NOT.
SO IF YOU TRY ASKING FOR HIM LATER...
...I WILL NOT GIVE HIM TO YOU.
DON'T TEST ME ON THIS.
AND NEVER LET US SPEAK OF IT AGAIN.
...IS...

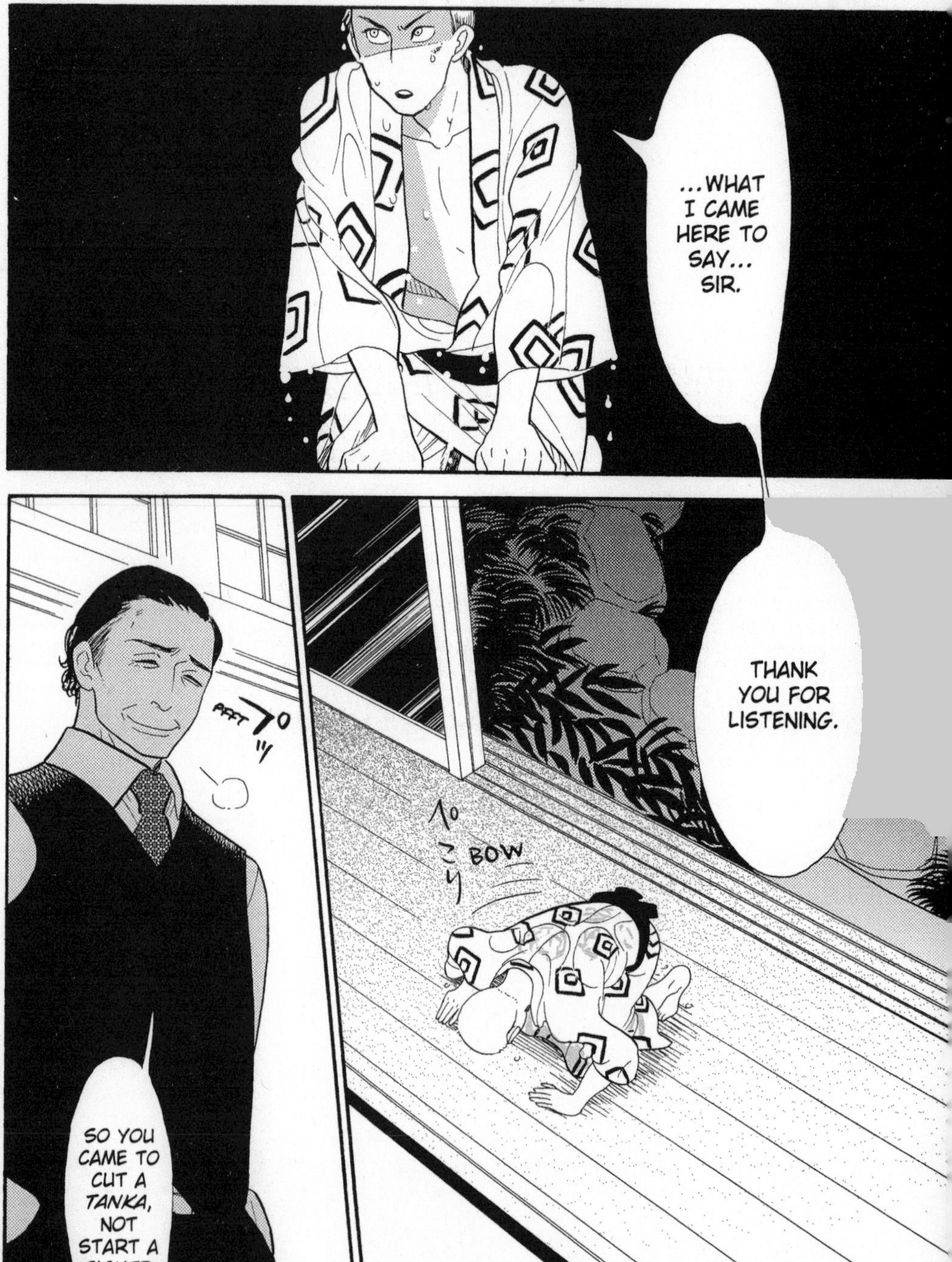
...WHAT I CAME HERE TO SAY... SIR.
THANK YOU FOR LISTENING.
ぺこり
BOW
PFFT
ブッ
SO YOU CAME TO CUT A *TANKA*, NOT START A FIGHT?

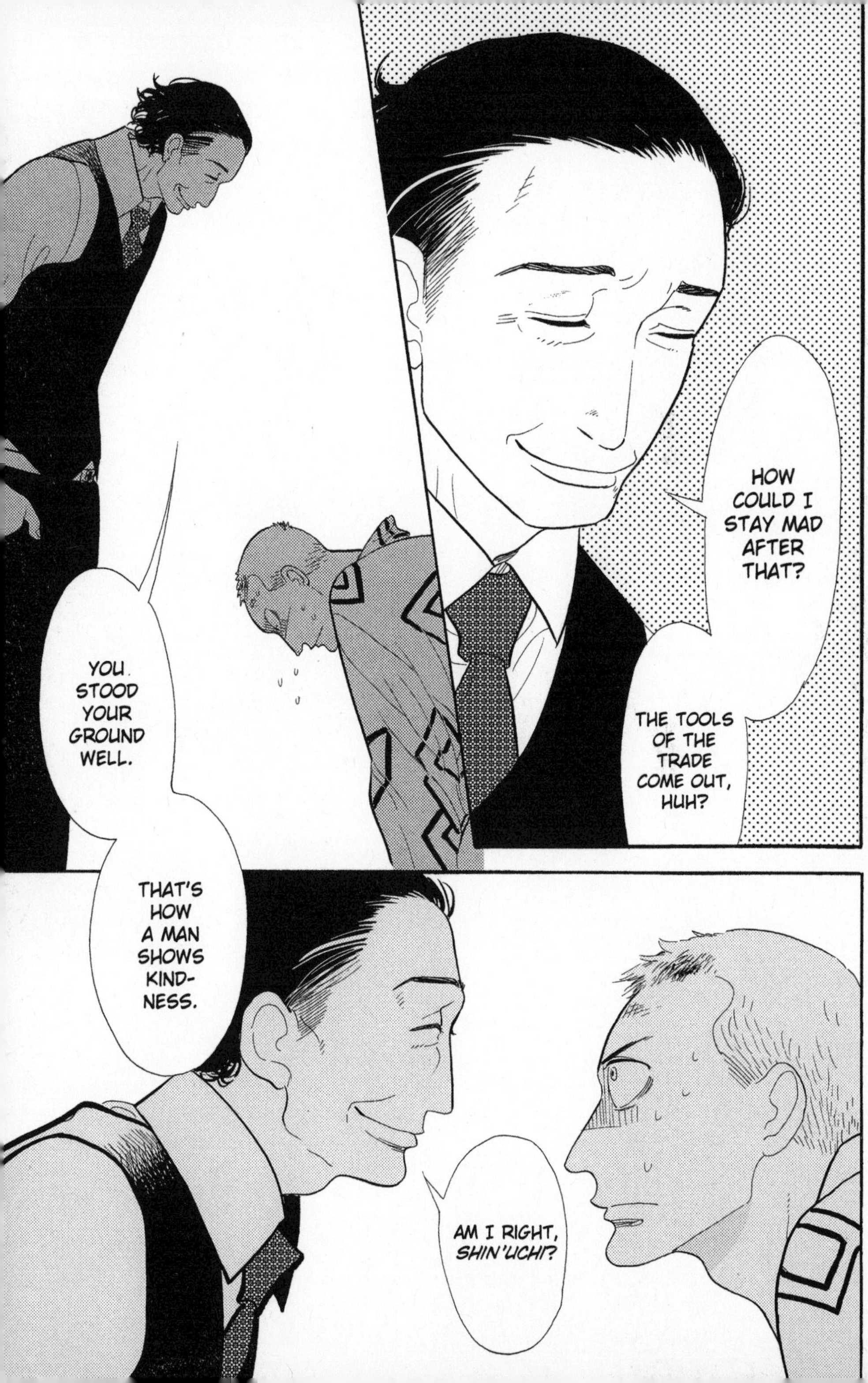
HOW COULD I STAY MAD AFTER THAT?
THE TOOLS OF THE TRADE COME OUT, HUH?
YOU. STOOD YOUR GROUND WELL.
THAT'S HOW A MAN SHOWS KINDNESS.
AM I RIGHT, *SHIN'UCHI*?

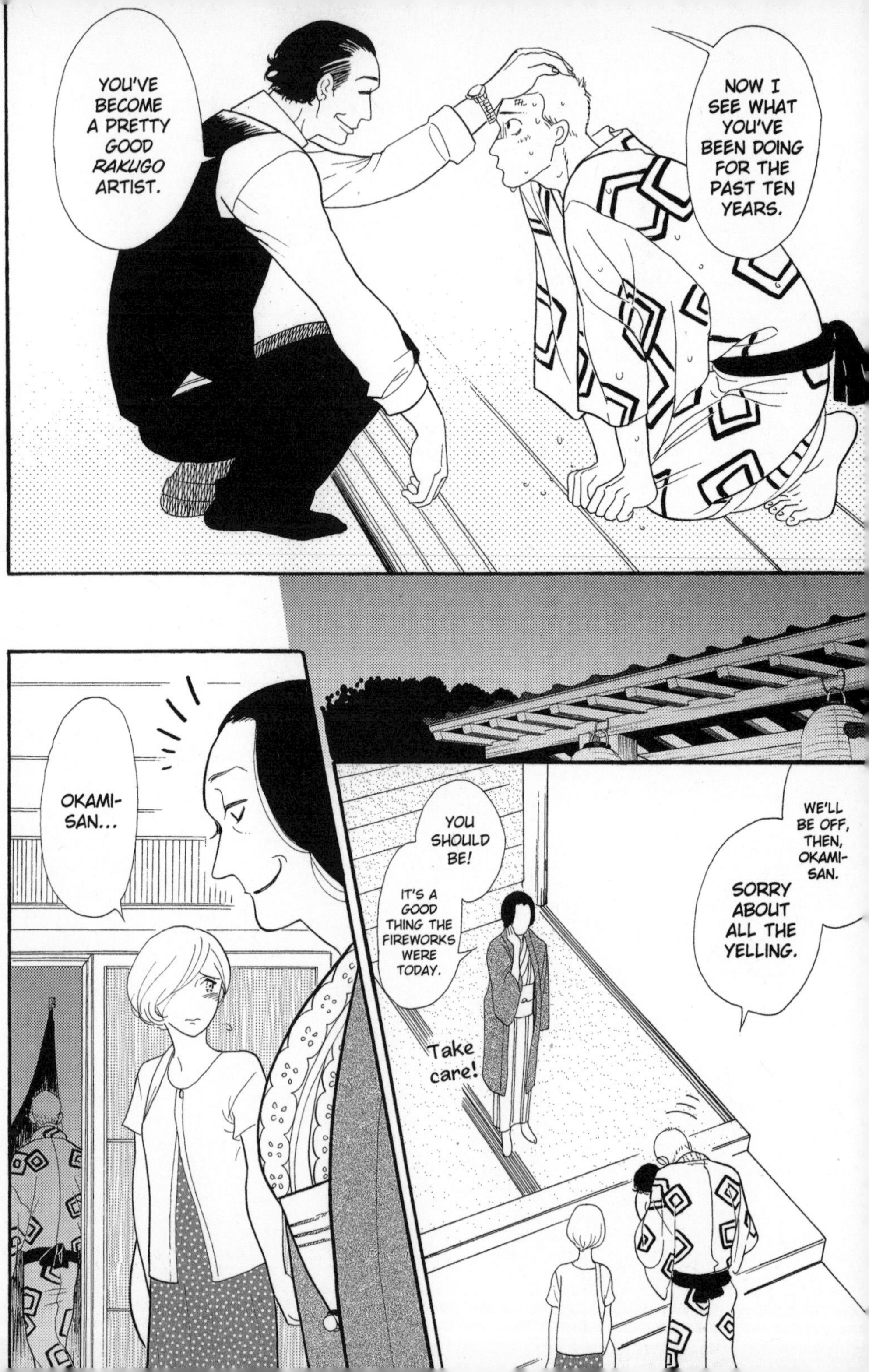
NOW I SEE WHAT YOU'VE BEEN DOING FOR THE PAST TEN YEARS.
YOU'VE BECOME A PRETTY GOOD *RAKUGO* ARTIST.
WE'LL BE OFF, THEN, OKAMI-SAN.
SORRY ABOUT ALL THE YELLING.
YOU SHOULD BE!
IT'S A GOOD THING THE FIREWORKS WERE TODAY.
Take care!
OKAMI-SAN...

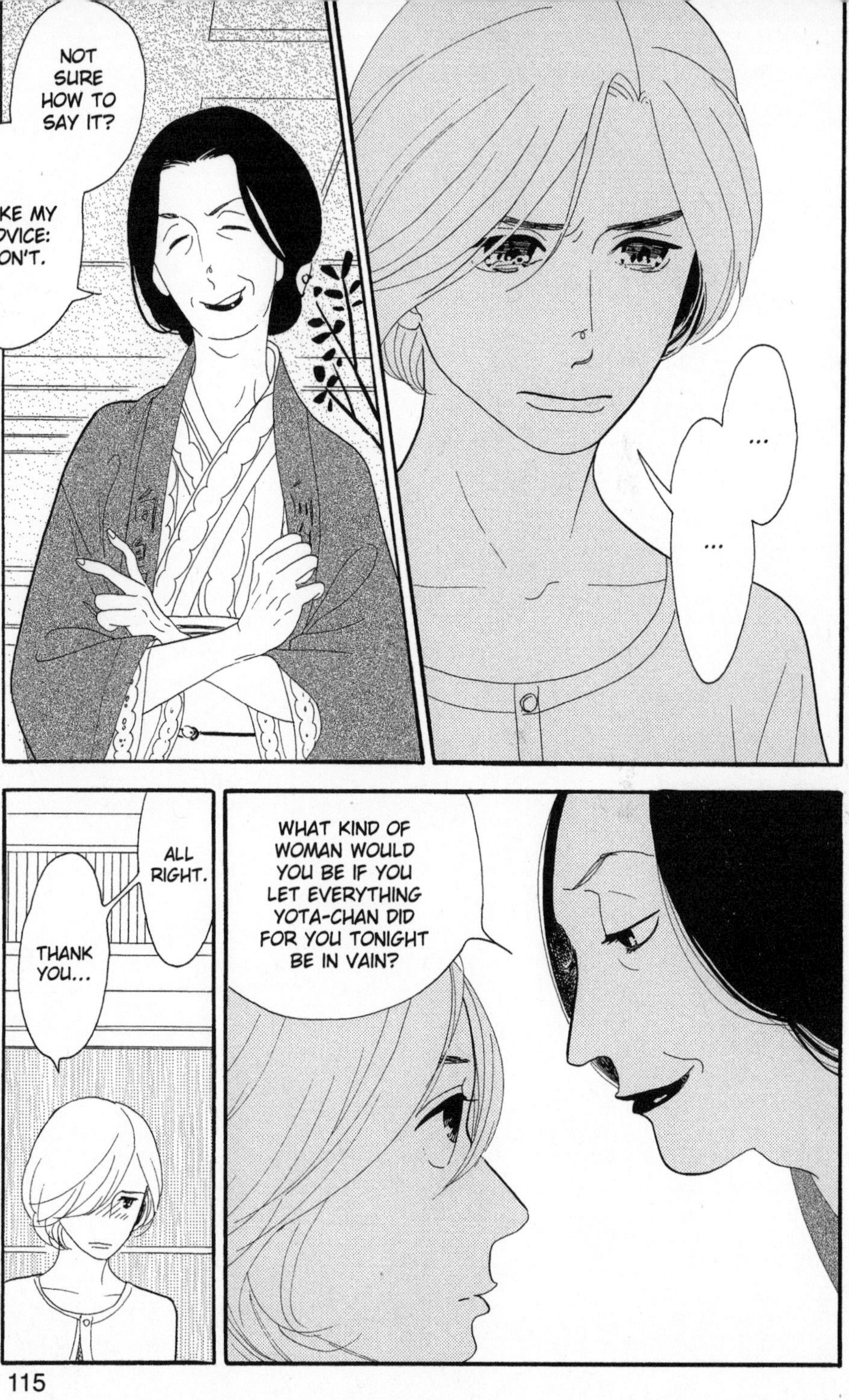
...
...
NOT SURE HOW TO SAY IT?
TAKE MY ADVICE: DON'T.
WHAT KIND OF WOMAN WOULD YOU BE IF YOU LET EVERYTHING YOTA-CHAN DID FOR YOU TONIGHT BE IN VAIN?
ALL RIGHT.
THANK YOU...

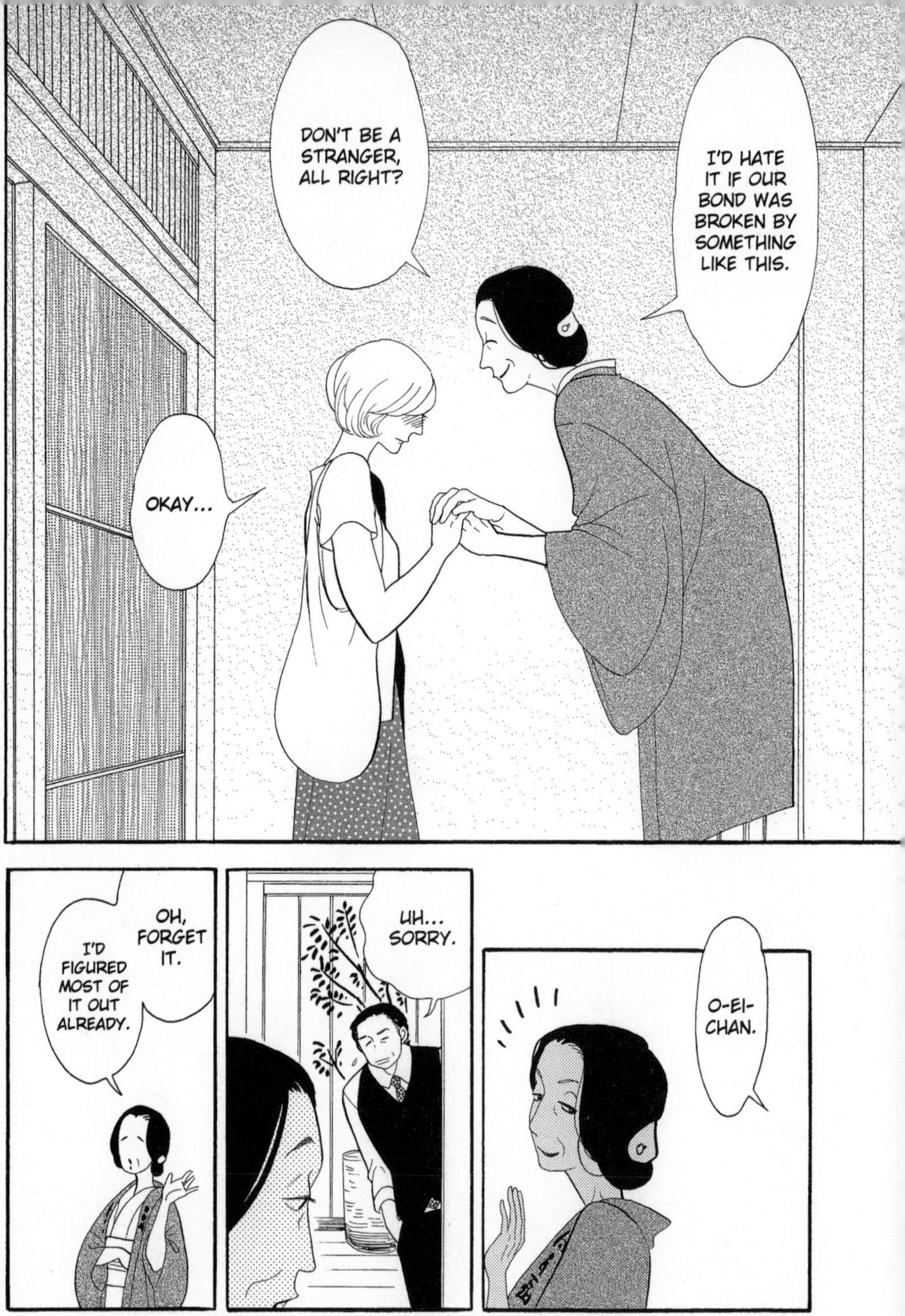
I'D HATE IT IF OUR BOND WAS BROKEN BY SOMETHING LIKE THIS.
DON'T BE A STRANGER, ALL RIGHT?
OKAY...
O-EI-CHAN.
UH... SORRY.
OH, FORGET IT.
I'D FIGURED MOST OF IT OUT ALREADY.

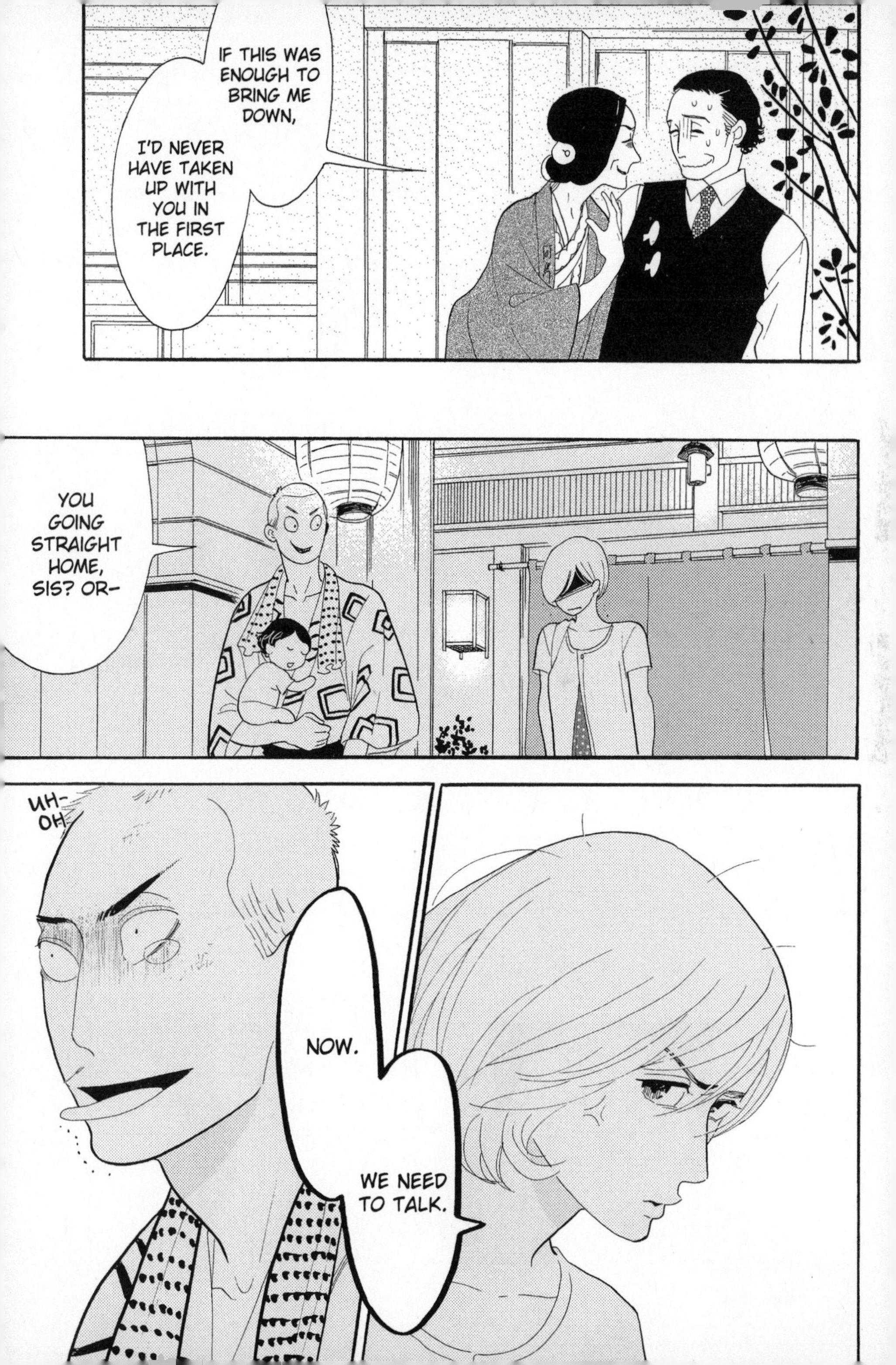
IF THIS WAS ENOUGH TO BRING ME DOWN,
I'D NEVER HAVE TAKEN UP WITH YOU IN THE FIRST PLACE.
YOU GOING STRAIGHT HOME, SIS? OR–
NOW.
WE NEED TO TALK.
UH-OH

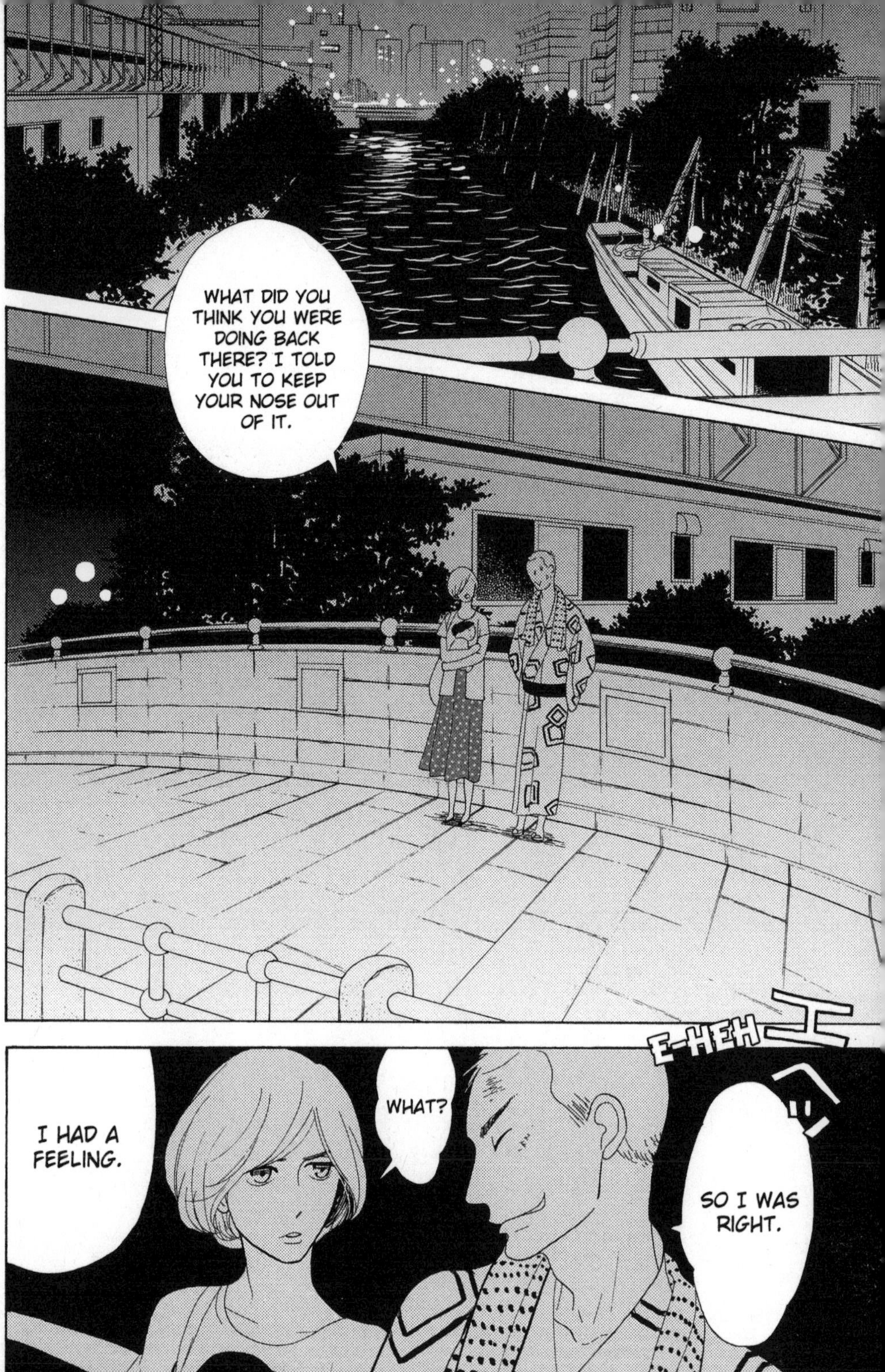
WHAT DID YOU THINK YOU WERE DOING BACK THERE? I TOLD YOU TO KEEP YOUR NOSE OUT OF IT.
E-HEH
SO I WAS RIGHT.
WHAT?
I HAD A FEELING.

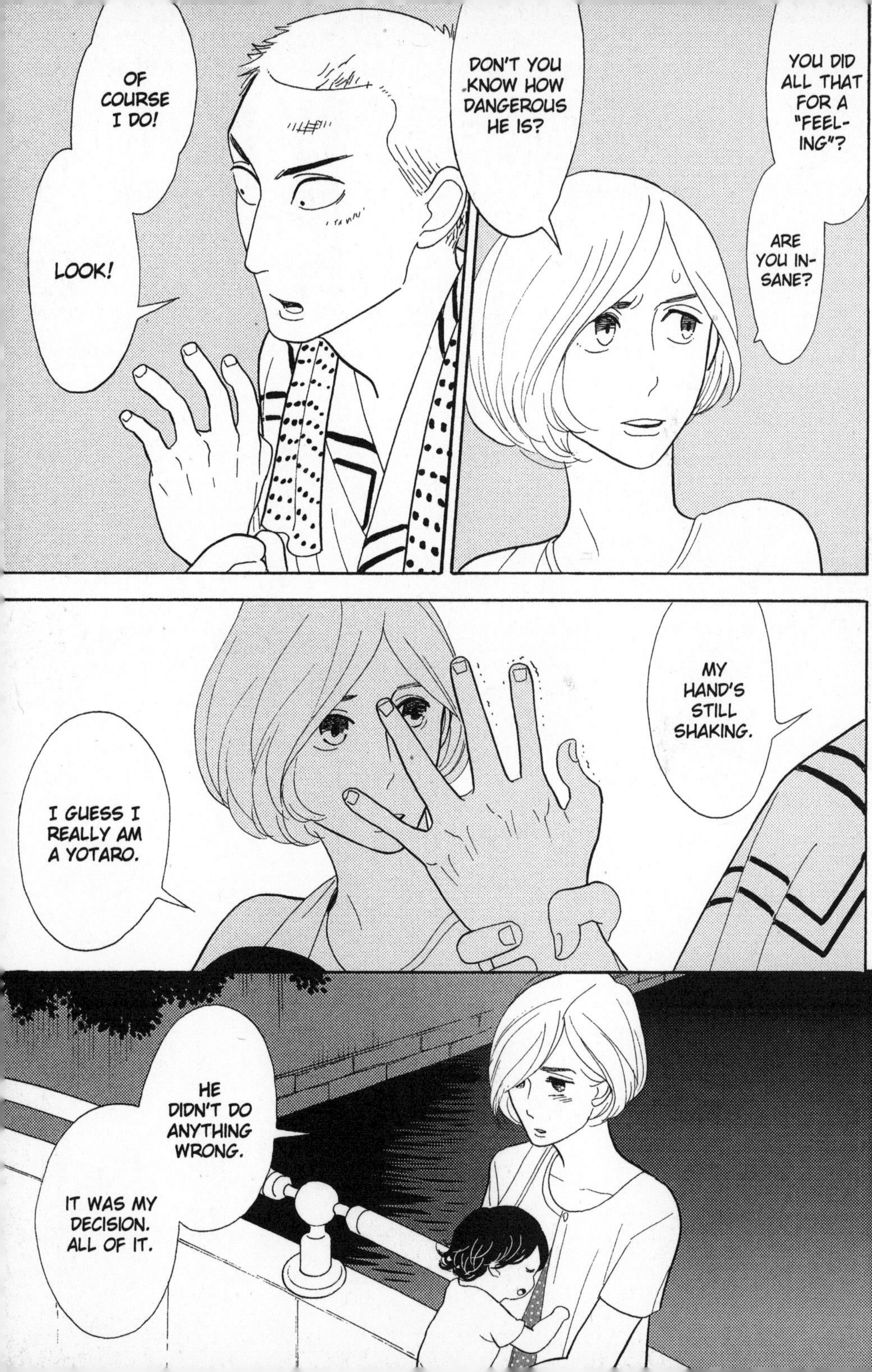
YOU DID ALL THAT FOR A "FEEL-ING"?
ARE YOU IN-SANE?
DON'T YOU KNOW HOW DANGEROUS HE IS?
OF COURSE I DO!
LOOK!
MY HAND'S STILL SHAKING.
I GUESS I REALLY AM A YOTARO.
HE DIDN'T DO ANYTHING WRONG.
IT WAS MY DECISION. ALL OF IT.

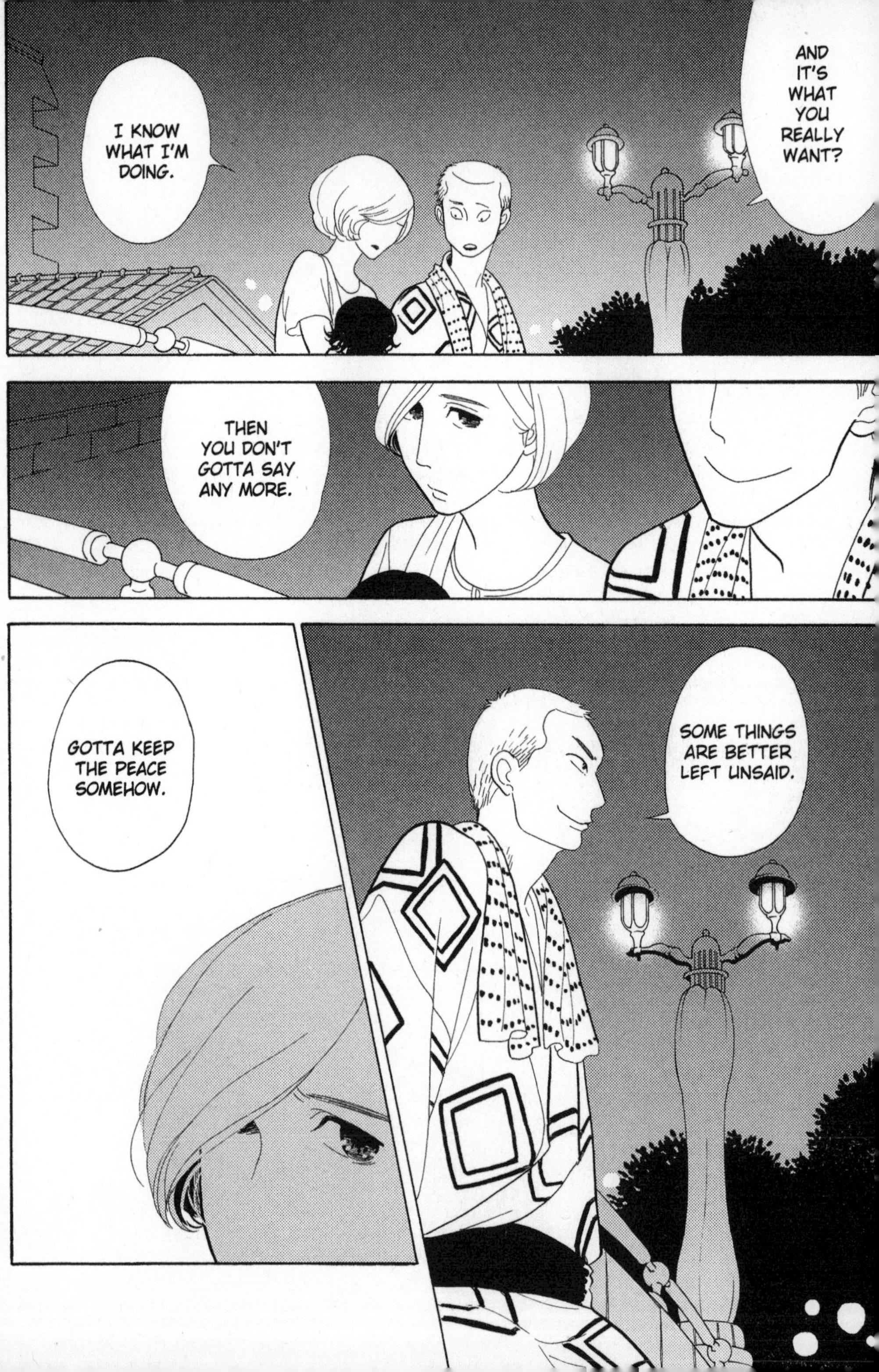
AND IT'S WHAT YOU REALLY WANT?
I KNOW WHAT I'M DOING.
THEN YOU DON'T GOTTA SAY ANY MORE.
SOME THINGS ARE BETTER LEFT UNSAID.
GOTTA KEEP THE PEACE SOMEHOW.

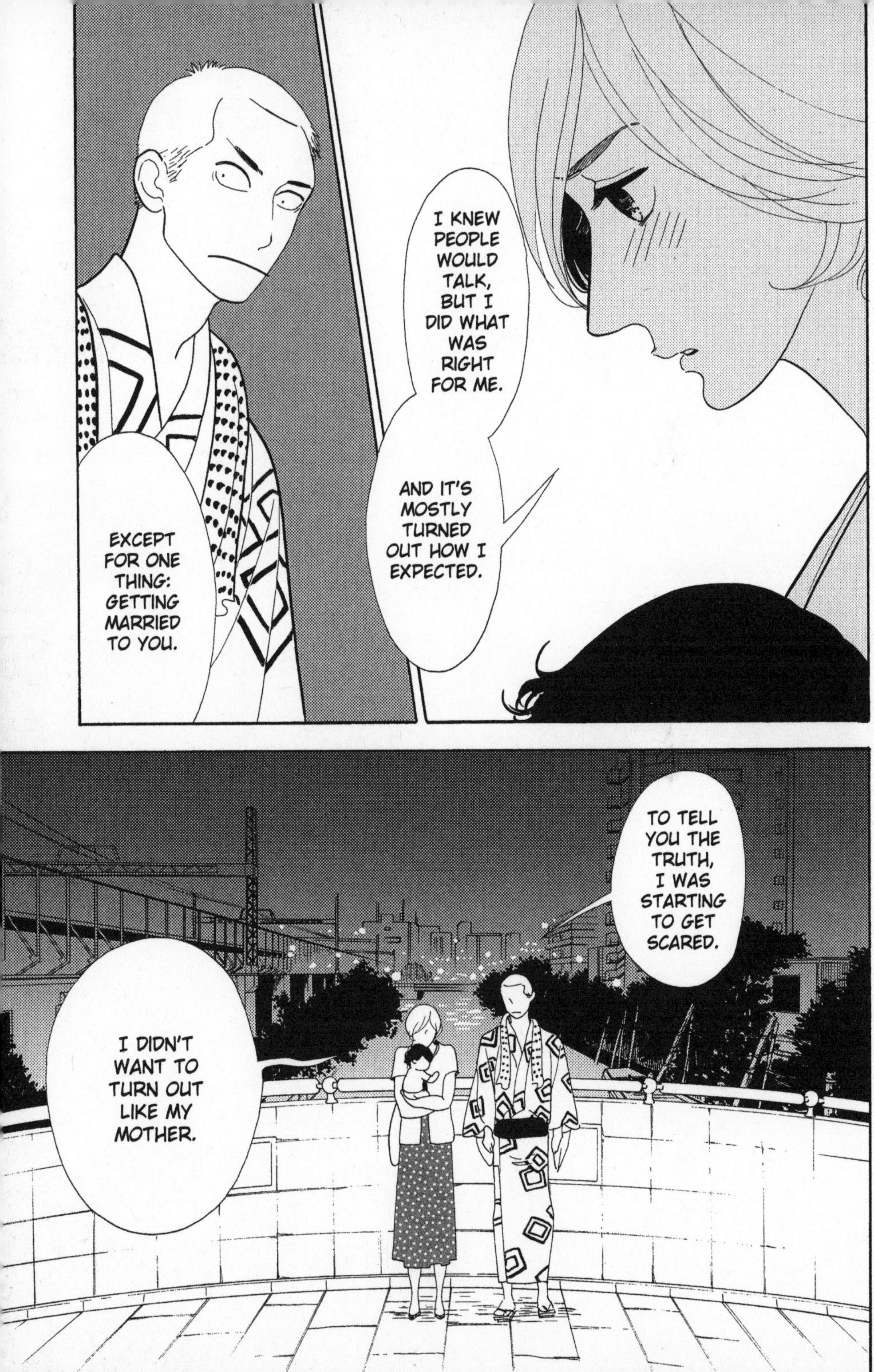
I KNEW PEOPLE WOULD TALK, BUT I DID WHAT WAS RIGHT FOR ME.
AND IT'S MOSTLY TURNED OUT HOW I EXPECTED.
EXCEPT FOR ONE THING: GETTING MARRIED TO YOU.
TO TELL YOU THE TRUTH, I WAS STARTING TO GET SCARED.
I DIDN'T WANT TO TURN OUT LIKE MY MOTHER.

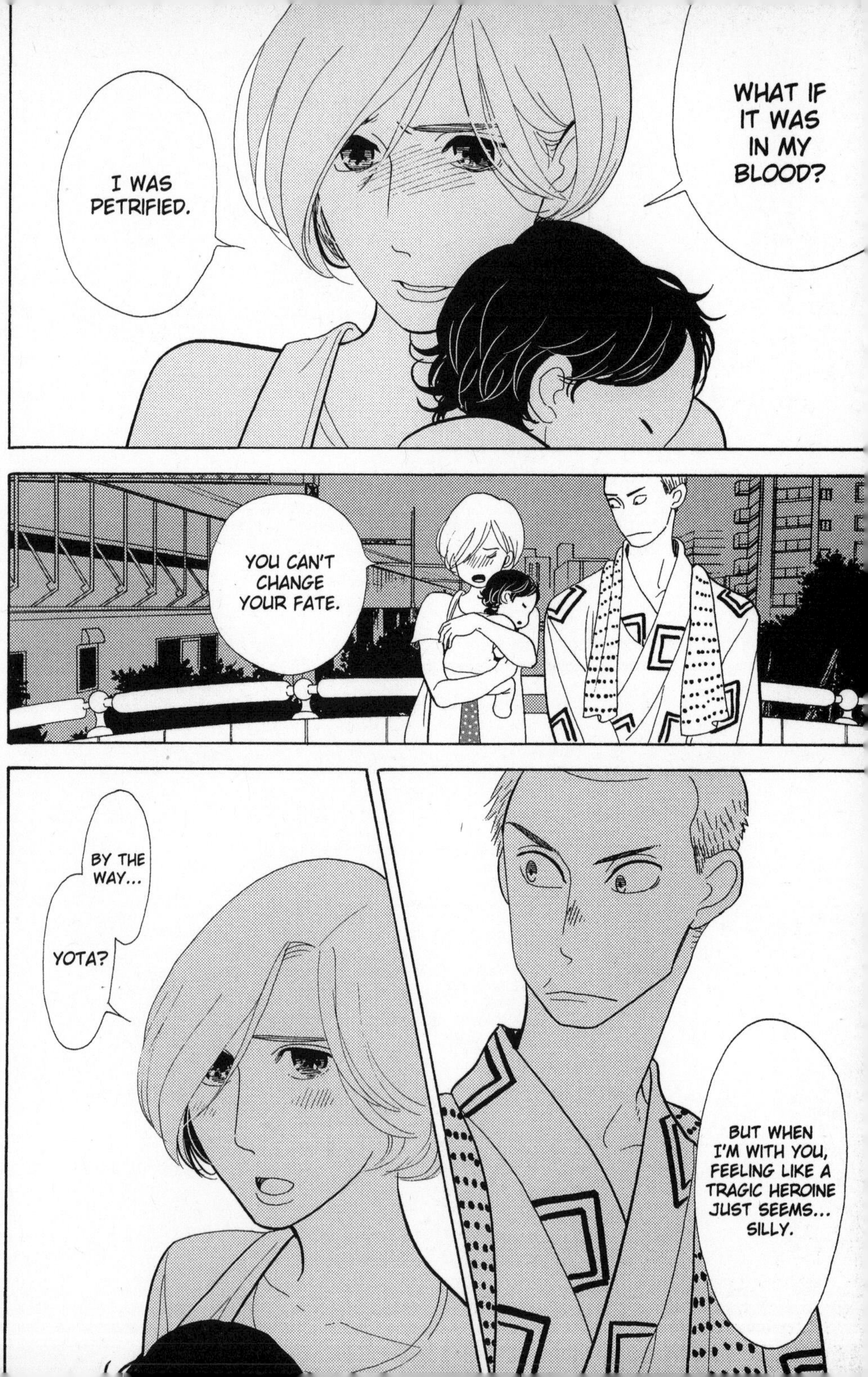
WHAT IF IT WAS IN MY BLOOD?
I WAS PETRIFIED.
YOU CAN'T CHANGE YOUR FATE.
BUT WHEN I'M WITH YOU, FEELING LIKE A TRAGIC HEROINE JUST SEEMS... SILLY.
BY THE WAY...
YOTA?

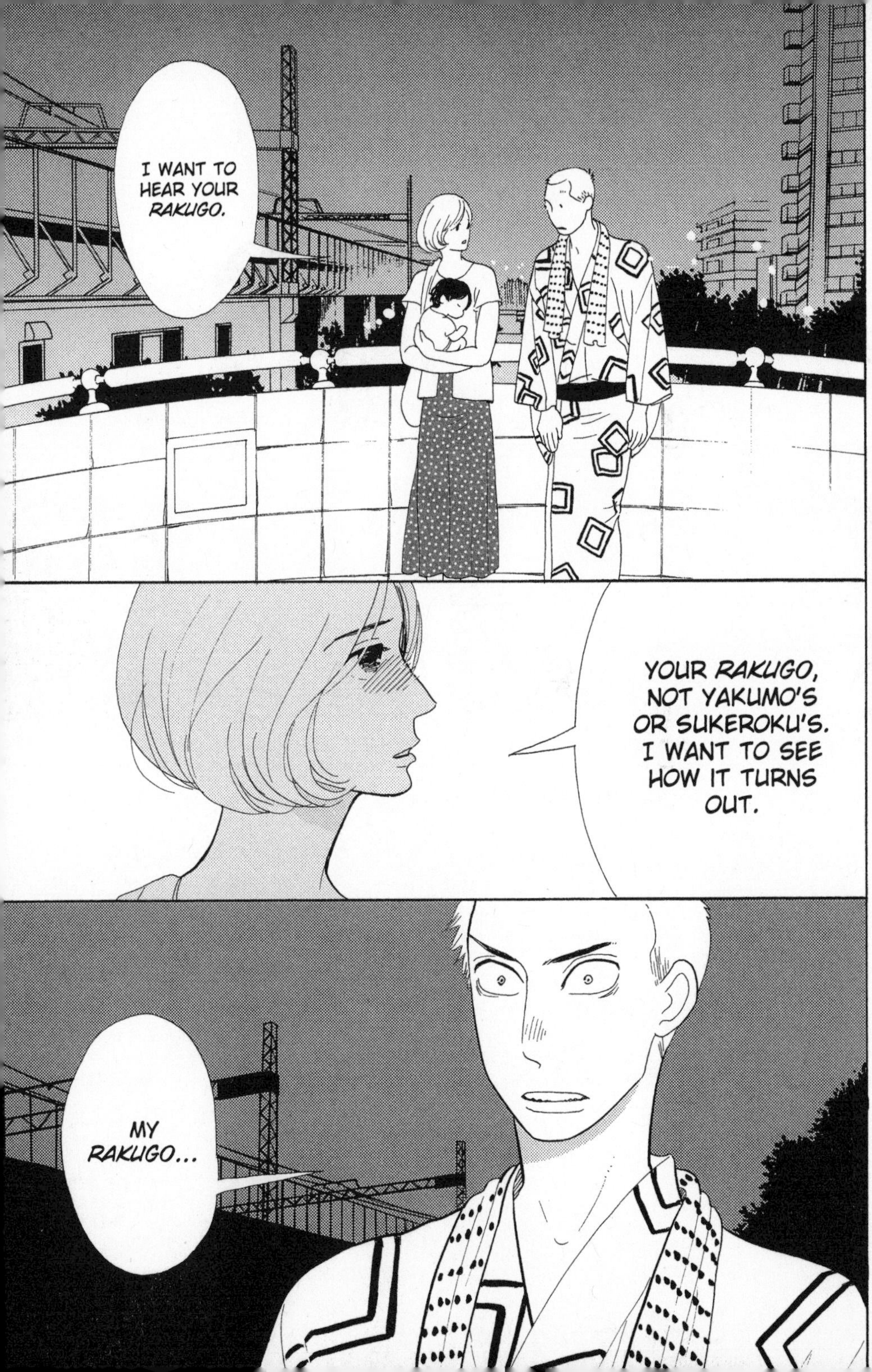
I WANT TO HEAR YOUR *RAKUGO.*
YOUR *RAKUGO,* NOT YAKUMO'S OR SUKEROKU'S. I WANT TO SEE HOW IT TURNS OUT.
MY *RAKUGO...*

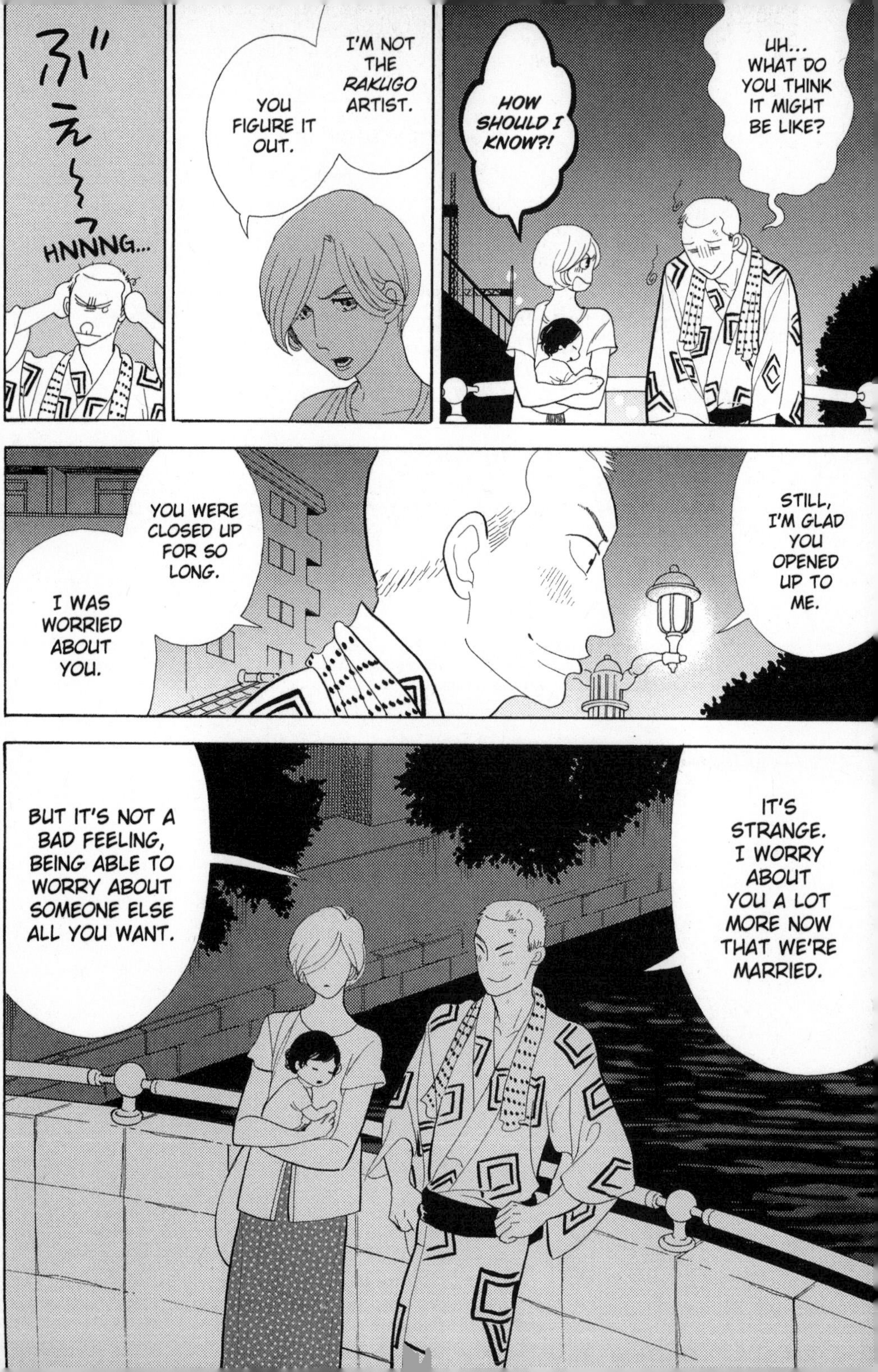
UH... WHAT DO YOU THINK IT MIGHT BE LIKE?
HOW SHOULD I KNOW?!
I'M NOT THE RAKUGO ARTIST.
YOU FIGURE IT OUT.
ぶえ〜〜っ
HNNNG...
STILL, I'M GLAD YOU OPENED UP TO ME.
YOU WERE CLOSED UP FOR SO LONG.
I WAS WORRIED ABOUT YOU.
IT'S STRANGE. I WORRY ABOUT YOU A LOT MORE NOW THAT WE'RE MARRIED.
BUT IT'S NOT A BAD FEELING, BEING ABLE TO WORRY ABOUT SOMEONE ELSE ALL YOU WANT.

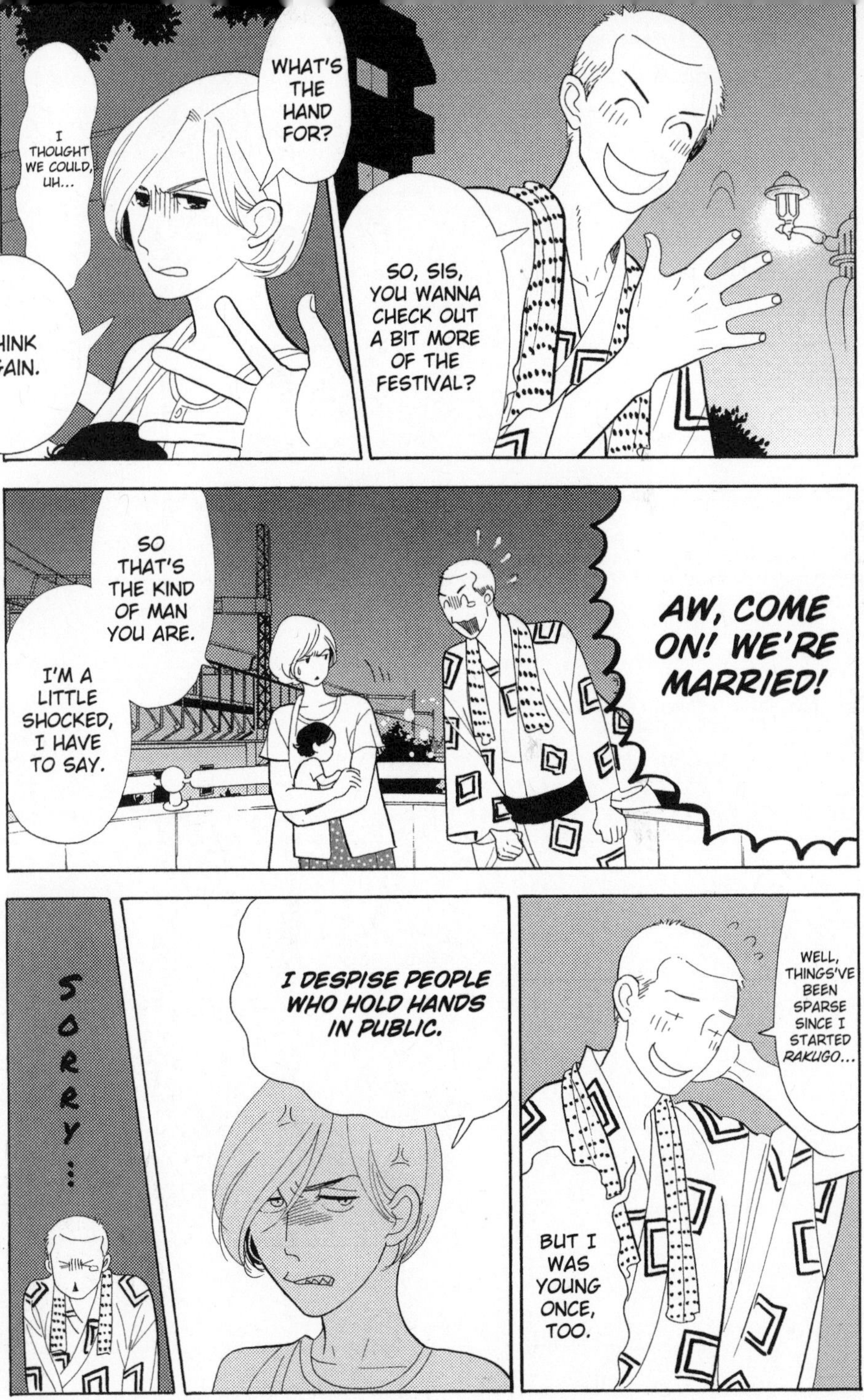
SO, SIS, YOU WANNA CHECK OUT A BIT MORE OF THE FESTIVAL?
WHAT'S THE HAND FOR?
I THOUGHT WE COULD, UH...
THINK AGAIN.
AW, COME ON! WE'RE MARRIED!
SO THAT'S THE KIND OF MAN YOU ARE.
I'M A LITTLE SHOCKED, I HAVE TO SAY.
WELL, THINGS'VE BEEN SPARSE SINCE I STARTED *RAKUGO*...
BUT I WAS YOUNG ONCE, TOO.
I DESPISE PEOPLE WHO HOLD HANDS IN PUBLIC.
SORRY...

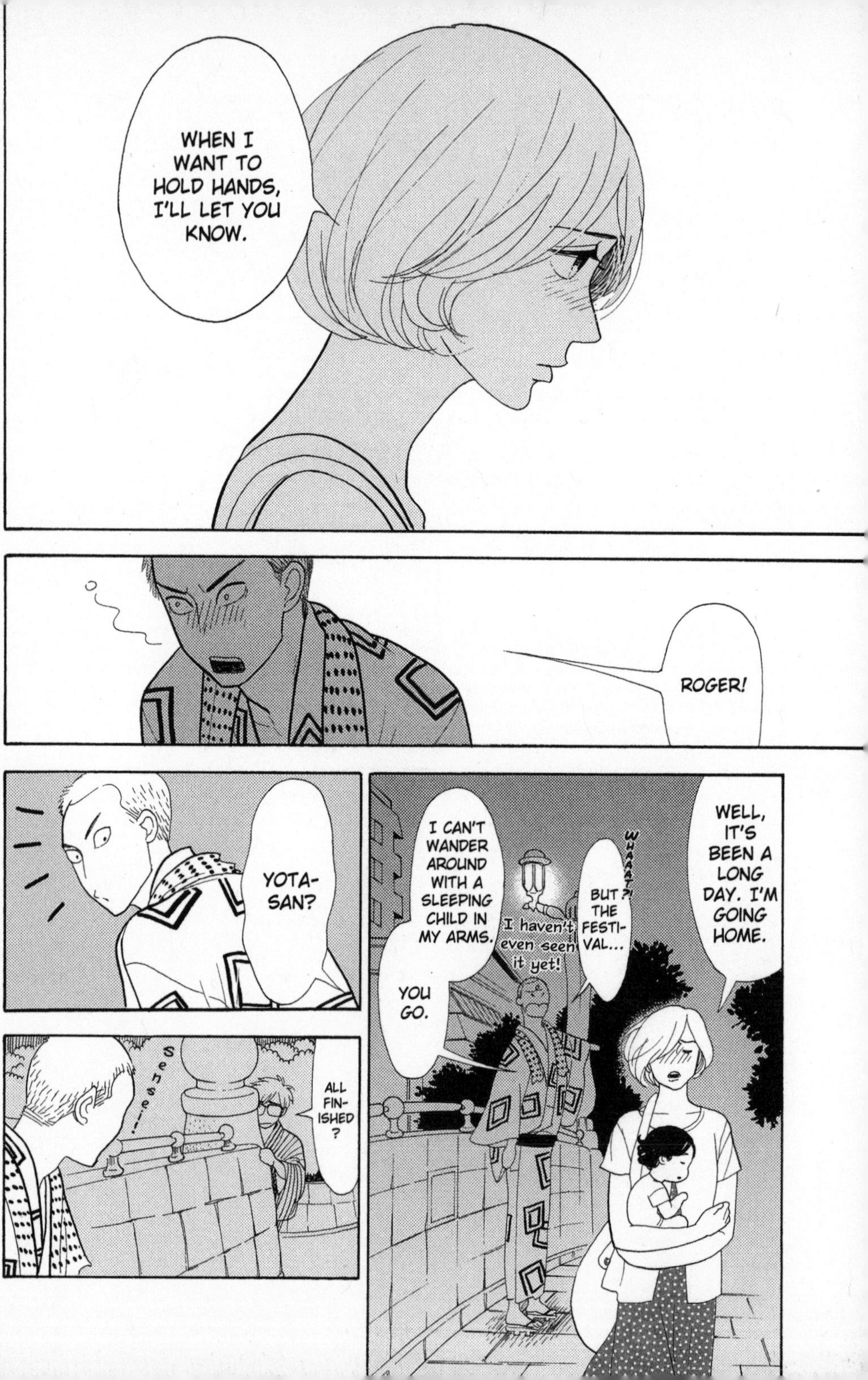
WHEN I WANT TO HOLD HANDS, I'LL LET YOU KNOW.
ROGER!
WELL, IT'S BEEN A LONG DAY. I'M GOING HOME.
BUT THE FESTIVAL...
WHAAAT?!
I haven't even seen it yet!
I CAN'T WANDER AROUND WITH A SLEEPING CHILD IN MY ARMS.
YOU GO.
YOTA-SAN?
Sensei...!
ALL FINISHED?

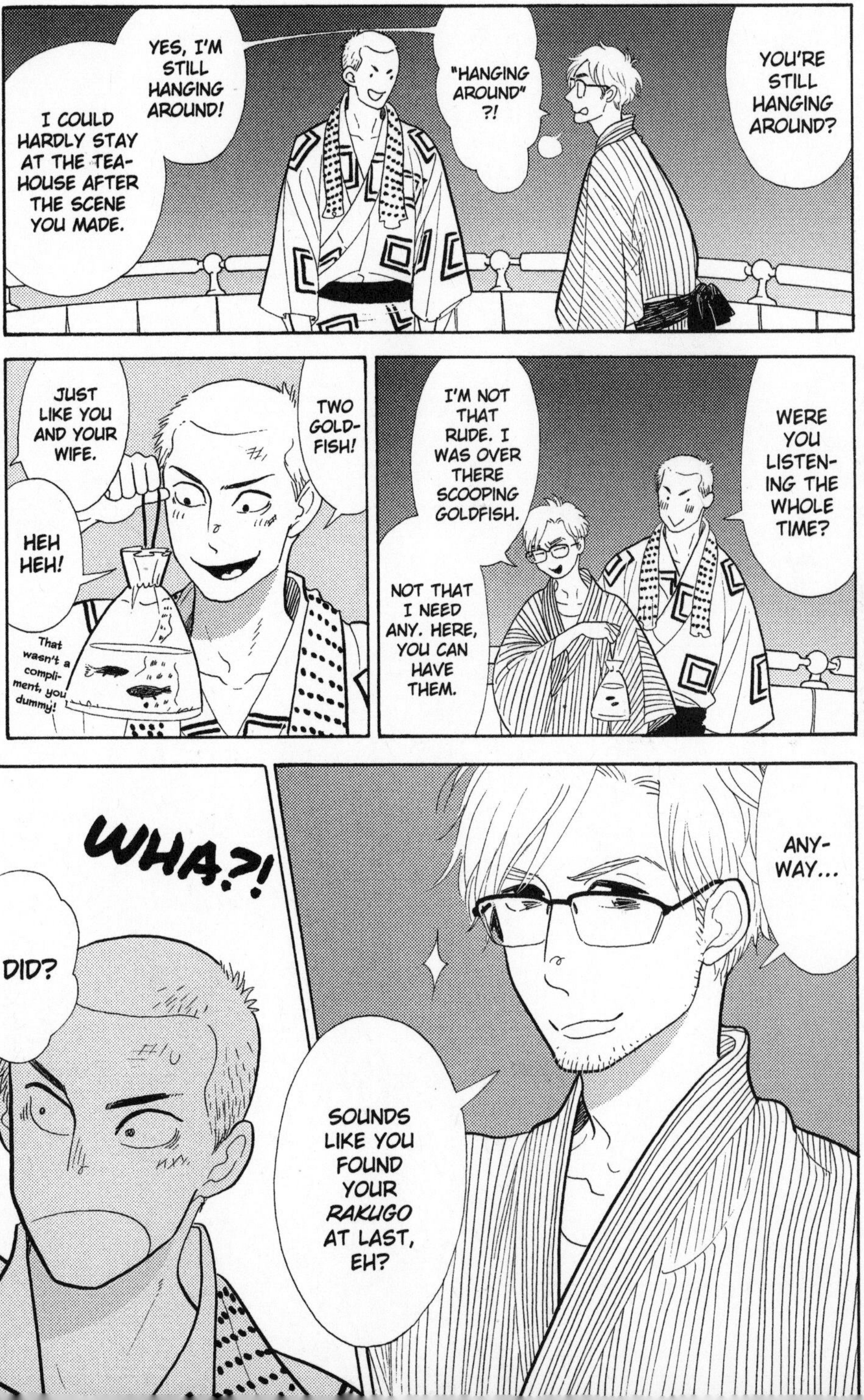
YOU'RE STILL HANGING AROUND?
"HANGING AROUND" ?!
YES, I'M STILL HANGING AROUND!
I COULD HARDLY STAY AT THE TEA-HOUSE AFTER THE SCENE YOU MADE.
WERE YOU LISTEN-ING THE WHOLE TIME?
I'M NOT THAT RUDE. I WAS OVER THERE SCOOPING GOLDFISH.
NOT THAT I NEED ANY. HERE, YOU CAN HAVE THEM.
TWO GOLD-FISH!
JUST LIKE YOU AND YOUR WIFE.
HEH HEH!
That wasn't a compliment, you dummy!
ANY-WAY...
SOUNDS LIKE YOU FOUND YOUR *RAKUGO* AT LAST, EH?
WHA?!
I DID?

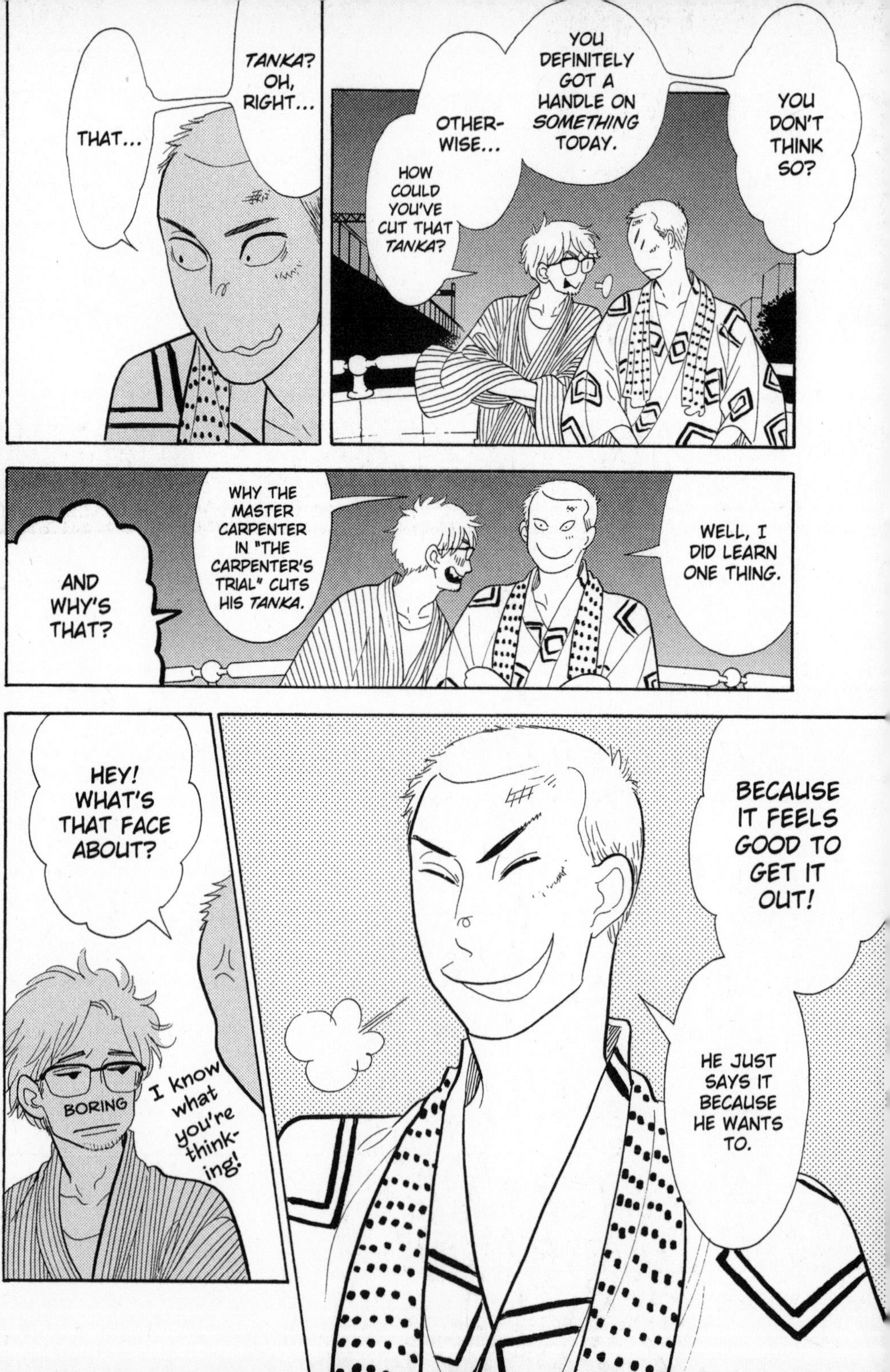
YOU DON'T THINK SO?
YOU DEFINITELY GOT A HANDLE ON *SOMETHING* TODAY.
OTHER-WISE...
HOW COULD YOU'VE CUT THAT *TANKA*?
TANKA? OH, RIGHT...
THAT...
WELL, I DID LEARN ONE THING.
WHY THE MASTER CARPENTER IN "THE CARPENTER'S TRIAL" CUTS HIS *TANKA*.
AND WHY'S THAT?
BECAUSE IT FEELS GOOD TO GET IT OUT!
HE JUST SAYS IT BECAUSE HE WANTS TO.
HEY! WHAT'S THAT FACE ABOUT?
BORING
I know what you're think-ing!

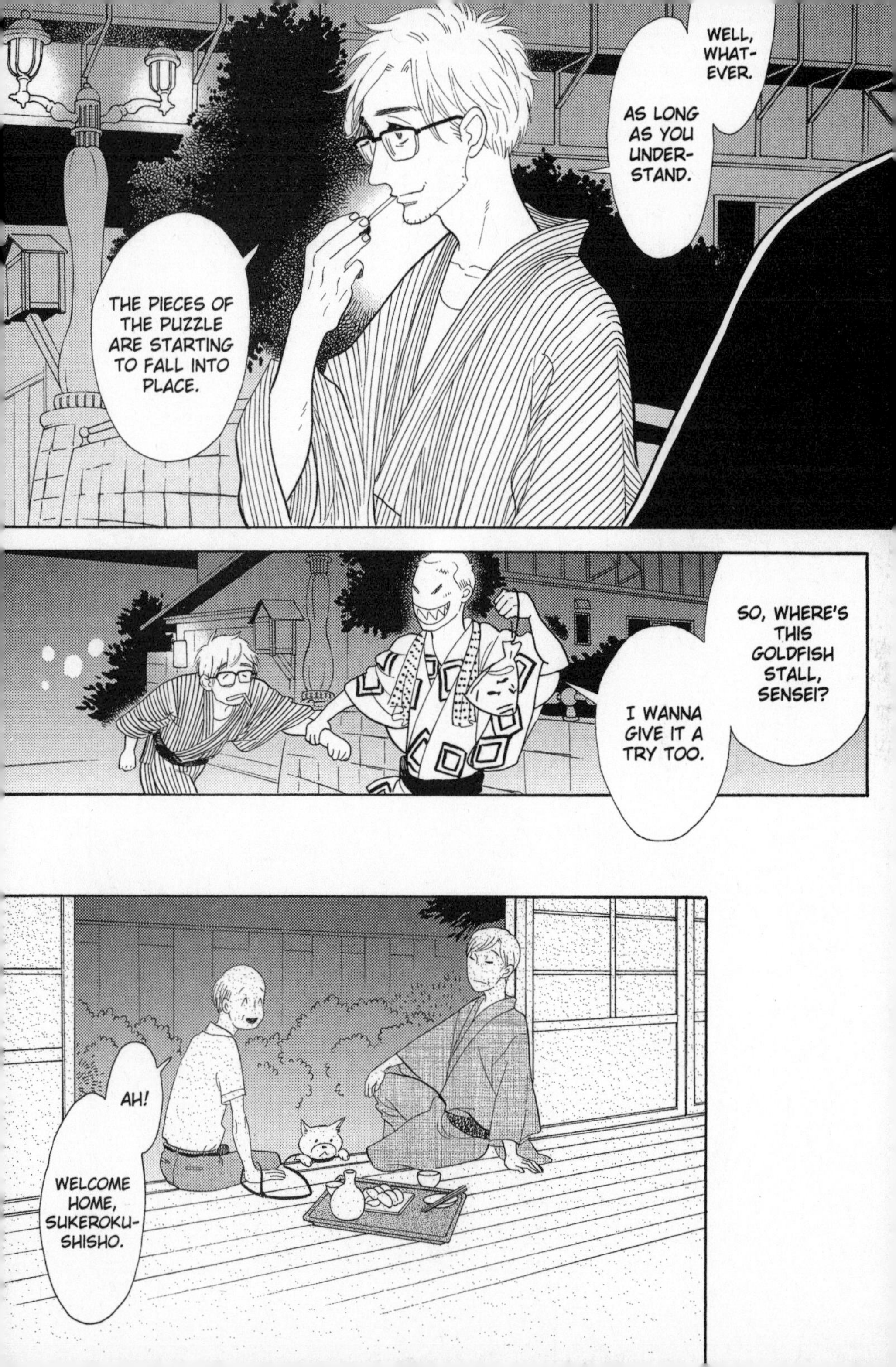
WELL, WHATEVER.
AS LONG AS YOU UNDERSTAND.
THE PIECES OF THE PUZZLE ARE STARTING TO FALL INTO PLACE.
SO, WHERE'S THIS GOLDFISH STALL, SENSEI?
I WANNA GIVE IT A TRY TOO.
AH!
WELCOME HOME, SUKEROKU-SHISHO.

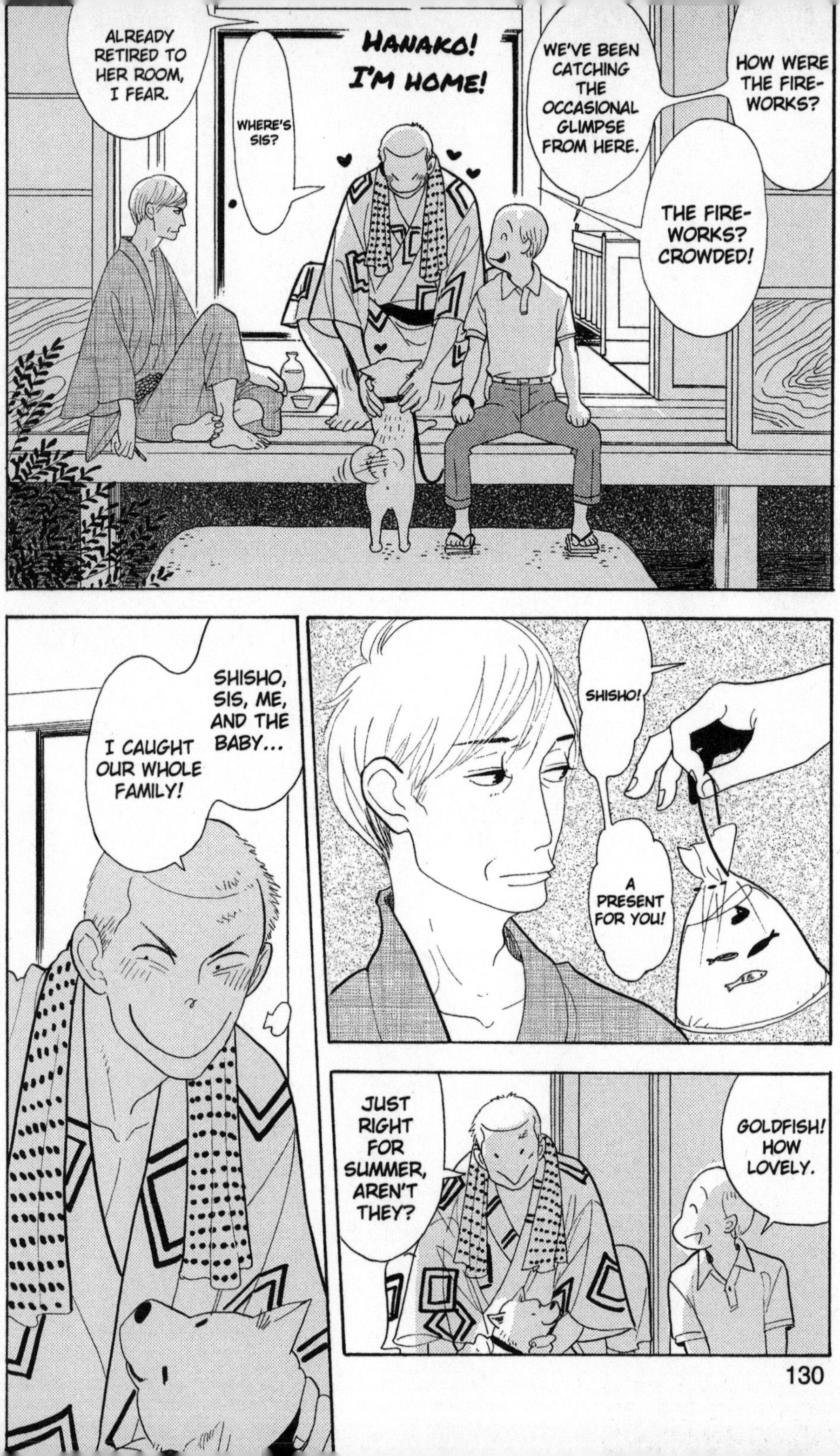
HOW WERE THE FIRE-WORKS?
THE FIRE-WORKS? CROWDED!
WE'VE BEEN CATCHING THE OCCASIONAL GLIMPSE FROM HERE.
HANAKO! I'M HOME!
WHERE'S SIS?
ALREADY RETIRED TO HER ROOM, I FEAR.
SHISHO!
A PRESENT FOR YOU!
GOLDFISH! HOW LOVELY.
JUST RIGHT FOR SUMMER, AREN'T THEY?
SHISHO, SIS, ME, AND THE BABY...
I CAUGHT OUR WHOLE FAMILY!

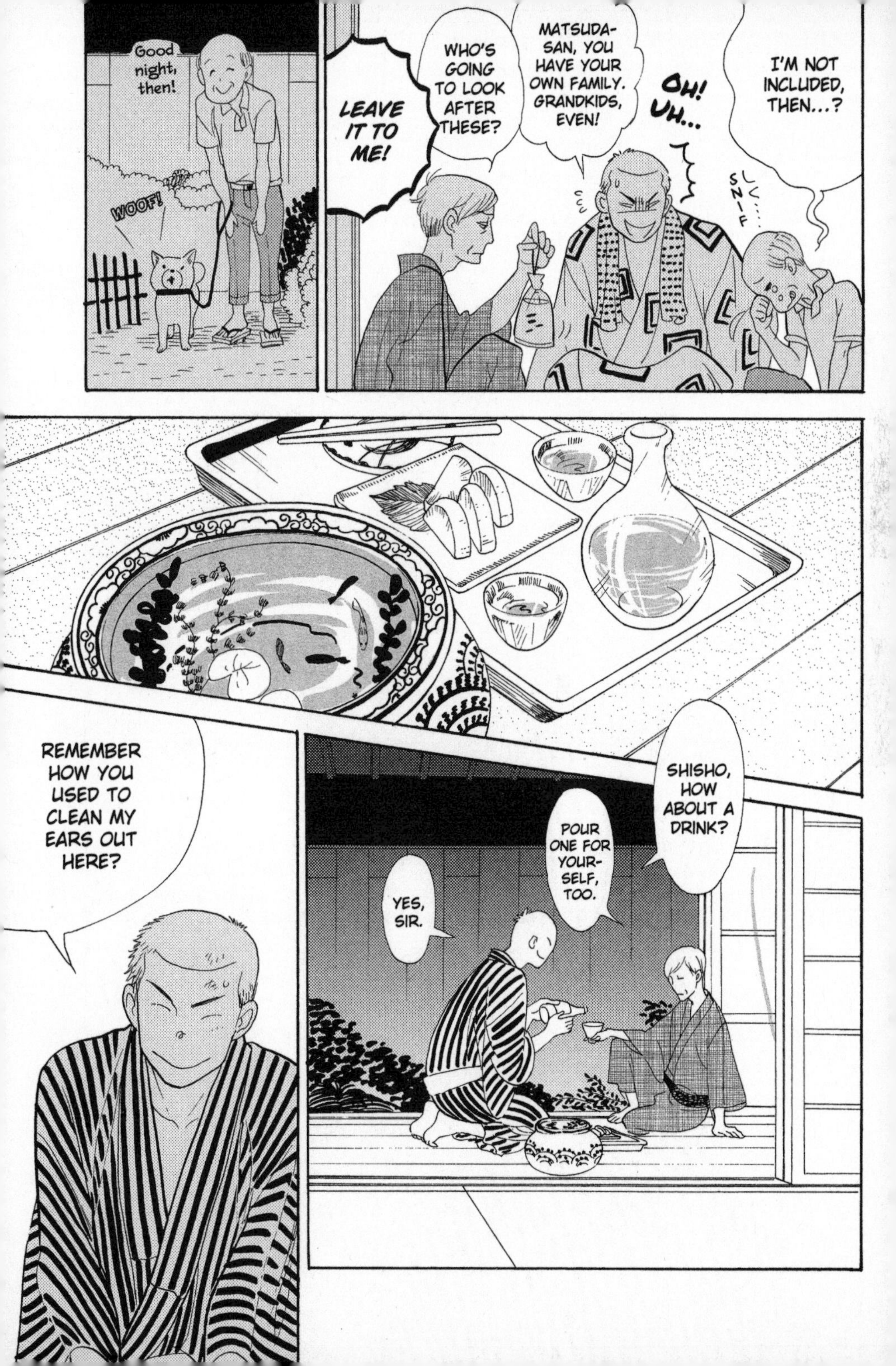
I'M NOT INCLUDED, THEN...?
SNIF
OH! UH...
MATSUDA-SAN, YOU HAVE YOUR OWN FAMILY. GRANDKIDS, EVEN!
WHO'S GOING TO LOOK AFTER THESE?
LEAVE IT TO ME!
Good night, then!
WOOF!
SHISHO, HOW ABOUT A DRINK?
POUR ONE FOR YOURSELF, TOO.
YES, SIR.
REMEMBER HOW YOU USED TO CLEAN MY EARS OUT HERE?

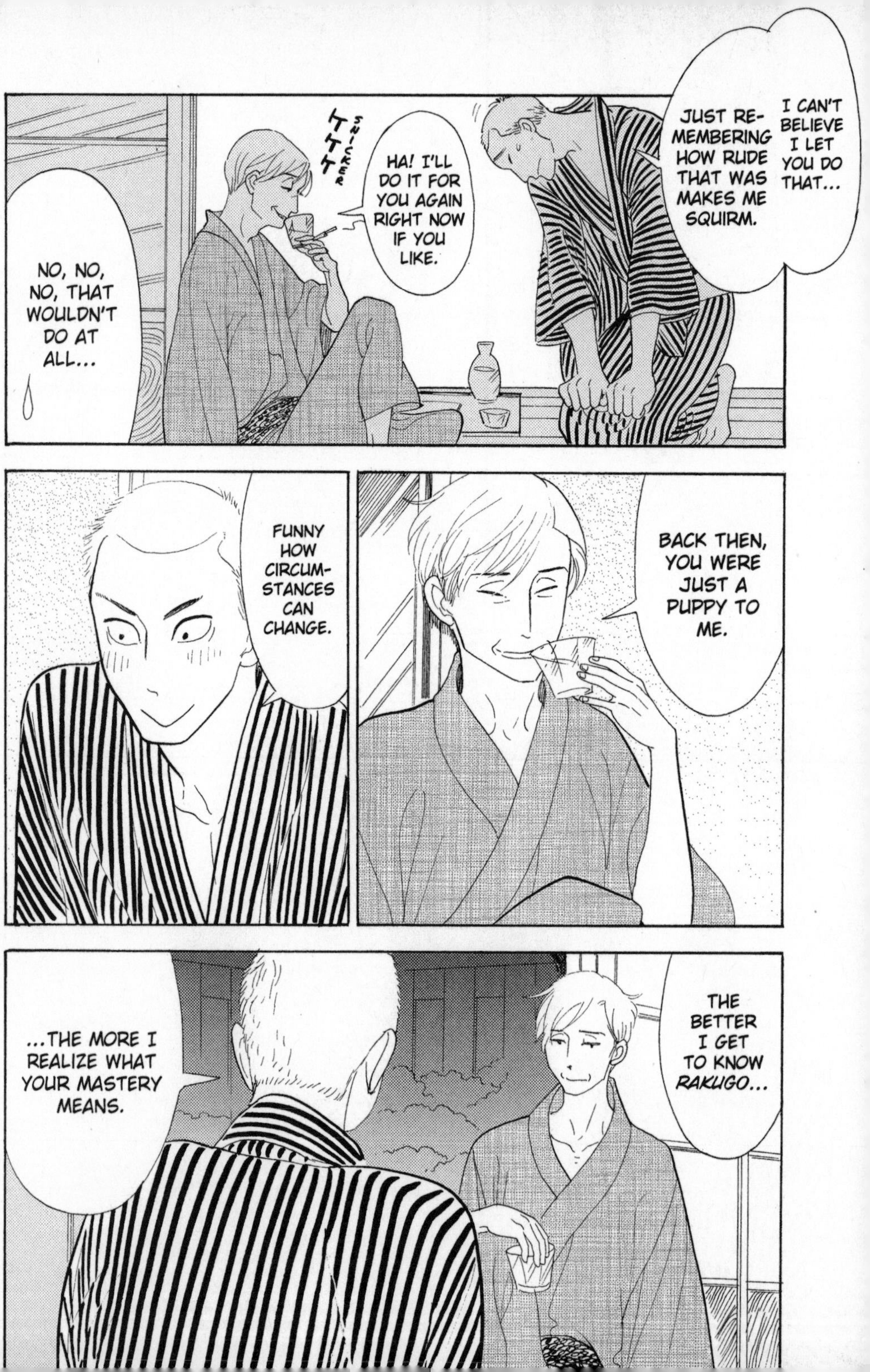
I CAN'T BELIEVE I LET YOU DO THAT...
JUST RE-MEMBERING HOW RUDE THAT WAS MAKES ME SQUIRM.
SNICKER
HA! I'LL DO IT FOR YOU AGAIN RIGHT NOW IF YOU LIKE.
NO, NO, NO, THAT WOULDN'T DO AT ALL...
BACK THEN, YOU WERE JUST A PUPPY TO ME.
FUNNY HOW CIRCUM-STANCES CAN CHANGE.
THE BETTER I GET TO KNOW *RAKUGO*...
...THE MORE I REALIZE WHAT YOUR MASTERY MEANS.

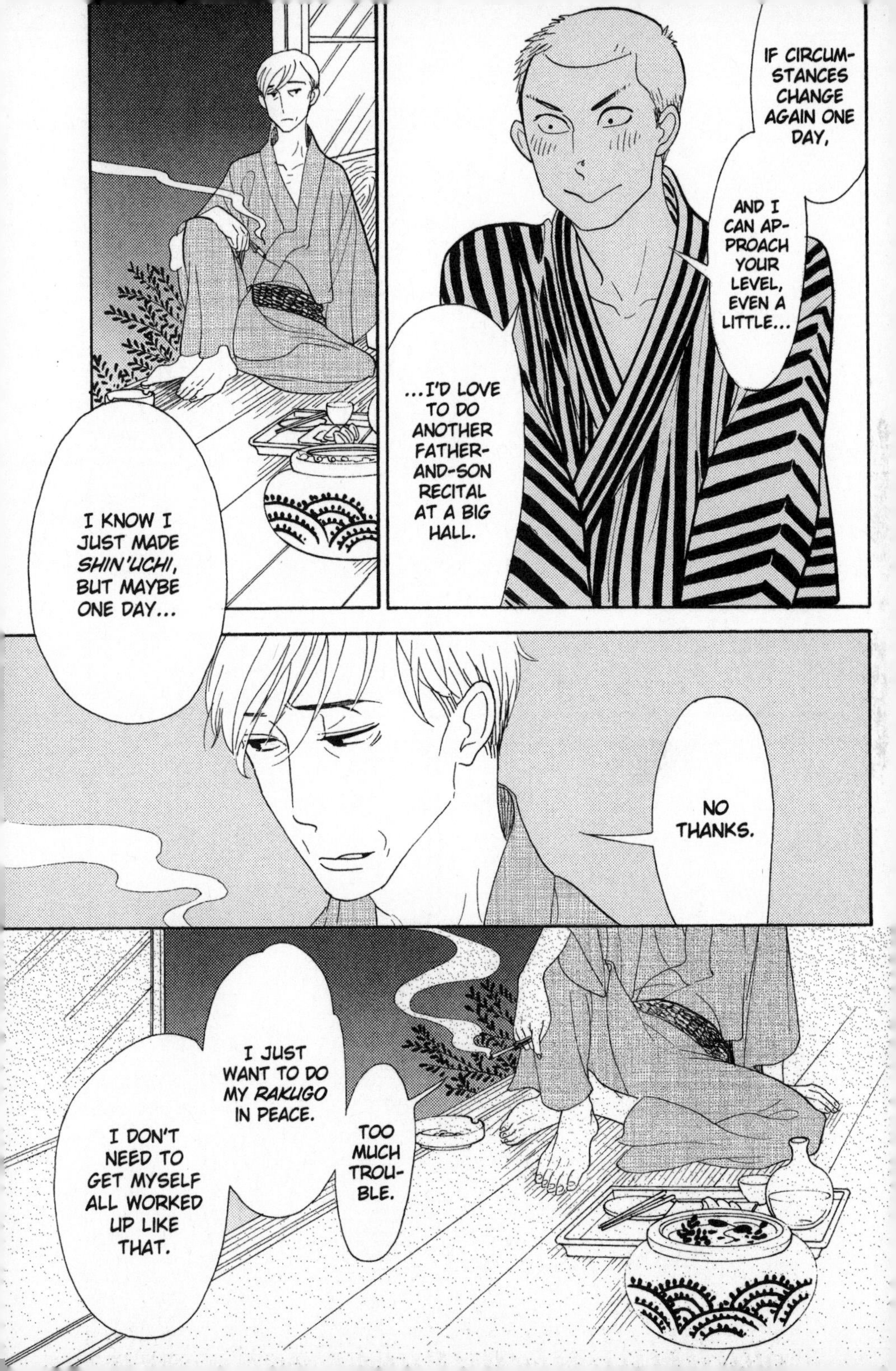
IF CIRCUM-STANCES CHANGE AGAIN ONE DAY,
AND I CAN AP-PROACH YOUR LEVEL, EVEN A LITTLE...
...I'D LOVE TO DO ANOTHER FATHER-AND-SON RECITAL AT A BIG HALL.
I KNOW I JUST MADE *SHIN'UCHI*, BUT MAYBE ONE DAY...
NO THANKS.
TOO MUCH TROU-BLE.
I JUST WANT TO DO MY *RAKUGO* IN PEACE.
I DON'T NEED TO GET MYSELF ALL WORKED UP LIKE THAT.

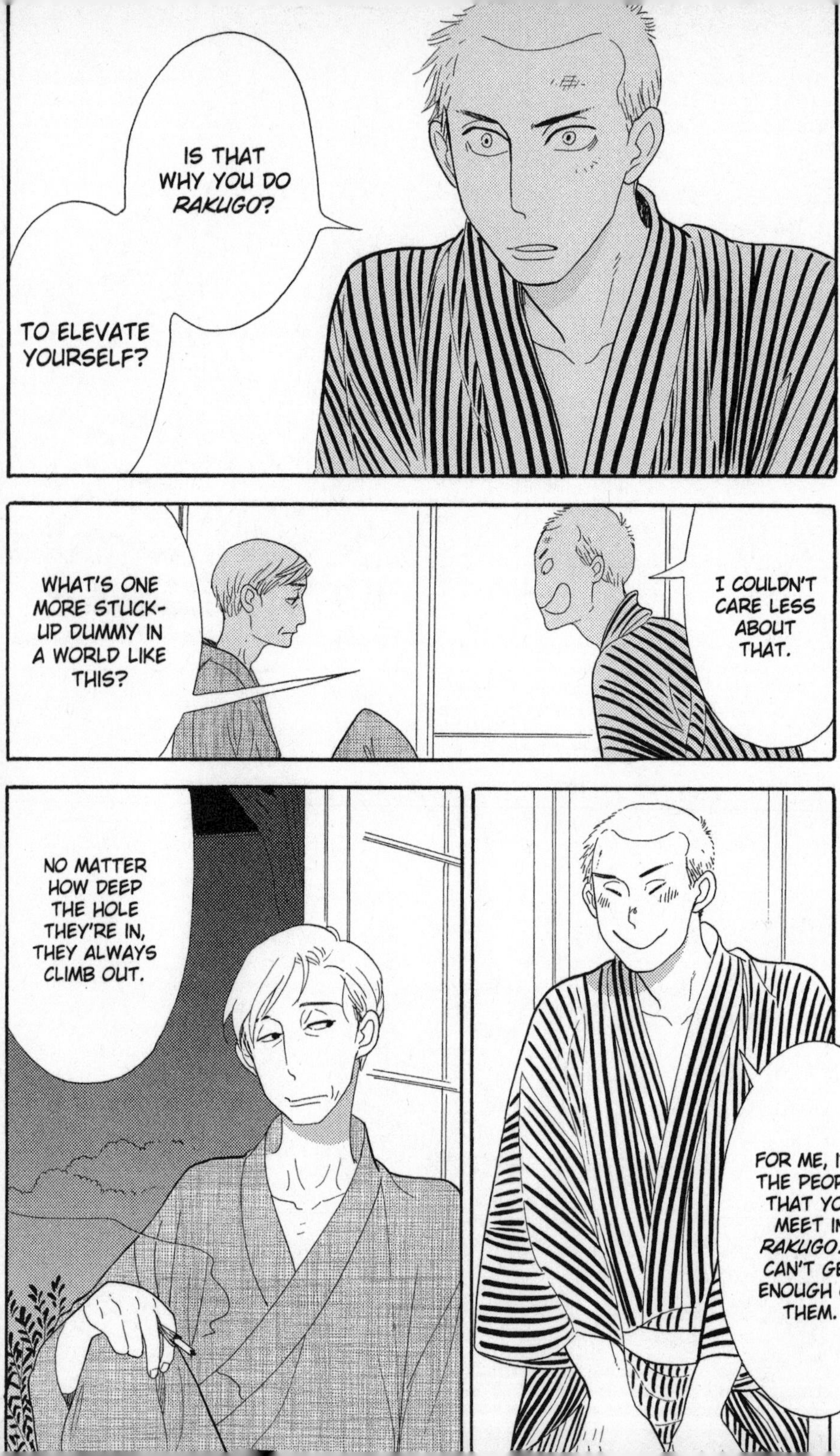
IS THAT WHY YOU DO *RAKUGO*?
TO ELEVATE YOURSELF?
I COULDN'T CARE LESS ABOUT THAT.
WHAT'S ONE MORE STUCK-UP DUMMY IN A WORLD LIKE THIS?
FOR ME, IT'S THE PEOPLE THAT YOU MEET IN *RAKUGO*. I CAN'T GET ENOUGH OF THEM.
NO MATTER HOW DEEP THE HOLE THEY'RE IN, THEY ALWAYS CLIMB OUT.

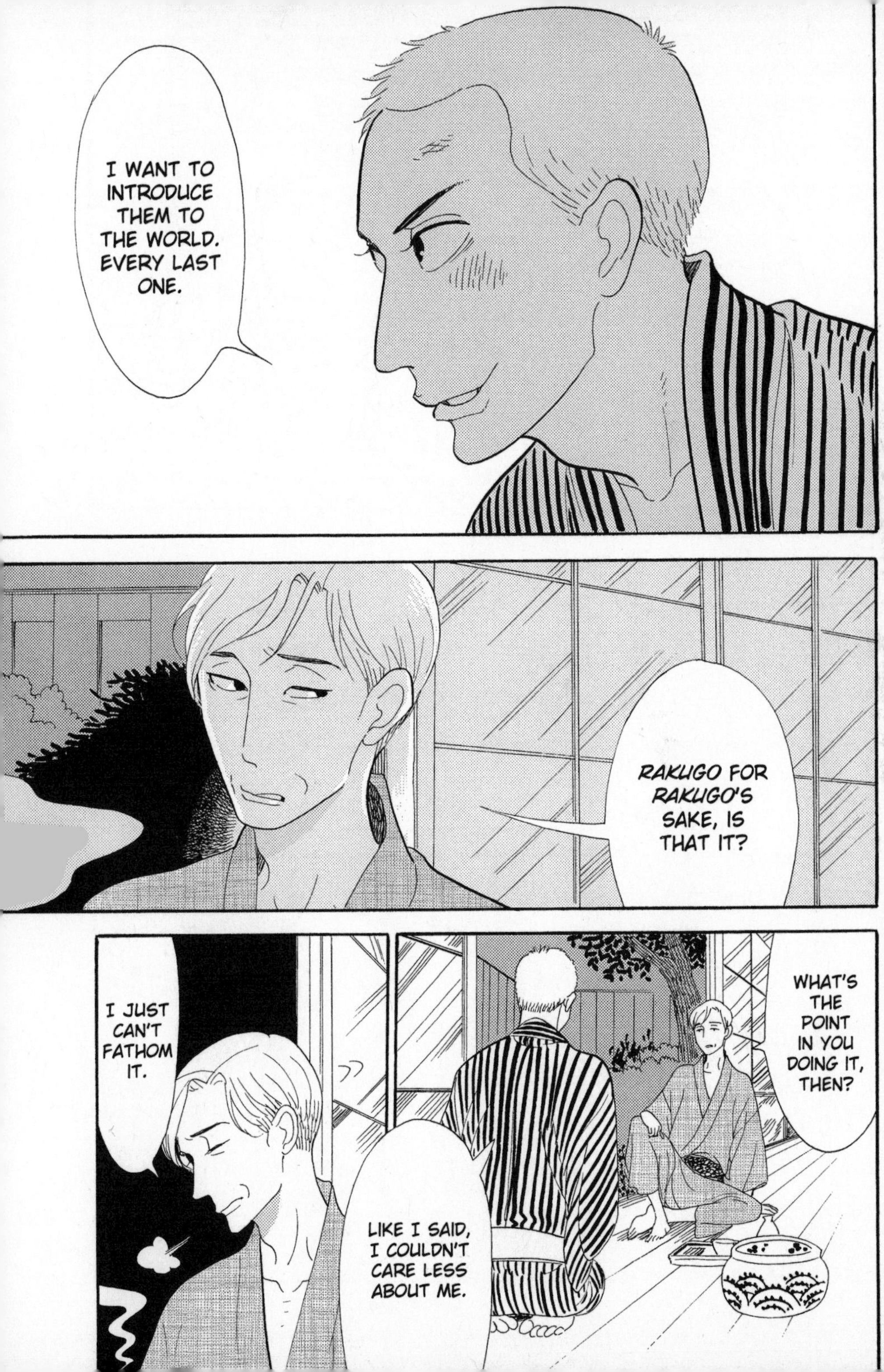
I WANT TO INTRODUCE THEM TO THE WORLD. EVERY LAST ONE.
RAKUGO FOR *RAKUGO*'S SAKE, IS THAT IT?
WHAT'S THE POINT IN YOU DOING IT, THEN?
LIKE I SAID, I COULDN'T CARE LESS ABOUT ME.
I JUST CAN'T FATHOM IT.

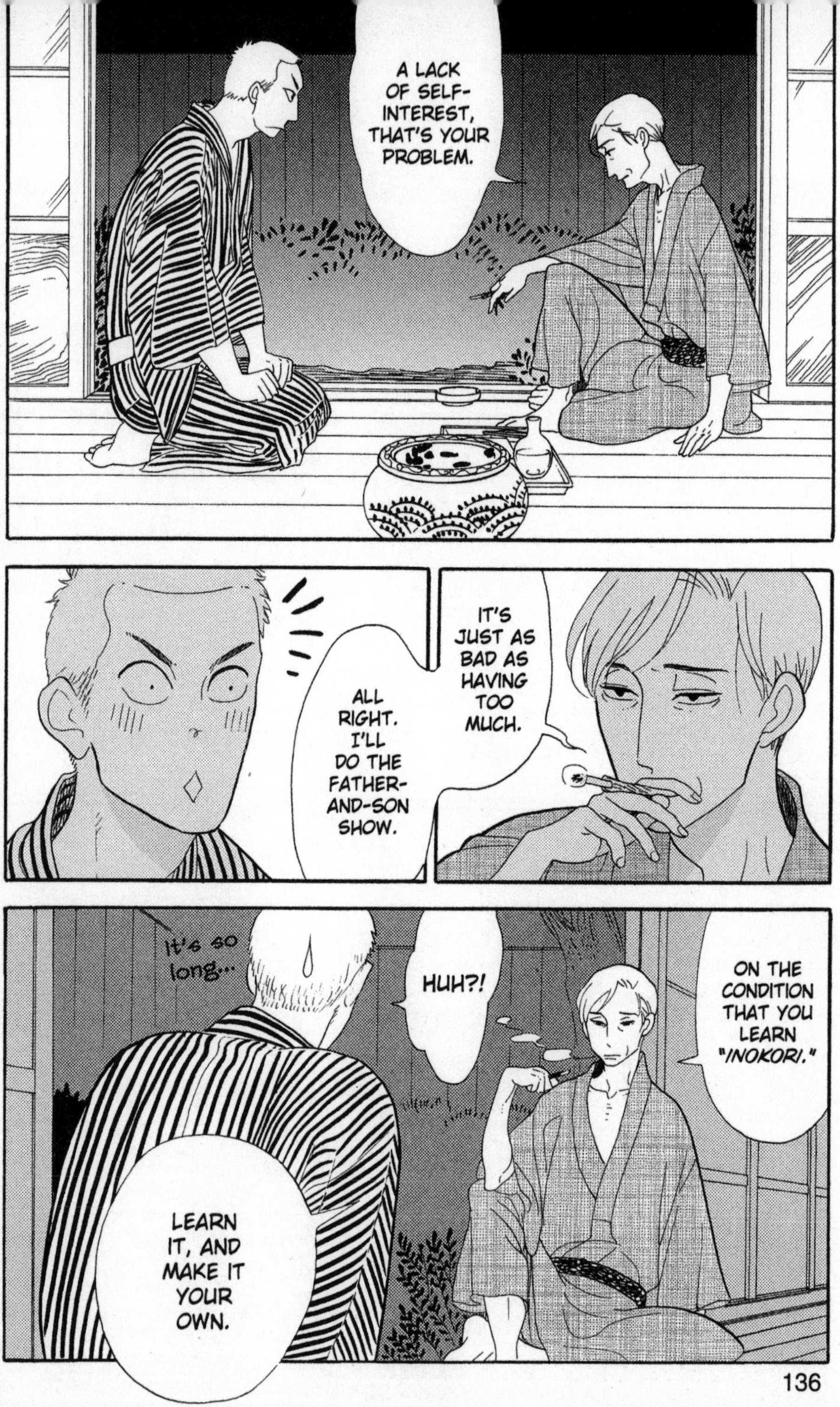
A LACK OF SELF-INTEREST, THAT'S YOUR PROBLEM.
IT'S JUST AS BAD AS HAVING TOO MUCH.
ALL RIGHT. I'LL DO THE FATHER-AND-SON SHOW.
ON THE CONDITION THAT YOU LEARN "INOKORI."
HUH?!
It's so long...
LEARN IT, AND MAKE IT YOUR OWN.

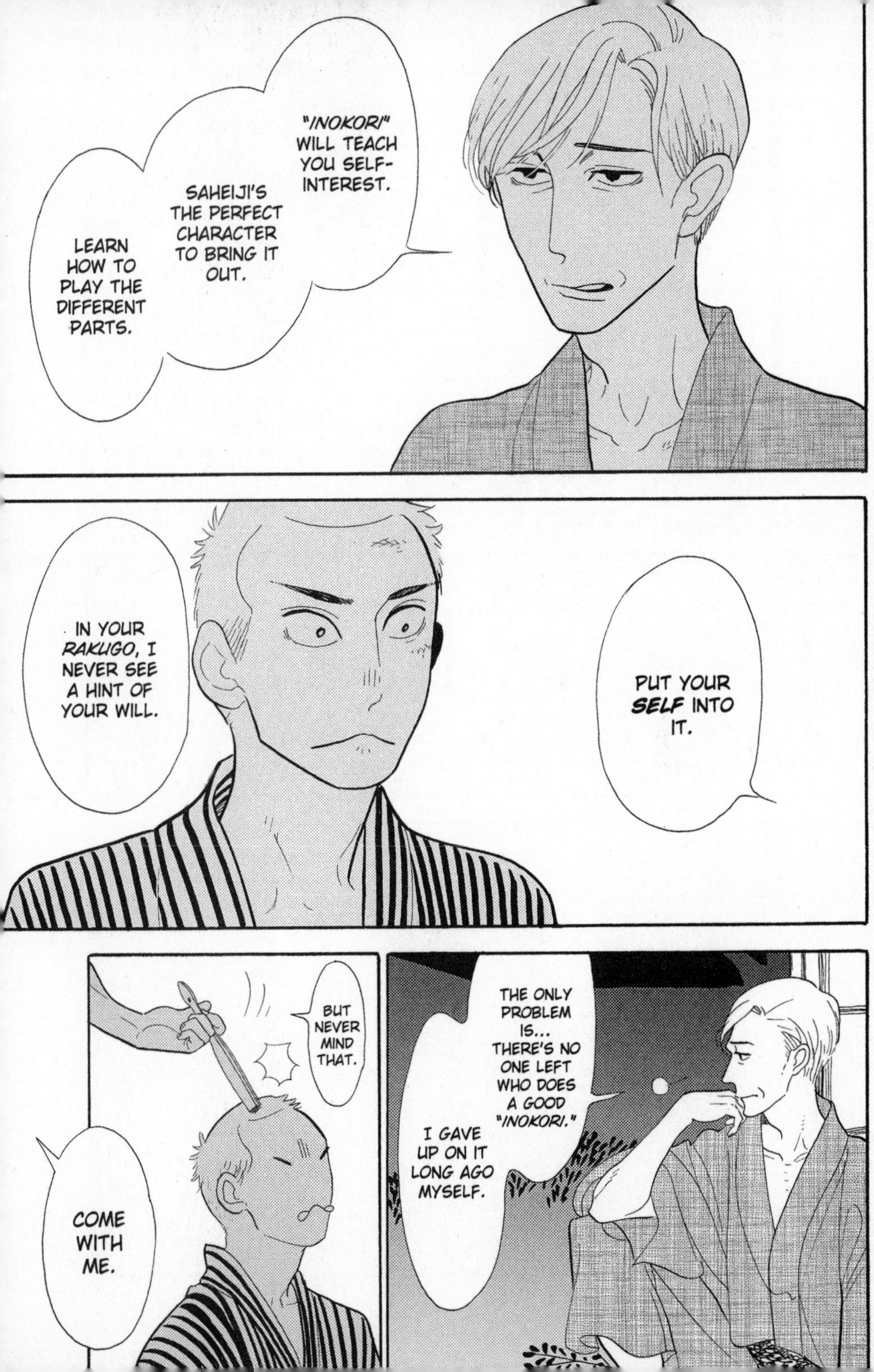
"*INOKORI*" WILL TEACH YOU SELF-INTEREST.
SAHEIJI'S THE PERFECT CHARACTER TO BRING IT OUT.
LEARN HOW TO PLAY THE DIFFERENT PARTS.
PUT YOUR ***SELF*** INTO IT.
IN YOUR *RAKUGO*, I NEVER SEE A HINT OF YOUR WILL.
THE ONLY PROBLEM IS... THERE'S NO ONE LEFT WHO DOES A GOOD "*INOKORI*."
I GAVE UP ON IT LONG AGO MYSELF.
BUT NEVER MIND THAT.
COME WITH ME.

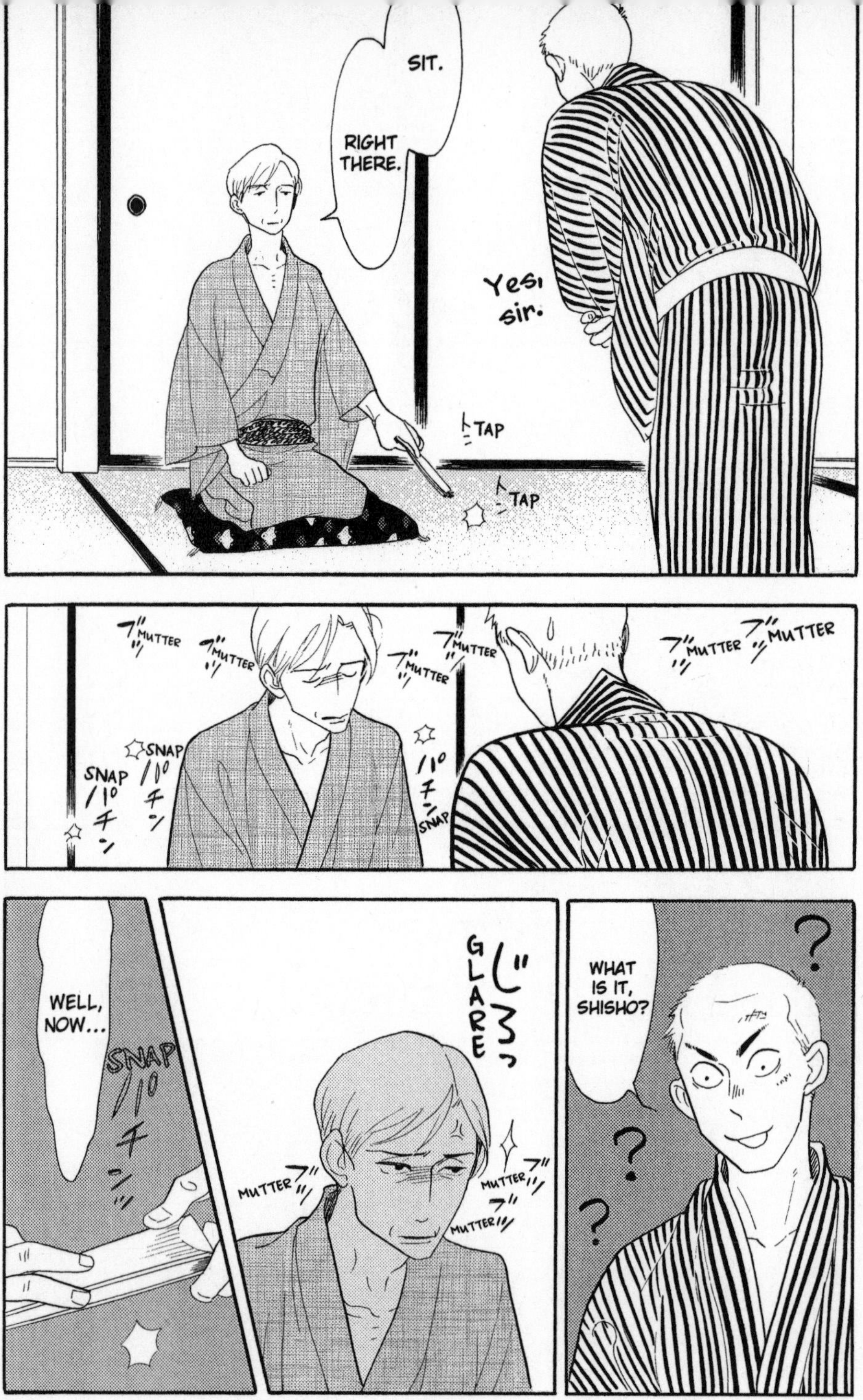
SIT.
RIGHT THERE.
Yes sir.
TAP
TAP
MUTTER
MUTTER
MUTTER
MUTTER
MUTTER
MUTTER
SNAP
SNAP
SNAP
WHAT IS IT, SHISHO?
GLARE
MUTTER
MUTTER
MUTTER
WELL, NOW...
SNAP

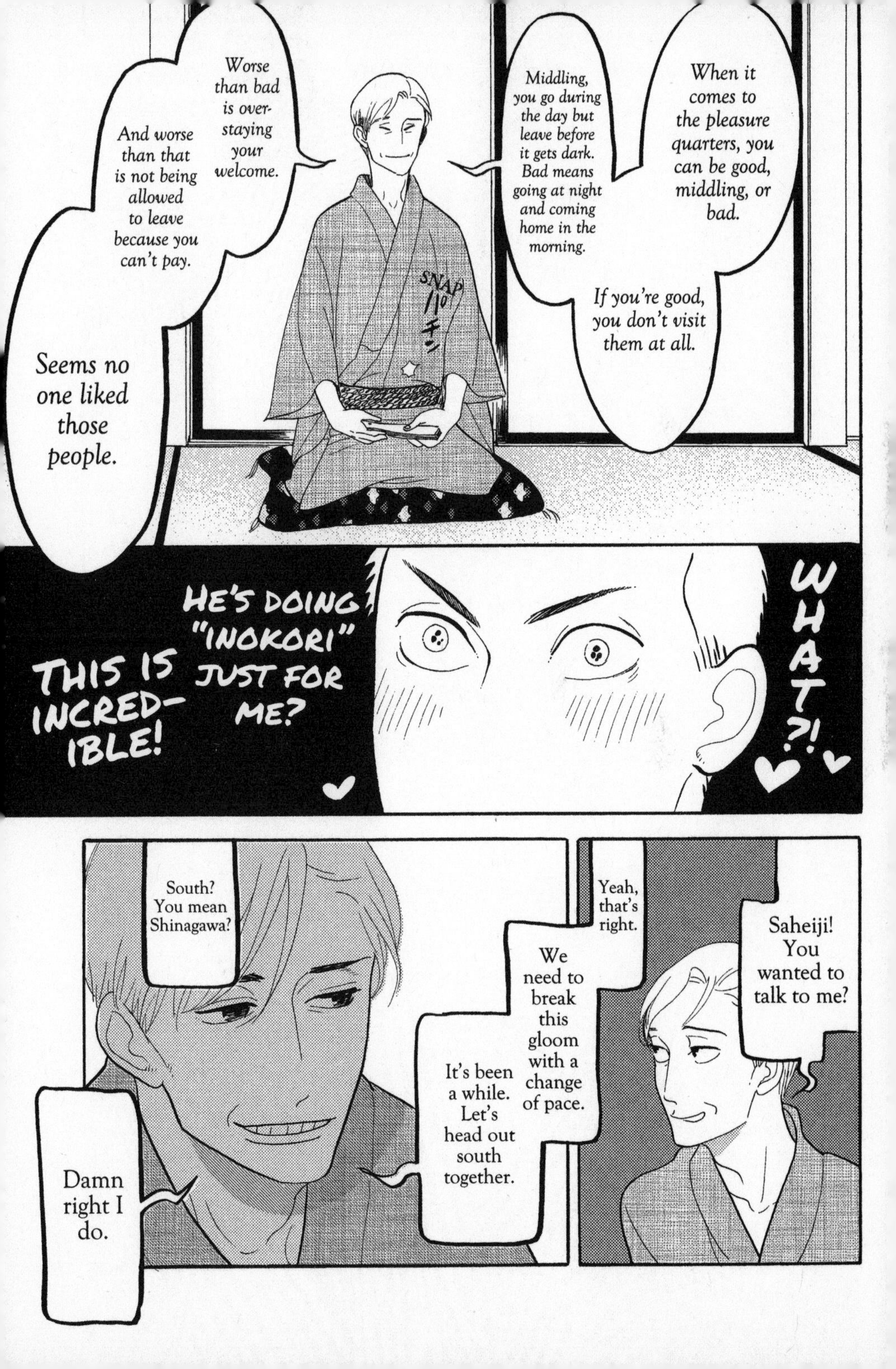

When it comes to the pleasure quarters, you can be good, middling, or bad.
If you're good, you don't visit them at all.
Middling, you go during the day but leave before it gets dark. Bad means going at night and coming home in the morning.
Worse than bad is over-staying your welcome.
And worse than that is not being allowed to leave because you can't pay.
SNAP
Seems no one liked those people.
WHAT?!
HE'S DOING "INOKORI" JUST FOR ME?
THIS IS INCRED-IBLE!
Saheiji! You wanted to talk to me?
Damn right I do.
It's been a while. Let's head out south together.
We need to break this gloom with a change of pace.
South? You mean Shinagawa?
Yeah, that's right.

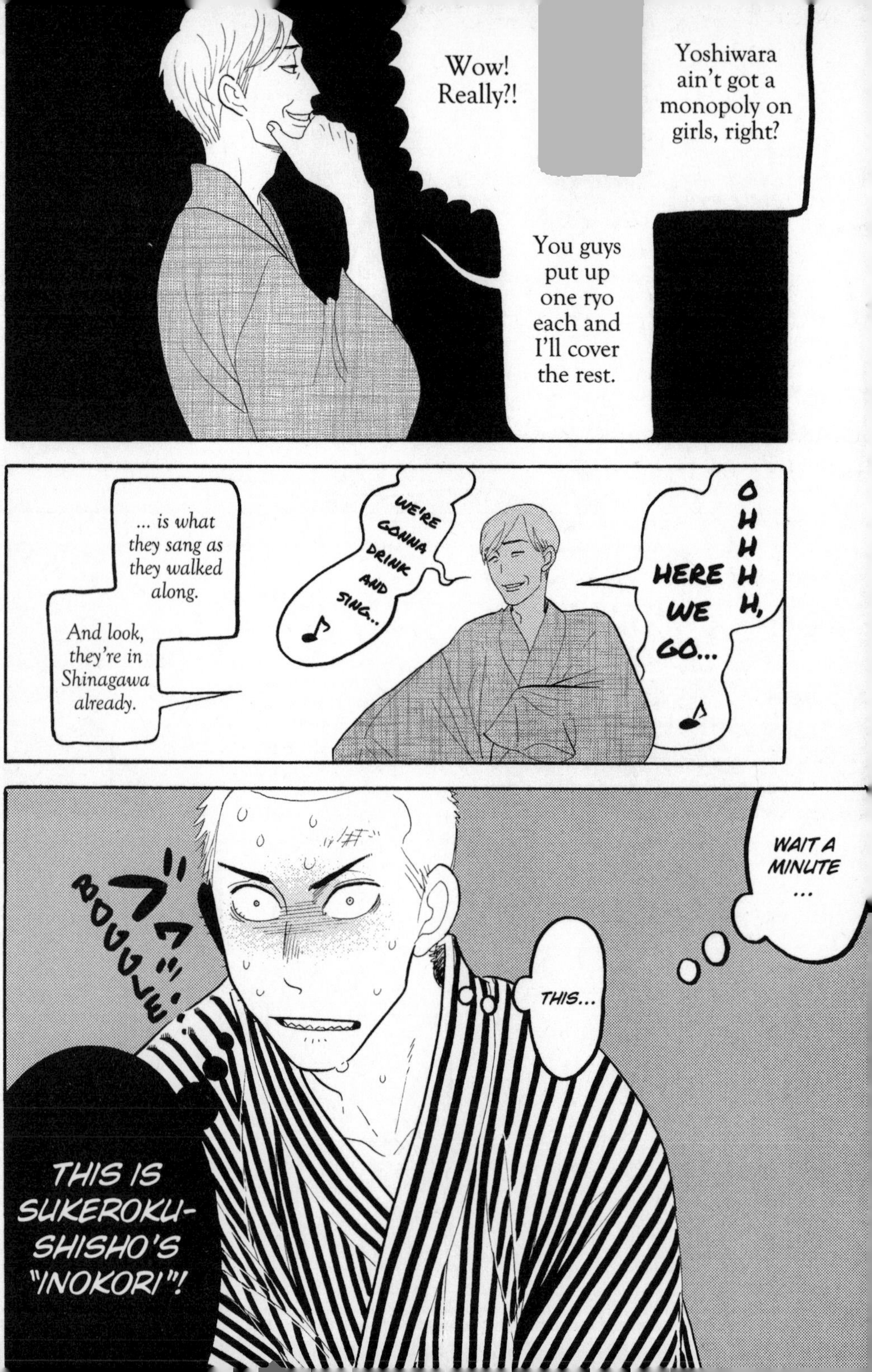
Yoshiwara ain't got a monopoly on girls, right?
Wow! Really?!
You guys put up one ryo each and I'll cover the rest.
OHHHH, HERE WE GO... ♪
WE'RE GONNA DRINK AND SING... ♪
... is what they sang as they walked along.
And look, they're in Shinagawa already.
WAIT A MINUTE ...
THIS...
BOUULE!
THIS IS SUKEROKU-SHISHO'S "INOKORI"!

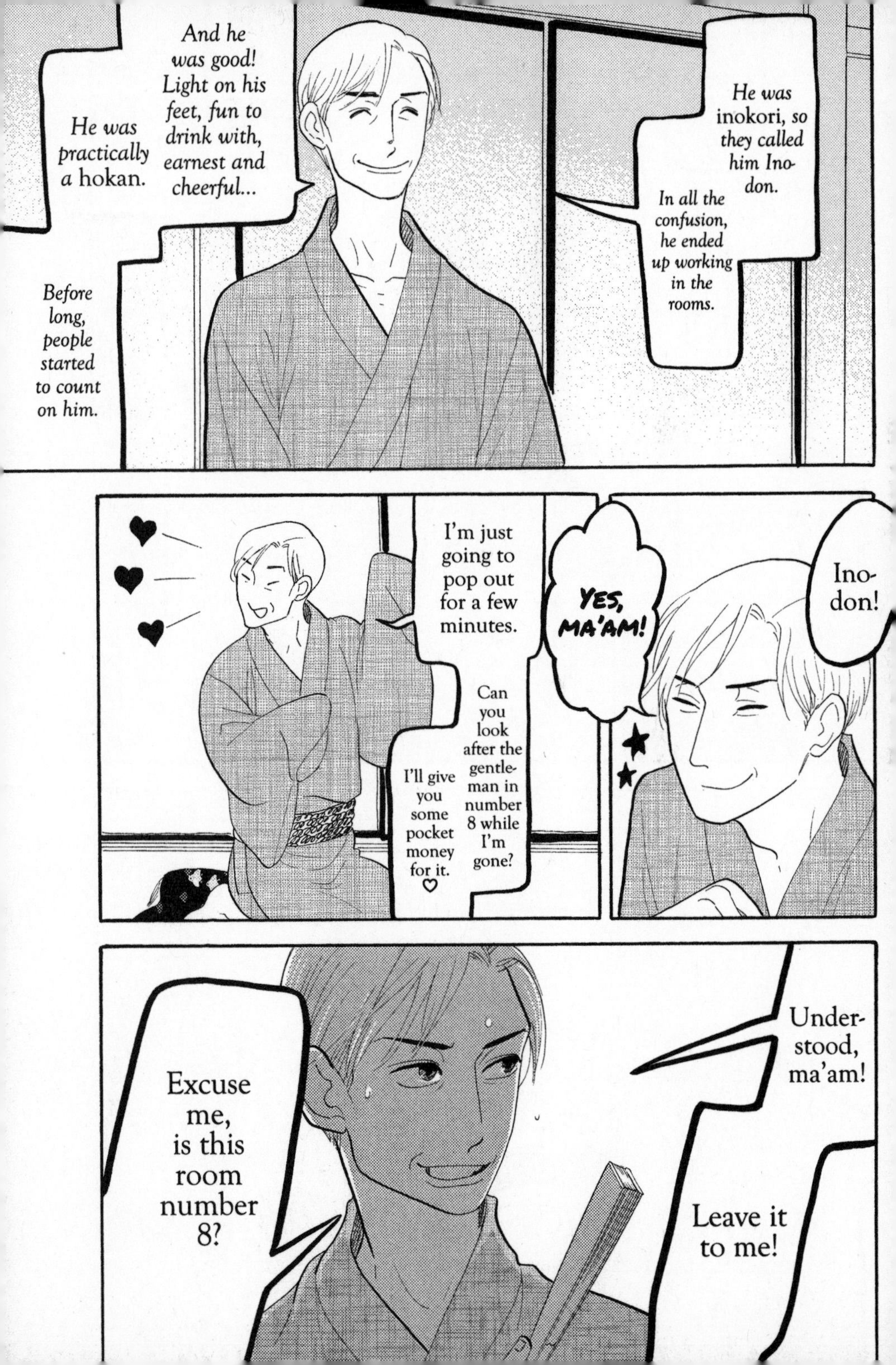
He was inokori, so they called him Ino-don.
In all the confusion, he ended up working in the rooms.
And he was good! Light on his feet, fun to drink with, earnest and cheerful...
He was practically a hokan.
Before long, people started to count on him.
Ino-don!
YES, MA'AM!
I'm just going to pop out for a few minutes.
Can you look after the gentleman in number 8 while I'm gone?
I'll give you some pocket money for it. ♡
Understood, ma'am!
Leave it to me!
Excuse me, is this room number 8?

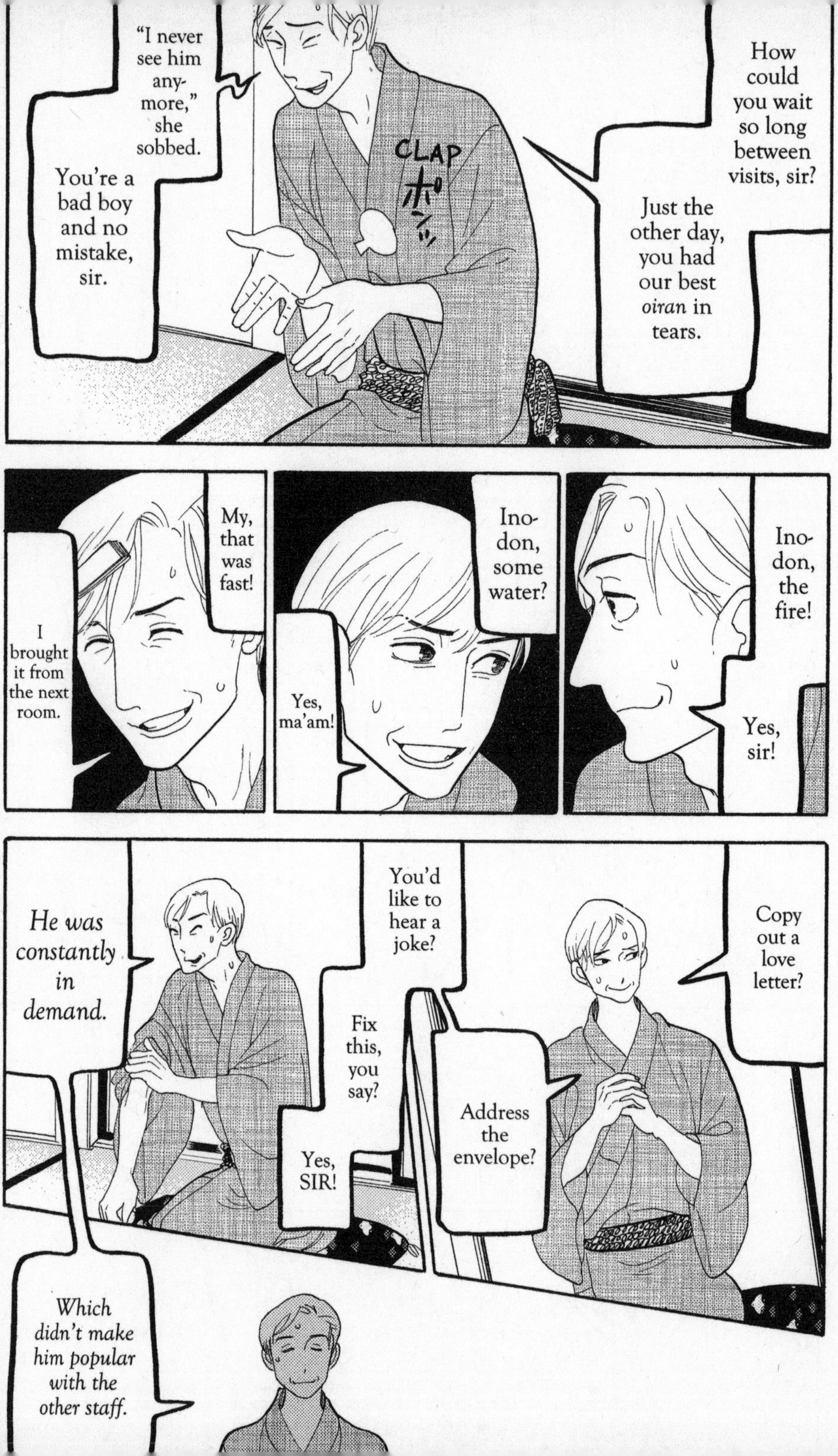
How could you wait so long between visits, sir?
Just the other day, you had our best *oiran* in tears.
"I never see him any-more," she sobbed.
You're a bad boy and no mistake, sir.
CLAP
ポン
Ino-don, the fire!
Yes, sir!
Ino-don, some water?
Yes, ma'am!
My, that was fast!
I brought it from the next room.
Copy out a love letter?
Address the envelope?
You'd like to hear a joke?
Fix this, you say?
Yes, SIR!
He was constantly in demand.
Which didn't make him popular with the other staff.

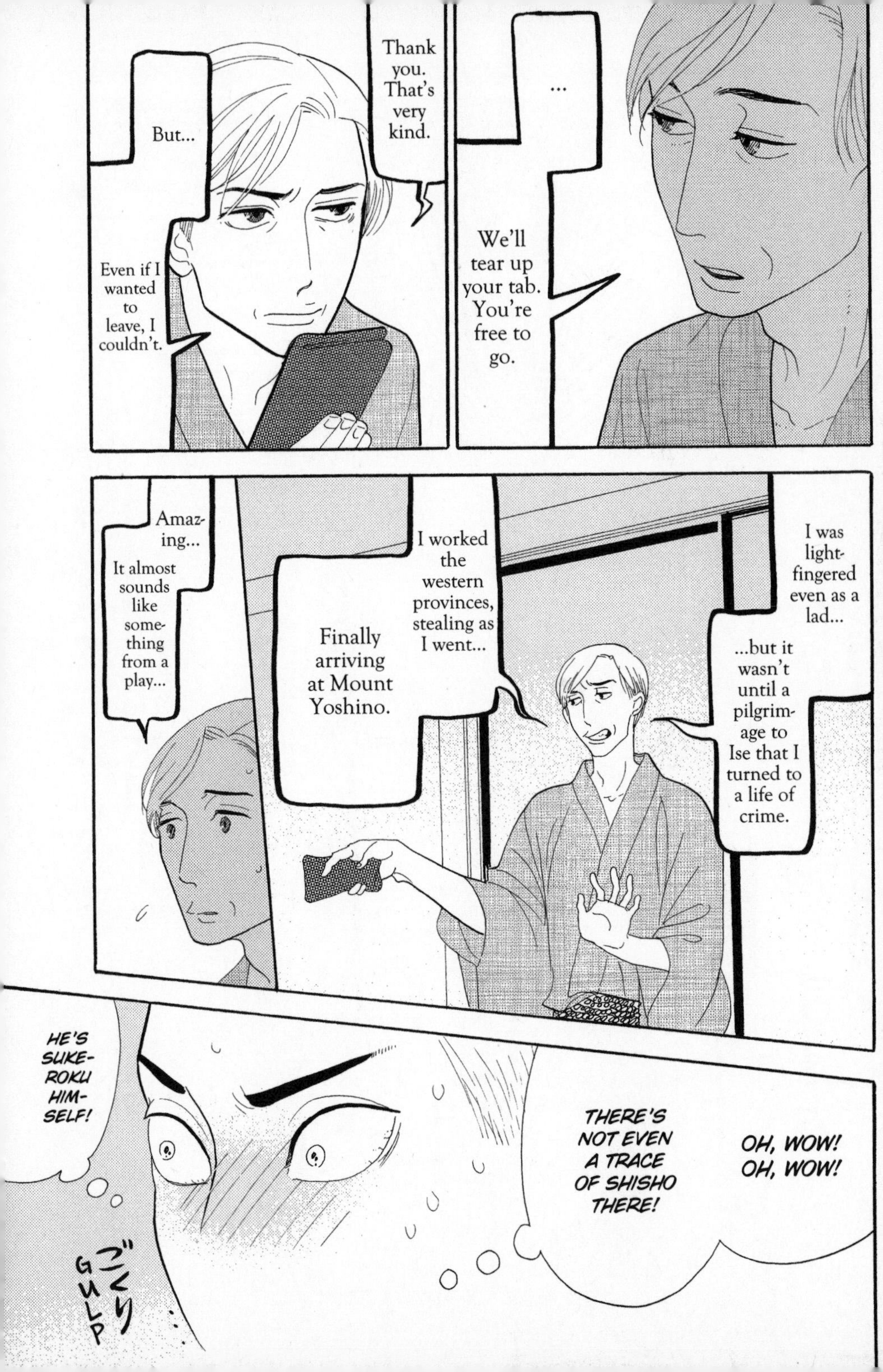
...
We'll tear up your tab. You're free to go.
Thank you. That's very kind.
But...
Even if I wanted to leave, I couldn't.
I was light-fingered even as a lad...
...but it wasn't until a pilgrimage to Ise that I turned to a life of crime.
I worked the western provinces, stealing as I went...
Finally arriving at Mount Yoshino.
Amazing...
It almost sounds like something from a play...
OH, WOW! OH, WOW!
THERE'S NOT EVEN A TRACE OF SHISHO THERE!
HE'S SUKE-ROKU HIM-SELF!
ごくり
GULP

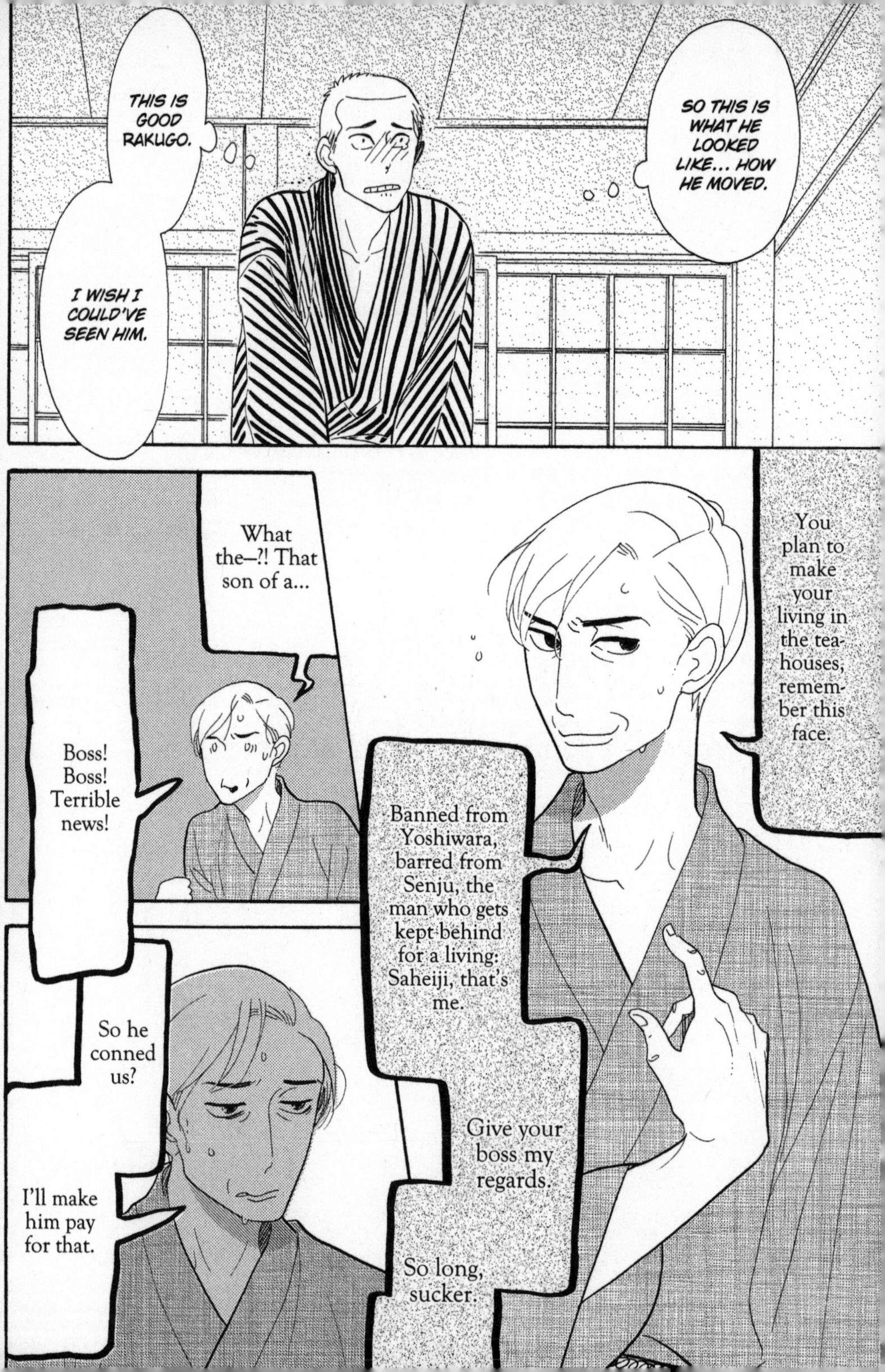
SO THIS IS WHAT HE LOOKED LIKE... HOW HE MOVED.
THIS IS GOOD RAKUGO.
I WISH I COULD'VE SEEN HIM.
You plan to make your living in the tea-houses, remember this face.
Banned from Yoshiwara, barred from Senju, the man who gets kept behind for a living: Saheiji, that's me.
Give your boss my regards.
So long, sucker.
What the–?! That son of a...
Boss! Boss! Terrible news!
So he conned us?
I'll make him pay for that.

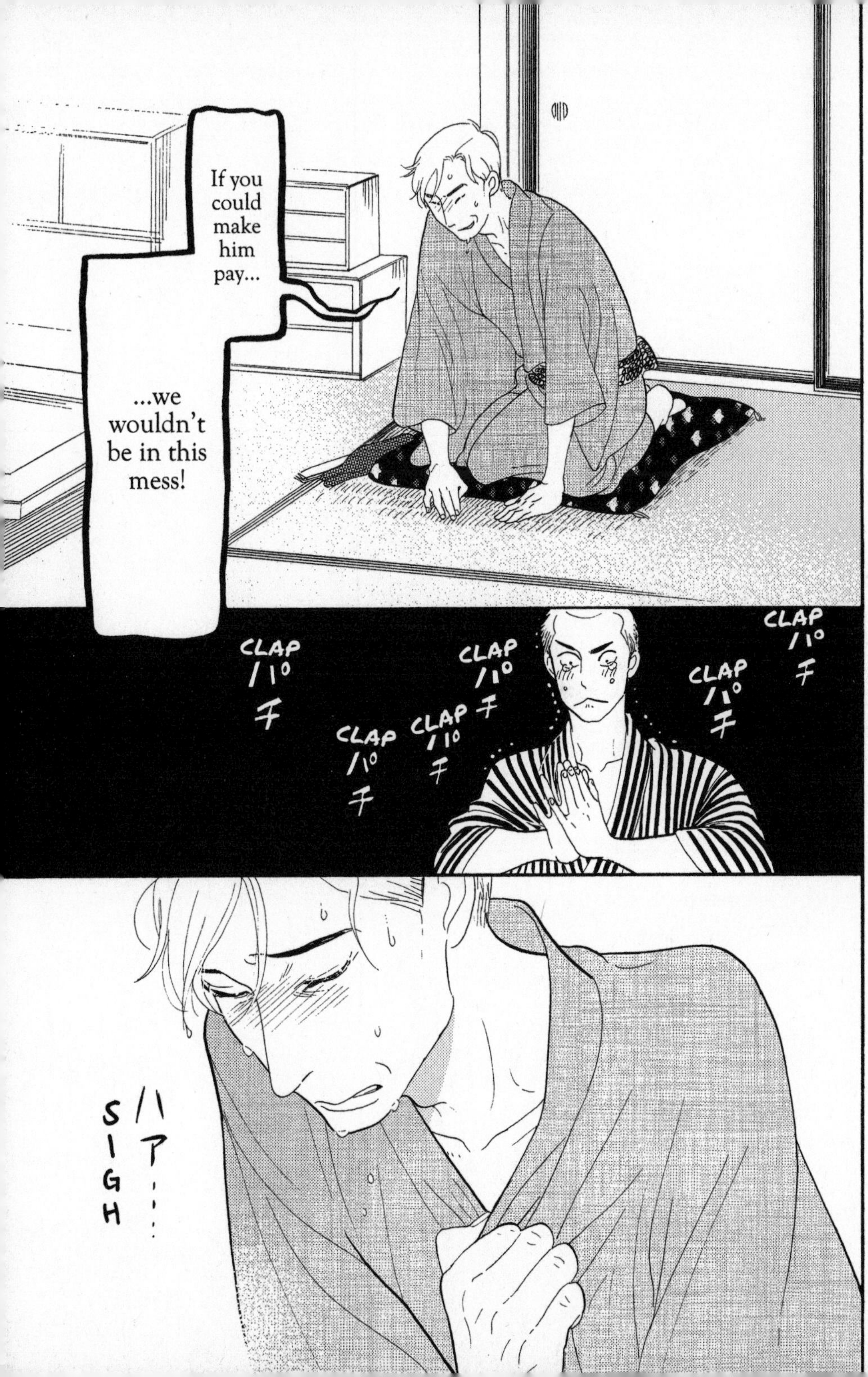
If you could make him pay...
...we wouldn't be in this mess!
CLAP
パチ
CLAP
パチ
CLAP
パチ
CLAP
パチ
CLAP
パチ
CLAP
パチ
SIGH
ハア…

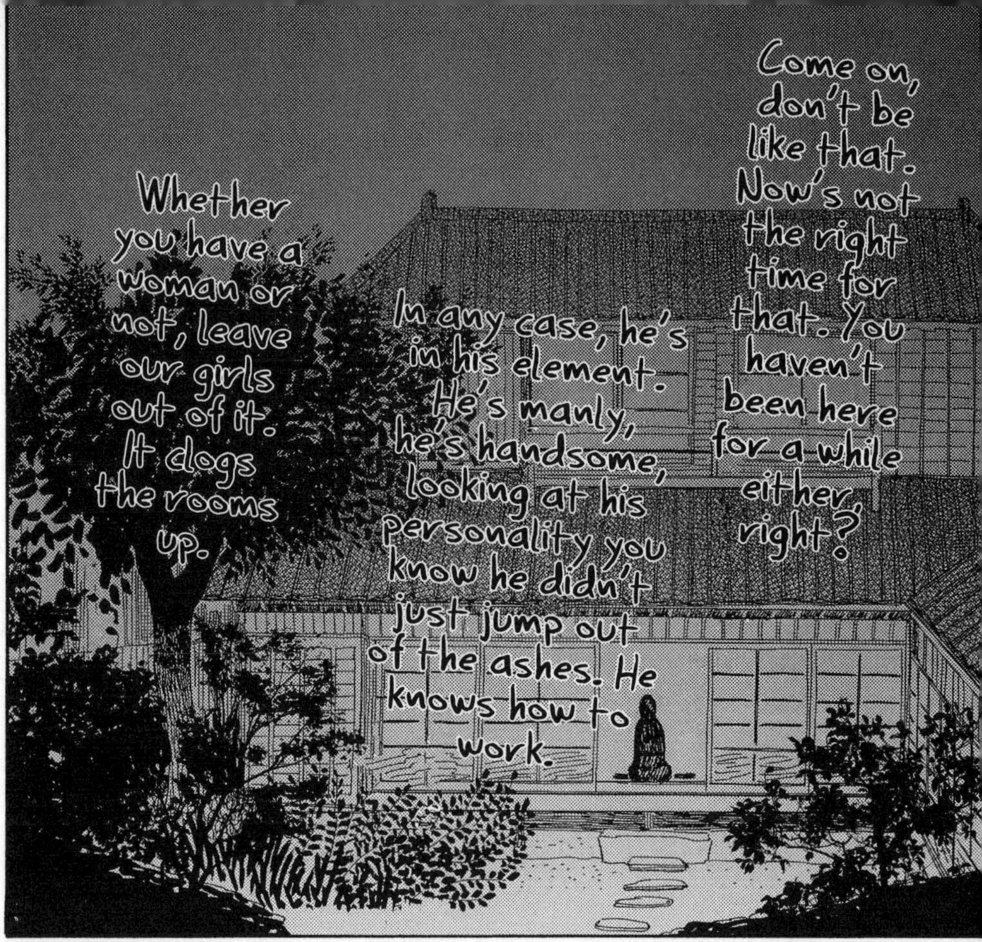
Come on, don't be like that. Now's not the right time for that. You haven't been here for a while either, right?
In any case, he's in his element. He's manly, he's handsome, looking at his personality you know he didn't just jump out of the ashes. He knows how to work.
Whether you have a woman or not, leave our girls out of it. It clogs the rooms up.

Note: *Sun* is a measurement that has been standardized in the common era to be around 3 cm, but historically was based on the width of a thumb knuckle.

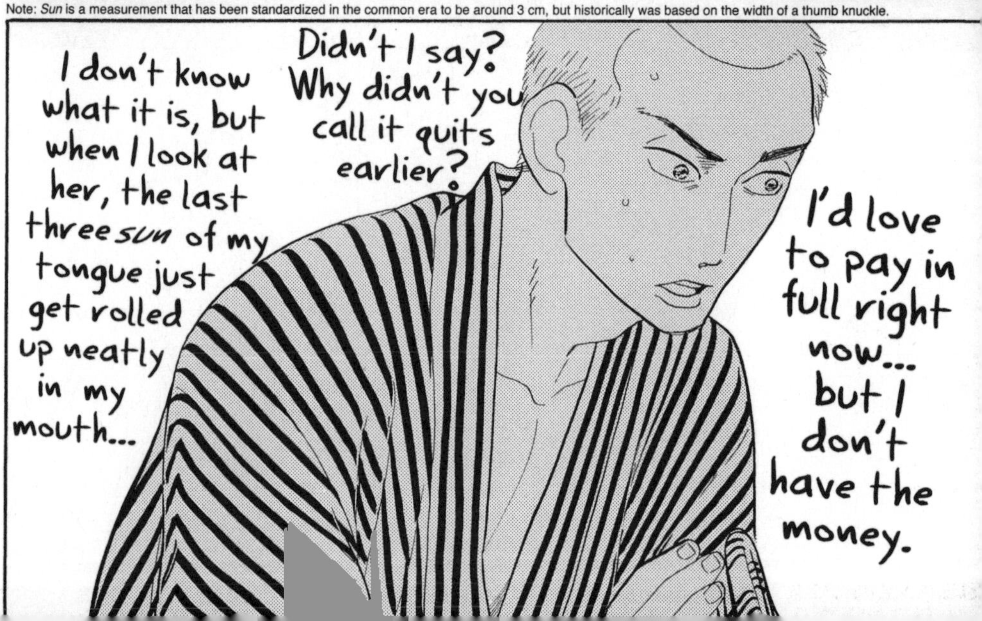
Didn't I say? Why didn't you call it quits earlier?
I'd love to pay in full right now... but I don't have the money.
I don't know what it is, but when I look at her, the last three *sun* of my tongue just get rolled up neatly in my mouth...

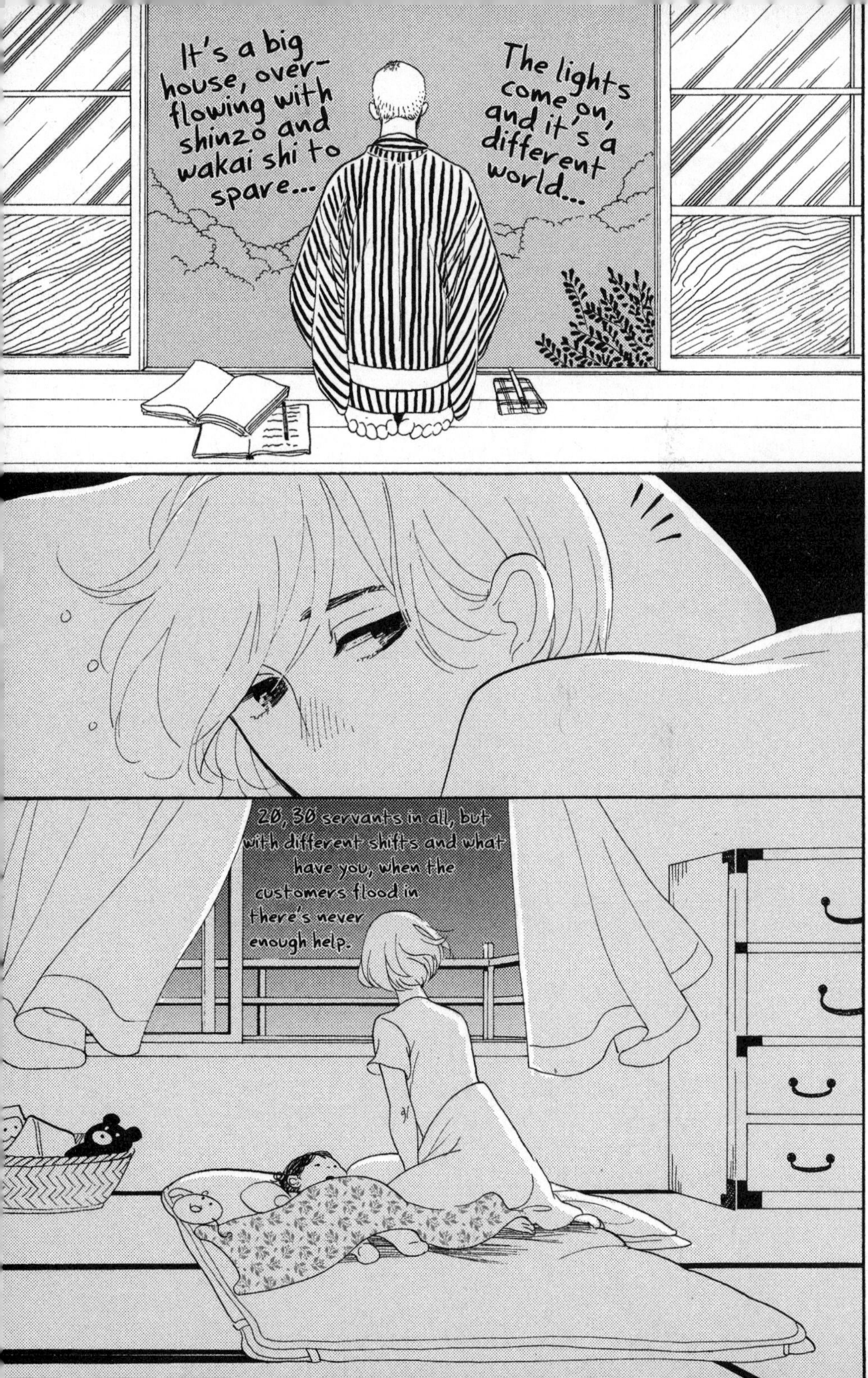
The lights come on, and it's a different world...
It's a big house, over-flowing with shinzo and wakai shi to spare...
20, 30 servants in all, but with different shifts and what have you, when the customers flood in there's never enough help.

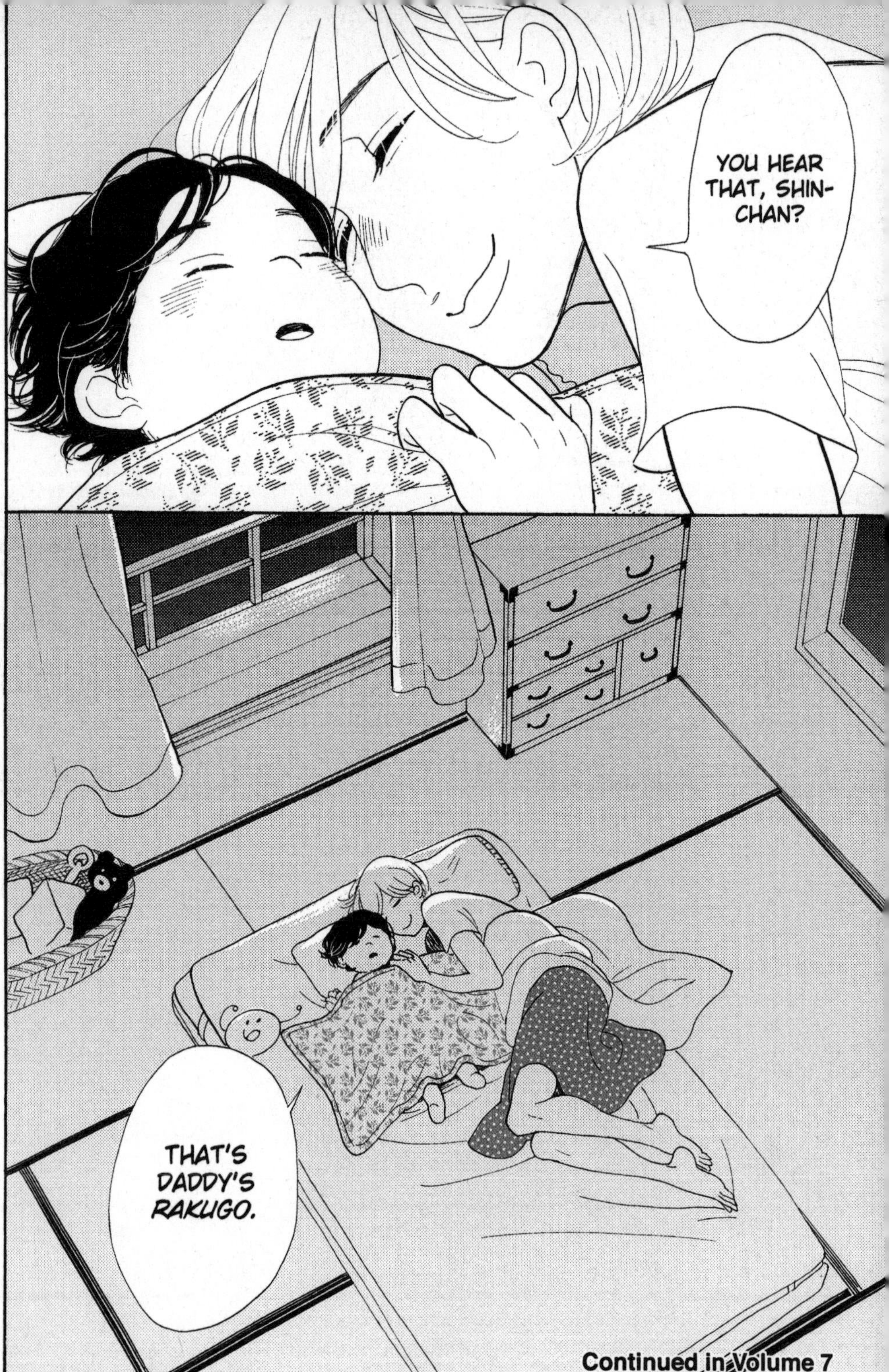
YOU HEAR THAT, SHIN-CHAN?
THAT'S DADDY'S RAKUGO.

Continued in Volume 7

Sources

Rakugo Zenshu (Complete Rakugo), vol. 2: Kin'ensha

Rakugo Hyakusen: Haru (One Hundred Rakugo Selections: Spring) / Chikuma Bunko: Chikuma Shobo

Tsukattemitai Rakugo no Kotoba (Rakugo Terms You'll Want to Use): Aspect

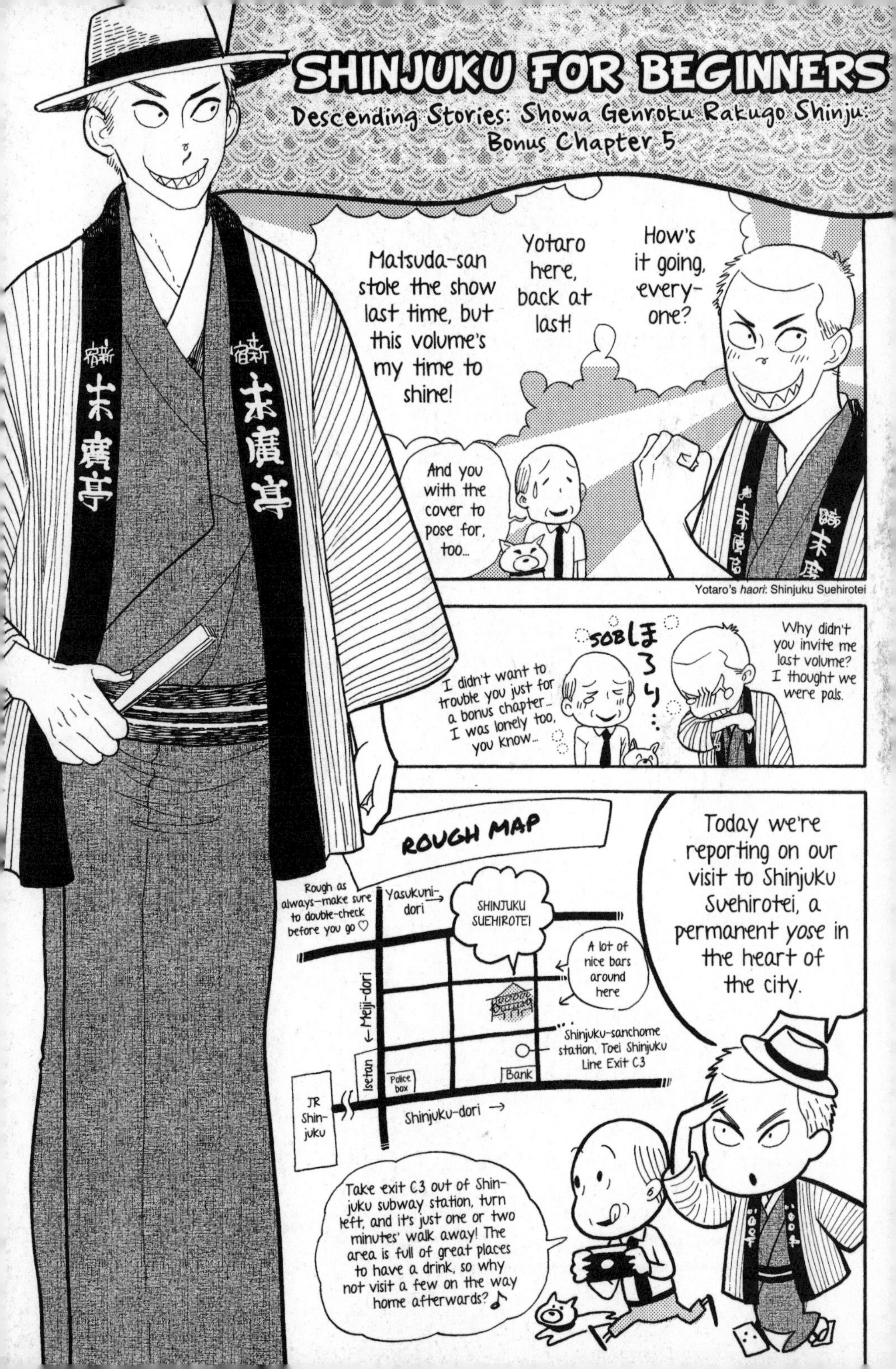
SHINJUKU FOR BEGINNERS
Descending Stories: Showa Genroku Rakugo Shinju: Bonus Chapter 5
How's it going, every-one?
Yotaro here, back at last!
Matsuda-san stole the show last time, but this volume's my time to shine!
And you with the cover to pose for, too...
Yotaro's haori: Shinjuku Suehirotei
Why didn't you invite me last volume? I thought we were pals.
SOB ほろり…
I didn't want to trouble you just for a bonus chapter... I was lonely too, you know...
Today we're reporting on our visit to Shinjuku Suehirotei, a permanent yose in the heart of the city.
ROUGH MAP
Rough as always—make sure to double-check before you go ♡
Yasukuni-dori
SHINJUKU SUEHIROTEI
A lot of nice bars around here
Meiji-dori
Shinjuku-sanchome station, Toei Shinjuku Line Exit C3
Isetan
Police box
Bank
JR Shin-juku
Shinjuku-dori
Take exit C3 out of Shin-juku subway station, turn left, and it's just one or two minutes' walk away! The area is full of great places to have a drink, so why not visit a few on the way home afterwards? ♪

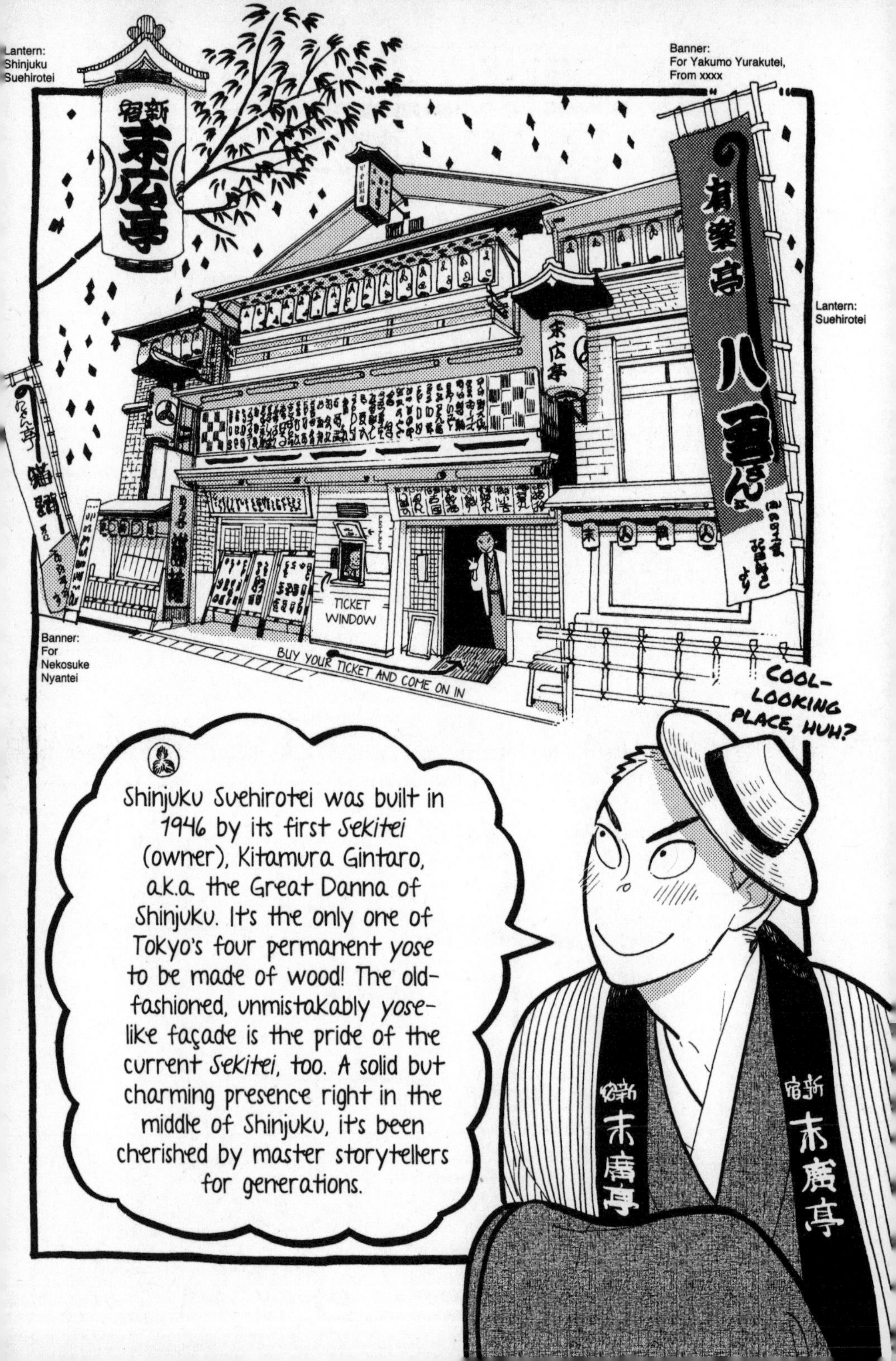
Banner:
For Yakumo Yurakutei,
From xxxx
有楽亭 八雲さん
Lantern:
Suehirotei
末広亭
Lantern:
Shinjuku
Suehirotei
新宿 末広亭
Banner:
For
Nekosuke
Nyantei
TICKET WINDOW
BUY YOUR TICKET AND COME ON IN
COOL-LOOKING PLACE, HUH?
Shinjuku Suehirotei was built in 1946 by its first *Sekitei* (owner), Kitamura Gintaro, a.k.a the Great Danna of Shinjuku. It's the only one of Tokyo's four permanent *yose* to be made of wood! The old-fashioned, unmistakably *yose*-like façade is the pride of the current *Sekitei*, too. A solid but charming presence right in the middle of Shinjuku, it's been cherished by master storytellers for generations.
新宿 末廣亭

INTERIOR VIEW

Stage
Yakumo
Box seats (38 seats)
Box seats (38 seats)
They'll lend you a cushion!
Theater seating (117 seats)
Shoes off and put away in the boxes provided.
If it's a full house, there are seats upstairs, too.

★Seats are normally unassigned. Sit wherever you like!

Souvenirs galore!

Suehirotei tenugui
Suehirotei fans
FULL HOUSE Suehirotei senjafuda
They're all so cute!♥
It's okay to eat and drink at the show. No alcohol or noisy snacks, though.

SHINJUKU

When my pleasant mood carried me across the threshold that mild spring afternoon, I found myself in an Edo spring... Season by season, unfolding like a picture scroll of the manners and customs of Edo, the arts of the *yose* are light shed on the hearts and homes of the nameless many of that lost age—they are silhouettes on the paper screen, and also the clamor of the harbor, the whisper of the wind. They transmit all the tastes of Edo to our own age... In this back alley just off the bustling avenue, Edo will be reborn.

(Excerpted from the introduction to Hitoshi Tomita's *Kikigaki Yose Suehirotei*, ("Recollections of Suehirotei.")

Translation Notes

"Shamisen with grumbling," page 8
A pun on the name of a *rakugo* story, *"Kogoto nenbutsu"* ("Mantra with grumbling").

Shubi Pine on the Sumida, page 11
A famous tree used as a landmark by people on their way to the Yoshiwara.

Special summer program, page 19
Literally a *"nōryō"* performance, using a word that means a "cool break from the summer heat." A riverside walk to enjoy the breeze and a fireworks display in the cool of evening are both examples of the *nōryō* concept.

Weekly Snap, page 20
In the original, *Shukan Meito*, literally "Weekly Mate." To judge by its appearance (and the advertisement seen in a train later), a low-brow tabloid-style magazine covering news, politics, and entertainment with a sensationalist slant. *Meito* has no particular connotations in Japanese, and was therefore changed to *Snap* in the translation as a rough equivalent more likely to be seen in the title of a magazine.

Glossary of terms used in the story, page 30
Nagajuban: A simple kimono-shaped garment worn beneath the kimono like underwear (usually!).
"Kappore": A flamboyant dance performed at parties and similar occasions.
Fundoshi: Traditional Japanese underwear.
Takashimaya: A department store (still open today).
Maruobi: A stiff *obi* of brocade fabric for formal occasions.

Kesa, page 32
The robes of a Buddhist priest.

A fox in my family…possessed by a girl, page 33
The bumbling Yotaro character in the *rakugo* story is mixing up his excuse, in reference to the traditional idea that people could be possessed by foxes, by accidentally claiming that a girl is possessing a fox instead.

Nishiki, page 35
Nishiki can refer to both brocade and to *nishiki-koi*, or the decorative *koi* carp often found in Japanese gardens—like the one seen on Yotaro's back.

Sate yoito korase… A-yoito! Sa, sa! Sa!, pages 36–37
Meaningless rhythm-keeping lyrics from *"Kappore."*

Zashiki, page 40
Literally the word for a Japanese-style room with tatami mats on the floor. By extension, a *zashiki* can refer to a private party held in such a room inside a teahouse or similar establishment, usually featuring paid entertainment.

Koi–Kin, page 45
A popular design for tattoos, combining a carp (*koi*) and the folk hero Kintaro. This combination dates back to the Edo period, when it was used to represent the wish that a boy would grow up big and strong—carp being a symbol of vigor, even appearing as "carp streamers" (*koinobori*) on Boy's Day, and Kintaro having been supernaturally strong even as a young boy.

Meiji, Taisho, pre-war Showa, page 50
Eras in modern Japanese history: 1868–1912, 1912–1926, and 1926 onwards, respectively.

Mush-mouthed, page 54
In the original, this corresponds to *chinketo*. Etymologically, this derives from something like "bizarre hairy foreigner," but it was used, as here, to refer to a person who speaks nonsense or refuses to listen to reason with no particular ethnic connotation.

Anyone who'd bow his head to you..., page 55
Literally "an older brother who'd bow his head to you is a bit different in accomplishment from (my/ this) older brother." In the *rakugo* story, this is Yotaro's boss getting angry at Yotaro's landlord on Yotaro's behalf.

Glossary of terms, page 56
Machiyaku: A town official.
Koyaku: Ointment. A pun on choyaku, another pronunciation of machiyaku.
Annya-monnya: A piece of gibberish roughly meaning a fool.

Tanka, page 57
Literally meaning "phlegm," this refers to a long stream of abuse hurled by a character in a *rakugo* story. This is known as *tanka wo kiru*, "cutting a *tanka*," an idiom which once might have had wider currency but is now generally associated with the *rakugo* world.

Stop saying "*da be*," page 59
Slightly rustic-sounding slang.

Jinku, page 59
A kind of popular song, usually in four lines with the moraic pattern 7-7-7-5.

He was this close to throwing me out, page 61
As echoed in Yotaro's gesture, the original Japanese is an idiom that literally means "my (near-decapitated) head was hanging from my neck by a single flap of skin."

Tamaya!, page 64
A fireworks guild in the Edo period. People would cheer for their favorite guilds during displays.

Danna, page 65
A patron. Originally a Buddhist term, and distantly related to the English word donor.

Okami-san, page 66
Female proprietor of a restaurant, teahouse, inn, etc.

Oyabun-san, page 71
Male head of a hierarchical organization such as a guild or gang, conceived of as a surrogate parent (*oya*) to his subordinates.

Mukudori-*gumi*, page 75
Yakuza gangs are known as *kumi* or *gumi*, in combination with the name of the group as seen here. Mukudori means "starling."

The forest around Mount Fuji, page 103
Known as the *jukai*, or "sea of trees." The dense volcanic forest is easy to get lost in and has gained some notoriety as a suicide destination.

Suppara-betcho, page 109
An insulting-sounding word with no actual meaning.

Horse's bone...cow's bone, page 109
Ways of referring to an unknown nobody.

Scooping goldfish, page 127
A common sight at Japanese festivals. These stalls have tubs full of goldfish, and sell small paper nets that visitors use to try to catch a fish to take home.

Glossary of terms, page 147
Shinzo: Trainee courtesans without their own room, above *kamuro* (child servants of courtesans) but not full-fledged *joro* (the general class of courtesans).
Wakai shi: In the context of the Yoshiwara economy, male servants.

For Yakumo Yurakutei, page 152
Banners like this are paid for by supporters and patrons to celebrate favored performers appearing in certain venues.

Shinjuku Suehirotei symbol, page 152
The symbol at the start of Yotaro's word balloon is a *maru mitsu-kashiwa*, "circled triple oak leaf," the crest of the Suehirotei.

Senjafuda, page 153
Slips of paper or stickers that were originally pasted to pillars in shrines or temples by visitors.

RAKUGO STORIES IN THIS VOLUME:

Daiku Shirabe (大工調べ) - The Trial of the Carpenter (page 55)
Inokori Saheiji (居残り佐平次) - Saheiji is Kept Behind (page 139)

It is said that the roots of the current *Rakugo Kyokai* Association can be traced to the Tokyo *Rakugo Kyokai* formed thanks to the efforts of Ryutei Saraku V following the 1923 Great Kanto Earthquake. Yanagiya Kosan IV was later appointed its chairman and established it anew as the *Rakugo Kyokai* Association. It received permission to become an incorporated association with the Agency for Cultural Affairs acting as its competent authority in 1977, and its stated goal was to "advance the spread of popular performing arts with a focus on classical *rakugo*, contributing to the cultural development of our country in the process." It later became the general incorporated association it is today in 2012. It conducts performances in four theatres (*yose*) in Tokyo, as well as in halls, assembly spaces, schools, and more around the country.

For an overview of the *Rakugo Kyokai* Association, please visit:
http://rakugo-kyokai.jp/summary/

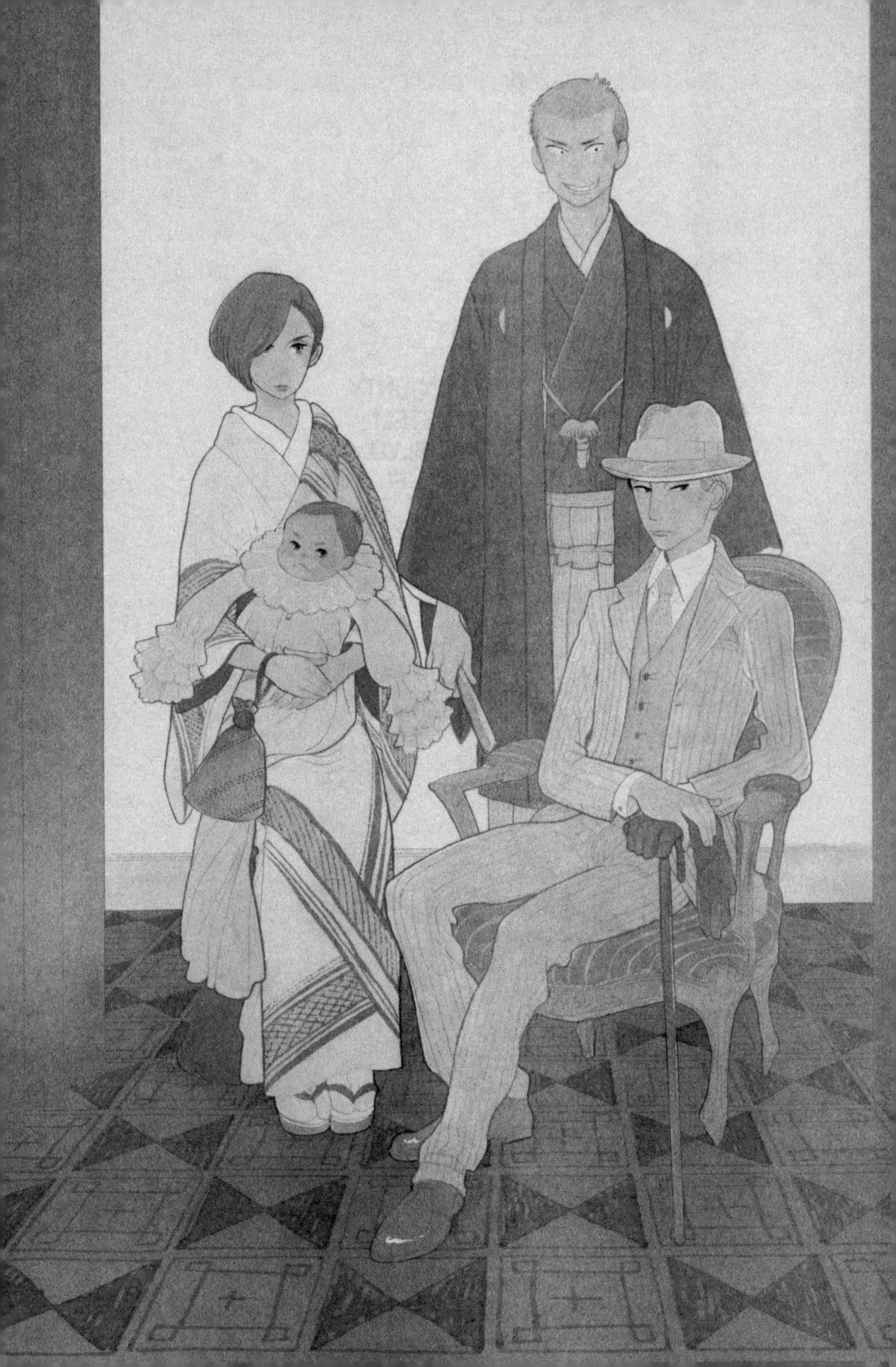

Descending Stories: Showa Genroku Rakugo Shinju volume 6 is a work of fiction. Names, characters, places, and incidents are the products of the author's imagination or are used fictitiously. Any resemblance to actual events, locales, or persons, living or dead, is entirely coincidental.

A Kodansha Comics Trade Paperback Original.

Published in the United States by Kodansha Comics, an imprint of Kodansha USA Publishing, LLC, New York.

Publication rights for this English edition arranged through Kodansha Ltd., Tokyo.

First published in Japan in 2014 by Kodansha Ltd., Tokyo.

ISBN 978-1-63236-544-6

Printed in the United States of America.

www.kodanshacomics.com

9 8 7 6 5 4 3 2 1

Translation: AltJapan Co., Ltd. (Matt Treyvaud, Hiroko Yoda, Matt Alt)
Lettering: Andrew Copeland
Editing: Lauren Scanlan
Rakugo term supervision: Rakugo Kyokai Association
Kodansha Comics edition cover design: Phil Balsman